D1087581

Market Risk Management for
Hedge Funds

For other titles in the Wiley Finance Series
please see www.wiley.com/finance

Market Risk Management for Hedge Funds

Foundations of the Style and Implicit Value-at-Risk

François Duc and Yann Schorderet

WILEY

A John Wiley & Sons, Ltd., Publication

Other Wiley Editorial Offices

John Wiley & Sons Inc., 111 River Street, Hoboken, NJ 07030, USA

Jossey-Bass, 989 Market Street, San Francisco, CA 94103-1741, USA

Wiley-VCH Verlag GmbH, Boschstr. 12, D-69469 Weinheim, Germany

John Wiley & Sons Australia Ltd, 42 McDougall Street, Milton, Queensland 4064, Australia

John Wiley & Sons (Asia) Pte Ltd, 2 Clementi Loop #02-01, Jin Xing Distripark, Singapore
129809

John Wiley & Sons Canada Ltd, 6045 Freemont Blvd, Mississauga, ONT, L5R 4J3, Canada

Wiley also publishes its books in a variety of electronic formats. Some content that appears in
print may not be available in electronic books.

Library of Congress Cataloging-in-Publication Data
Duc, François
   Market risk management for hedge funds : foundations of the style and implicit value-at-risk /
François Duc and Yann Schorderet.
     p. cm.
   Includes bibliographical references and index.
   ISBN 978-0-470-72299-2
  1. Hedge funds.   2. Risk management.   3. Hedge funds—Evaluation.   4. Investment
analysis—Mathematical models.   I. Schorderet, Yann. II. Title.
   HG4530.D83 2008
   332.64'524—dc22

                          2008039311

British Library Cataloguing in Publication Data
A catalogue record for this book is available from the British Library

ISBN 978-0-470-72299-2 (HB)

Typeset in 11/13pt Times by Aptara Inc., New Delhi, India
Printed and bound in Great Britain by TJ International Ltd, Padstow, Cornwall, UK

To Karine and Chloé the two loves of my life.

To Professor Gilbert Ritschard, I am grateful (to him) for inculcating the joy of learning process in statistics and for his continuous friendship.

F.D.

To my parents, who always support me in my endeavours in arts and sciences.

Y.S.

Various forms of scepticism [. . .] deny that we can have any reliable access to an objective reality, and which therefore reject the possibility of knowing how things truly are. These 'antirealist' doctrines undermine confidence in the value of disinterested efforts to determine what is true and what is false, and even in the intelligibility of the notion of objective inquiry.

Harry G. Frankfurt

Depuis quelques années, on ne parle plus de programmation, mais de prospective. Sans doute, il y a là un progrès. On a compris qu'il n'est plus possible de prévoir l'avenir en poursuivant l'expérience du passé. Mais on n'a pas encore compris que l'on ne peut aussi imaginer prospectivement l'avenir qu'à partir des éléments de notre présent, ce qui veut dire que ces éléments seront toujours incomplets et que seule la marche en avant nous permettra d'en découvrir d'autres. Or, ces éléments-là changeront complétement la vue prospective élaborée dans un moment déjà révolu. Il nous est interdit de faire de la prospective. Nous devons nous contenter d'une 'proximospective' pour échapper à la rétrospective. Notre rôle est limité: [. . .] il consiste à avancer pas à pas vers un but que nous ignorons, en ne cessant de faire les hypothèses de travail que notre expérience croissante nous permet de formuler.

Henri Laboritt

Contents

Acknowledgements

The idea of this book emerged during an informal discussion in May 2005 with Jan Erik Frogg – Head of Alternative Investments at Union Bancaire Privée (UBP) – on how some of the more recent developments in Risk Management techniques can improve the portfolio management of funds of hedge funds. The authors want to thank him for his initial input as well as for his continuous support.

If almost all the material comes from the collaboration between the two authors from 2006 to mid-2007, Chapter 5 is the result of the collaboration between the UBP Structural Risk Team headed by Paul Olin, UBP Risk Advisory Team, and Ferry Wahl from UBP Qualitative Research. The two authors want to warmly thank all contributors to this work, and particularly Paul Olin for his valuable inputs.

Moreover, other materials come from various 'UBP Industry Review and Outlook' publications: section 2.3.1 was written by Naboth Nyamazana and section 2.3.2 was written by Mason Mallory both of whom are members of the UBP Structural Risk Team while the description of the model in section 10.2 was written by Francesco Carollo and Yves Hennard from the UBP Alternative Investments Quantitative Team. We would like to thank all these people and UBP to allow us to use this material for this book.

In addition, we owe special thanks to the members of the 2005–2007 UBP Geneva Portfolio Management, namely Lara Sevanot Davis, Shoaib Khan, Robert Khoury and Kris Raecke. Not only was it a real pleasure for the two authors to work on a day-to-day basis with these senior investment professionals but their intensive use of risk budgeting tools since the end of 2005 contributed to the improvement of the approach.

A lot of credit in our research writing has to be attributed to experienced professionals in the traditional and alternative investment industry, namely Christophe Bernard, Daniel de Picciotto, Jan Erik Frogg, Dominique Leprevots, Laurent Reiss and Patrick Rey, as well as to communication professionals, namely Bertrand Bricheux, Jérôme Koechlin and Riccardo Payro. Our gratitude goes also to some friends working in the investment industry (Mariam Ben Hammoud, Michel Chardon, Jean-Pierre Durante, David Friche and Cédric Zuffrey) who have made useful comments on some parts of the draft manuscript and to Marie-Julie Beauverd and Anne Simond for proof reading.

We also want to thank Laurent Barras from Imperial College London for heated discussion on the art of modelling and for initiating the implementation at UBP of the Diez de los Rios and Garcia (2006) model, Francesco Carollo for building the software used to estimate the coefficients of the Diez de los Rios and Garcia (2006) model performed in Chapter 13, Yves Hennard from the UBP Alternative Investments Quantitative Team for providing the classification mapping process of the database and Phillipe Huber from Cinetics SA for computing the latent factors used in Chapter 3 when working at UBP. Moreover, we wish to acknowledge Professor Narayan Vaik and Professor David Fung for instructive discussions during the 2008 Hedge Fund Programme at London Business School.

Obviously, it is also a real pleasure for the authors to acknowledge all the people inside or outside UBP who spent some time working on the UBP hedge fund Value-at-Risk since 2000, especially the UBP Risk Management Team and the UBP Alternative Investments Team. The English version of this text benefited from the invaluable contribution of Barbara Caffin, Hubert Pawlak and Emmanuel Malfait.

The opinions expressed in this book represent solely our viewpoint and may not reflect the opinions or activities of any organization with which we are associated. All errors and omissions remain our own responsibility.

Finally, we owe the biggest debt of gratitude to our respective spouses and to all our friends for their thoughtful gestures during the writing process, especially 'la bande des 7 témoins', Angel Carreras, Michel Chardon, Claude-Alain Duc, Anaï Ledermann, Benoît Lorenzini, Rémy Perraudin and Cédric Zuffrey.

1

Introduction

For a long time, the measurement of market risk in relation to hedge funds was considered of secondary importance. Alternative funds were initially the preserve of a few wealthy investors whose very personal relationships with the fund managers were more important than a statistical evaluation of risk. These historical investors in hedge funds maintained that the main source of returns was the talent of the fund manager, and that quantitative risk measures would inevitably fail to take into account the complexity of a particular manager's strategy and skill. In 2007, with over 10 000 hedge funds available, identifying each manager as having a specific style and denying the existence of a set of risk factors common to certain subsets of alternative strategy styles can no longer be justified. Moreover, nowadays all major institutional investors have significant exposure to hedge funds. The exception has become the rule and consolidation of market risk at the portfolio level – a standard practice for institutional investors – therefore requires the application of a simple and easily understandable synthetic risk indicator such as Value-at-Risk.

Another justification for the limited use of risk measures for hedge funds in the past also relies on the importance of qualitative due diligence in the risk management process. Before any investment is made in a hedge fund, caution dictates that an analysis of structural and operational risks should be carried out: several studies have shown that between 40 and 60 percent of hedge fund company failures are attributable to poor control of operational risk. Extensive due diligence, carried out by a dedicated team of operational risk specialists, is therefore crucial. Furthermore, investing in an alternative fund basically means delegating both the portfolio management and the associated risk management. It is therefore necessary to qualitatively evaluate the investment strategy, underlying positions, amount of leverage, credit risk, stop-loss limits, level of diversification and risk control tools and processes used by the fund manager.

But a structural and qualitative analysis, although vital, is not sufficient: the financial market instability of recent years, and the complexity of hedge fund strategies, demand regular risk monitoring after the investment has been made. The quantitative measurement of hedge fund risks is an essential part of this monitoring process since it is systematic, continuous and can be automated – unlike qualitative monitoring, which requires frequent, meticulous analysis and on-site assessments.

The implementation of a robust Value-at-Risk approach raises however two main difficulties. First, neither volatility, nor downside deviation nor even the derived Value-at-Risk methods are reliable and robust market risk measures for hedge funds. Volatility is based on the principle that hedge fund returns are normally and symmetrically distributed, and consequently, that investors are no more concerned about losses than gains. As for downside deviation, although this takes into account the asymmetry of returns, it does not provide a full description of fat tail returns that are typical for hedge fund performance. These criticisms have resulted in the need for the development of more robust market risk measures for hedge funds that allow for the modelling of fat tail returns, hence the implementation of more sophisticated Value-at-Risk methods than the traditional variance–covariance Value-at-Risk.

Second, the underlying risks of an investment strategy may be overlooked if the concept relies solely on hedge fund returns (because of the sample selection), while a model measuring the sensitivity of historical returns to market indices does not take into account the key features of alternative funds: an investment strategy involving active management of traditional assets with a risk management overlay. The debate around hedge fund clones that occurred at the end of 2006 and was carried out throughout 2007 revealed that no academic consensus was reached on an explanatory model for alternative investment strategies using traditional assets as factors. Moreover, the absence of a benchmark and the high level of investment freedom available to hedge fund managers ends up with a highly heterogeneous universe of funds. As a consequence, the hedge funds industry is currently characterized by the absence of an efficient and standard classification of alternative investment styles.

Given the current state of knowledge, the pragmatic solution for a quantitative measure of hedge funds' market risk consists in giving up the explicit side of the model and focusing on an efficient measure. The model should not try to explicitly explain the kind and level of exposure to traditional risk factors, but simply measure the sensitivity to risk factors that implicitly contain various types of exposures to traditional assets. Taking into account the high level of heterogeneity of the hedge funds universe, the selection of a few relevant implicit risk factors should be performed within a large number of latent variables (Best Choice Models).

The first step towards this type of pragmatic model was the application of the Sharpe (1988) Style Analysis to hedge funds, providing a Value-at-Risk based on the sensitivity of hedge funds to the CS/Tremont hedge fund indices. The Alternative Style Value-at-Risk was introduced by Lhabitant (2001) and Lhabitant (2002a). Developed for practical use when François-Serge Lhabitant was working at Union Bancaire Privée (UBP), the Alternative Style Value-at-Risk also became an academic success.

Contrary to what is often believed, the Style Value-at-Risk for hedge funds is not really a style drift model.[1] This would require both an accurate classification system and representative indices. But mixing these indicators through a Style Model enables us to build a basket of non-linear and dynamic exposures to traditional risk factors that matches more efficiently the exposures of any given hedge fund. As far as hedge funds are concerned, the main advantage of the style approach comes from its implicit aspects.[2]

The second step in the construction of a pragmatic Value-at-Risk for alternative investments consists of fully developing both the implicit and the automated selection aspects of the style approach. However, the level of complexity of implicit models may quickly increase and, as a consequence, practitioners tend to avoid them. This concern of maintaining a practical and simple risk measure led to the consideration of an automated selection approach or, more accurately, a Best Choice Implicit Model based on the inverse of a clustering analysis combined with a Principal Component Analysis. This is the implicit model presented here.

The target of this book is both to present a clear exposure of the fundamentals for a quantitative risk measure for hedge funds and to cover the technical aspects of the Style Value-at-Risk and the Implicit Value-at-Risk applied to hedge funds.[3] Quantitative methods are a powerful tool to test a fundamental theory but may shrink to a poor, biased and

---

[1] Even though style analysis may be interpreted as a style drift model when analysing funds of hedge funds as an external investor (i.e. without the strategy transparency) and not as a portfolio manager.

[2] Actually, this is also, but to a lesser extent, one of the most appealing features of the traditional style model.

[3] The high level of transparency on a methodology first developed for investment purposes of the second largest allocator to hedge funds (namely UBP – Union Bancaire Privée) is motivated by our strong interest in participating to the elaboration of a standard in risk measurement for hedge fund investors. Indeed, the absence of a common point of reference makes comparisons between different products and different approaches regarding alternative investments difficult.

non-robust approach when used to extract a theory from financial data. Quantitative methods blindly applied to hedge fund performance could lead to misrepresentation of risks embedded in such investment vehicles. As an example, investors who were excessively focusing on the stability of the returns of hedge funds having a short volatility position or collecting a high liquidity premium were quite surprised in 1994 and in August 1998. In order to avoid the pro forma effect and provide some perspectives of good forecasting power and out-of-the-sample robustness, any proposition for a risk indicator for the alternative funds should not be the sheer product of data mining. Remembering the paradigm shift that the investment industry witnessed during the last seven years and providing a clear exposure of the alternative funds universe is a prerequisite of any technical note on Value-at-Risk applied to hedge funds. Furthermore, only diamonds are forever and models work only within certain environments. As a matter of fact, if an efficient classification of alternative investment styles, as well as a robust family of passive indices, are proposed in the future, the models proposed in this book will lose their relevance. Finally, despite outstanding books on absolute return investments such as Ineichen (2003), Jaeger (2002), Lhabitant (2006a), Rahl (2003) and Reynolds Parker (2000), hedge funds still suffer from various misconceptions. Our choice was to deliberately expose straightforward considerations even though they might hurt some traditional beliefs. Obviously, we would expect puzzled readers to refer to the above references.

The book is thus divided into three parts. The first provides the fundamentals for the Style and Implicit Value-at-Risk through the practitioner's vision of the alternative industry. Chapter 2 describes the effect of the ongoing institutionalization of the hedge funds industry. Chapter 3 examines one of the most important feature of an absolute return industry, i.e. the high level of heterogeneity. Chapter 4 addresses the issue of the active and passive[4] hedge funds indices. The failure of both approaches to provide a good representation of the hedge funds universe is the very root of the motivation for a Value-at-Risk based on a Best Choice Implicit Factor Model. Chapter 5 provides a qualitative insight of the four dimensions of risk management for an investor in hedge funds.

The second part of this book is devoted to the Style Value-at-Risk. Chapter 6 presents the original model as well as an out-of-the-sample

---

[4] Often referred as hedge funds clones.

backtest. Chapter 7 proposes a new parameterization of the Style Model. Chapter 8 addresses the issue of annualization of any risk measure for hedge funds and illustrates a fundamental difference between traditional and alternative investments.

The last part of this book presents the Best Choice Implicit Model. In Chapter 9, the limits of the Style Analysis are addressed and the Best Choice Implicit Value-at-Risk is introduced. Chapter 10 addresses the issue of cloning hedge funds returns within the Best Choice Implicit Model framework, while Chapter 11 details the Risk Budgeting approach that can be used with those types of models. Finally, Chapter 12 examines the forecasting power of the Value-at-Risk exceptions monitoring and Chapter 13 provides some adjustments of the Value-at-Risk that are particularly relevant during a financing crisis, such as the one prevailing during the second half of 2007 and in 2008.

Part I

Fundamentals for Style and Implicit Value-at-Risk

2
Ongoing Institutionalization

The early 2000s witnessed the bursting of one of the biggest financial bubbles. Contrary to what is often believed, this was not the technology bubble, but the (symmetric) benchmarking/relative performance bubble.

Initiated in the 1970s and imposed during the 1990s to the financial industries, the benchmark approach forced in some ways portfolio managers to perform an index replication approach: returns being always compared with benchmark indices, even active long-only managers tend to minimize their tracking error. Cremer and Petajisto (2006) show that nearly one-third of them were simply benchmark duplicators. Israelsen and Cogswell (2007) verified for a sample of 232 large cap US equity mutual funds, that the use of tracking error was simply counter-productive. Indeed, as pointed out by Goltz (2007), minimizing the tracking error leads to non-optimal risk management as the implicit target is to minimize negative spread as well as positive spread, i.e. reduce the outperformance over the benchmark. The suboptimality of the relative performance approach was obvious during the bear equity market at the beginning of the 2000s: investors who saw their savings nest egg shrink to half its size between 2000 and 2002 because they had invested only in equity indices, while, on the same markets, long/short managers who registered gains would be the last to argue with that. This sounded like the end of the misunderstanding that the global market was not risky. Finally, combined with the development and the success of exchange-traded funds, the relative performance approach led exactly to the opposite of what was initially targeted: in order to beat the benchmark, some funds used the more recently developed instruments to perfectly match the benchmark and allocated their tracking error budget to assets outside the benchmarks: the liquidity crisis of the summer of 2007 showed that very large and well-established money market funds were dramatically exposed to subprime.

Suboptimal and risky, denying the improvements brought by the financial innovation or, if not, unable to guarantee the respect of the mandate, the benchmark/relative performance approach started to lose the favour of institutional investors in the 2000s. This return to absolute performance benefited the hedge fund industry: all the managers forced to mimic a benchmark during the 1990s constituted a reserve of professionals ready to launch their own funds as soon as the demand for absolute return emerged. Obviously, this is what happened from 2000 to 2005 when the number of hedge funds grew in line with inflows in the alternative industry, as shown in the first two sections of this chapter.

In order to meet the requirements of institutional investors, the alternative industry performed some important structural changes. The institutionalization process of the hedge fund industry reached a crucial point in 2006 and the most significant transformations put in place during 2006–2007, discussed in section 2.3, clearly indicates that the alternative industry is reaching maturity. The traditional financial industry also adapted itself to the new environment and more and more traditional absolute performance vehicles were launched. For instance, the 130/30 funds were created in 2004 and in three years pulled in more than 100 billion in dollars and about 40 billion in Europe. But, as a matter of fact, it was really the practice of investment that changed during the 2000s. In November 2006, Blake Grossman, chief executive of Barclays Global Investors, the world's biggest money manager, said in a *Financial Times* interview

> The notion that there is a traditional way of investing that is long only, and then there is hedge funds, is crazy. [. . .] If you look out five years, there will be much less of a divide between what is considered a hedge fund and what is considered a traditional strategy.

Other signs of convergence between the traditional and the alternative industry are given in Cowell et al. (2007). The authors predict the 2007–2008 credit crisis, this will probably reduce the convergence between traditional and alternative investments, but will not reverse the trend.

> The investment industry will continue to consolidate with M&A activity occurring within and across all segments of the sector as organizational convergence mirrors product convergence.

In 2007, apart from some politics for demagogical reasons (see section 2.4), and some journalists, nobody denies any longer the hedge funds' importance in the improvement of both market efficiency and portfolio management.

However, the pace at which the benchmarking bubble inflates reveals investors' reluctance to give up an approach that enables valuations and comparisons between their investments. Indeed, for the whole period, the absolute return industry performed in a traditional long-only way, with alternative investments or mixing both approaches, and the current challenge remains to find out a way to judge the performance of its managers. Obviously, this subject is beyond the scope of our publication, but in the success of investable indices and the launch of hedge fund clones[1] we can see a clear sign of this resistance. Just like people believe in UFOs, investors 'want to believe' in the illusions conveyed by those types of investment vehicles.

Whatever the difficulty of defining a reference for the absolute return approach as a whole, there currently exists one type of investment vehicle that exhibits quite standardized mandates: the multi-strategy funds of funds. For those kinds of products, institutional investors[2] have imposed comparisons between competitors. Combined with the institutionalization of the hedge fund industry (i.e. of the underlying investments of the multi-strategy funds of funds), this practice recently increased the level of homogeneity between the multi-strategy funds of funds, as shown in the last section of this chapter.

2.1 HEDGE FUND INDUSTRY SIZE AND ASSET FLOWS

In absolute and relative terms, 2006 was a banner year for the hedge funds industry driven by strong net flows but also outstanding performance across the hedge funds universe. In 2006, the estimated gross hedge fund returns approached 15%, contributing close to half of the 32.5% asset growth for that year. The strong performance trend continued in the first half of 2007 and, not surprisingly, net flows through June further accelerated from the previous year. Current industry assets are estimated at close to USD 1.75 trillion dollars (Table 2.1).

While hedge fund assets continue to grow, the increase in the number of hedge funds and funds of funds has slowed down significantly. This is a clear signal of the ongoing institutionalization of the industry. Indeed, the investor base has changed over the past few years with funds of funds, endowments, pension funds, and other institutional investors surpassing high net worth individuals as the largest investors in hedge funds. The increase in the number of institutional investors allocating capital to hedge funds should be viewed positively as most such investors

---

[1] See Chapter 4.

[2] Which can also be seen as a sign of reluctance to give up benchmarking approach.

Table 2.1 Estimated asset growth and the estimated number of hedge funds and funds of funds from 1990 to Q2-2007

	Estimated assets in millions	Estimated asset flow in millions	Estimated number of funds	Estimated number of fund of funds
1990	38 910		530	80
1991	58 370	8 463	694	127
1992	95 720	27 861	937	168
1993	167 790	36 918	1 277	237
1994	167 630	−1 141	1 654	291
1995	185 750	14 698	2 006	377
1996	256 720	57 407	2 392	389
1997	367 560	91 431	2 564	426
1998	374 770	4 406	2 848	477
1999	456 430	55 340	3 102	514
2000	490 580	23 336	3 335	538
2001	539 060	46 545	3 904	550
2002	625 554	99 436	4 598	781
2003	820 009	70 635	5 065	1 232
2004	972 608	73 585	5 782	1 654
2005	1 105 385	46 907	6 667	1 997
2006	1 426 710	126 474	7 241	2 221
Q1-2007	1 604 600	60 222	7 321	2 254
Q2-2007	1 754 214	58 663	7 460	2 307

Source: HFR

have a depth of resources to perform due diligence reviews on hedge funds thereby improving the governance and transparency of hedge fund managers. But this created a trend towards large and established firms. One can say that hedge fund investing matured in 2006. The number of funds with assets exceeding 1 billion dollars has risen fast and the Billion Dollar Club no longer offers much exclusivity. The new frontier is now being explored by a number of firms with assets worth 20 billion dollars, with a few even close to 30 billion dollars. The growth of large hedge funds continued in 2007 at an even faster pace with the top three hedge fund managers all exceeding 30 billion dollars during the first half of the year. A number of top hedge fund firms have also begun to market traditional long-only funds, slowly developing their organizations into fully fledged asset managers.

On the other hand, the total number of new fund launches has dropped meaningfully over the past two years after peaking in 2005. Statistics show that during 2006 start-up activity fell by 25%. Given the first half of 2007 run rate, 2007 should experience a similar decline from the previous year. We estimate that start-up funds received approximately

10–15% of the 118 billion dollars of net flows so far this year (2007). Moreover, as large firms continue to grow, small firms find it harder to attract funds from the increasingly well-educated investor base, and the number of funds shutting down has risen since 2005. For 2007, the hedge fund attrition rate is expected to rise to 12%.

2.2 STYLE DISTRIBUTION

The Credit Suisse/Tremont Hedge Fund Index is the first family of asset weighted indices. The composite index is a basket of 10 alternative styles, namely, Convertible Arbitrage, Short Bias, Event-Driven, Global Macro, Long/Short Equity, Emerging Markets, Fixed Income Arbitrage, Market Neutral, Managed Futures and Multi-Strategy. As of September 2007, the CS/Tremont Index is composed of 455 hedge funds extracted from a database of approximately 5000 funds. According to the promoters, the 'Index represents at least 85% of assets under management in a selection universe for each sector'. So CS indices are appropriate to proxy the style evolution of the biggest funds, i.e. those that will benefit more significantly from the ongoing institutionalization. Table 2.2 exhibits the evolution of the weighting of the alternative styles within the global index from 1997 to 2006.

Since the end of the equity bear market of the early 2000s, assets primarily flew into four groups, Long/Short, Event-Driven, Global Macro and Multi-Strategy funds, which made up over 75% of the industry in 2007. One major reason of this bifurcation is capacity. Macro managers, as well as multi-strategy funds in the arbitrage and event-driven space, due to their often global and multi-disciplinary approach to investing,

Table 2.2 Annual style distribution within the CS/Tremont Hedge Fund Index in percent (%)

	1997	1998	1999	2000	2001	2002	2003	2004	2005	2006	Q2-07
Convert arb.	3.2	3.4	3.4	4.7	6.9	7.4	7.1	4.7	2.4	2.7	2.3
Short bias	0.4	0.6	0.6	0.5	0.2	0.7	0.5	0.5	0.6	0.5	0.5
Emerging mkt	6.6	2.9	2.2	1.6	1.6	2.1	2.4	3.7	5.2	6.9	6.8
Market ntl	1.2	3.1	4.0	5.7	7.1	7.4	5.5	4.4	4.1	5.0	4.7
Event-driven	13.5	17.4	16.1	18.9	25.3	24.2	20.5	21.6	24.2	23.5	25.1
Fixed income	8.4	6.8	5.8	5.1	5.1	5.4	8.5	7.8	7.5	6.3	5.7
Global macro	42.4	35.5	24.4	11	11.3	12.2	11.7	12.7	11.7	11.0	10.6
Long/Short	22.3	27.5	40.70	50.2	39.5	34	27.4	26.3	27.3	29.4	29.4
CTA	2	2.8	2.6	2.0	2.3	3.1	5.1	5.8	5.4	4.8	4.4
Multi-strat.	0.1	0.1	0.1	0.3	0.6	3.5	11.5	12.6	11.7	10.0	10.2

Source: www.hedgefundindex.com

offer significant scalability, with the largest funds above 30 billion dollars. At the same time, Long/Short Equity funds continue to proliferate and the aggregate capacity offered by more than 3000 funds globally is substantial while the hedge funds of emerging markets are back to their level before the 1998 crisis. In contrast, most individual relative value strategies face significant constraints, with many of the best funds having closed to new investors. While capacity remains available, it is limited and often accessible to long-standing well-connected allocators.

2.3   2006–2007 STRUCTURAL DEVELOPMENTS

Due to the rapid ongoing institutionalization, the industry has evolved in a number of ways which include the geographic spread of hedge fund managers, the listing of hedge fund managers on public stock exchanges, the varying use of independent administration, changes in the composition of the fund boards of directors, investment in trade processing computer systems, the increasing attention given to pricing issues and to side pockets.

2.3.1   Geography, Listing, Independent Arbitrators and Back Office

North America has been the historical domicile for most hedge fund managers. However, there has currently been an increase in hedge fund managers setting up offices in London and Geneva, and in some other European countries. In 2007, for a small sample of eligible funds (about 250) for institutional investors (i.e. funds succeeding to comply with a deep due diligence), 63% of the funds are managed from North America, 34% from Europe, and 3% from Asia Pacific and Latin America.

Over the past years, several hedge fund managers have been listing on public exchanges. The main reason cited for such listings is the need to retain staff by giving them share options in the listed management company. The listing of managers can be viewed as a sign that the industry has matured. Moreover, the success of such listings can be viewed as evidence of the market's confidence in the long-term viability of individual hedge funds.

The number of funds that are opting to be independently administered, as opposed to self-administration, has recently increased, especially in the US. This increase can be explained by the demands from institutional investors and the general realization that independent administration is the best practice. On the other hand, some large institutional hedge fund managers moved away from independent administration to self-administration owing to either the high volume of daily transactions or the complexity of the strategy and instruments traded. These managers have built extensive back offices with separate reporting lines for independence. Moreover, a number of administrators are moving away from providing net asset value light services, preferring to provide solely full net asset value services as a mean of managing their risk to hedge funds.

The majority of changes to a fund board of directors during the past year involved fund directors that were affiliated to the manager resigning and being replaced by independent directors. The resignations were explained as necessary to remove potential conflicts of interest and also to preserve the offshore status of the fund. In the next couple of years we are likely to see this trend continuing with the fund directors that are affiliated to the fund administrator giving way to independent directors. Most of the administrators were discontinuing the provision of directors service line to avoid potential conflicts of interests.

Moreover, several managers have invested in integrated front and back office trade processing systems. For funds that trade large volumes of over-the-counter credit derivatives, the major concern has been the backlog in trade confirmations that has been widely reported in the public press. Attempts have been made to alleviate the situation by partially automating the trade confirmation process for the over-the-counter derivatives. The automation of the over-the-counter confirmation process is still in its infancy and not all participants in the process have started using the available tools. The challenge for the next few years is to develop the systems further to facilitate straight through processing and minimize the re-keying of trades.

2.3.2 Pricing and Side Pockets

Pricing and side pockets have been the most discussed topics in hedge funds over the last years. This has been prompted by the increase in the number of illiquid and difficult-to-price over-the-counter transactions executed by hedge funds. Several organizations have produced guidance material in relation to pricing best practice. Pricing best practice includes the drafting of pricing policies covering all instruments traded, implementing independent back office price checks on front office pricing for in-house profit and loss account, independent administrator pricing for month-end net asset value calculations, and obtaining multiple quotes for illiquid or difficult-to-price instruments. Some managers trading illiquid instruments such as loans and private equity have engage independent pricing agents to periodically verify the pricing determined by the manager.

On the other hand, the use of side pockets has become more common. Side pockets are used to separate longer-term investments, generally called special investments in a hedge fund's private placement memorandum, from the typical investments held by the hedge fund. The types of investments held in side pockets may include private investments in public entities (PIPEs), private equity, real estate, or other illiquid and likely hard-to-value investments. Investments in side pockets are made when an investment manager identifies an opportunity to make an investment in a more illiquid investment class, and exchanges a pro-rata portion of each investor's shares into a share class organized for side pockets. Hedge fund managers typically account for these investments under a separate share class, in order to establish terms that are more suitable for the liquidity and pricing limitations of these investment classes.

The terms customarily used for side pockets include exempting the investments from performance fees until the underlying assets are sold, recording the underlying assets at cost for purposes of calculating management fees and reporting net asset values, and prohibiting redemptions from the share class attributed to side pockets until the underlying investment has been liquidated or becomes unrestricted. Carrying side pockets at cost allows hedge fund managers to avoid attempting to price the underlying investments, which may not have a readily available market value. By prohibiting redemptions, hedge fund managers avoid having to potentially sell a long-term investment at a steep discount in order to meet immediate liquidity needs.

Side pockets are normally limited by the private placement memorandum to 20% of a hedge fund's net asset value, but they rarely comprise more than 5% of a hedge fund's assets. Investors cannot purchase investments in a side pocket directly, and are normally not given the option to abstain from investing in side pockets if they are invested in the normal share class.

As approximately 15% of the funds had the ability in 2007 to use side pockets, concerns have arisen about an investment manager's potential misuse of the investment class and the related accounting practices. In particular, the policy of reporting the investments at cost troubles some investors, as they are not able to get a full picture of their investment performance. Furthermore, some commentators believe that hedge fund managers may designate underperforming investments as side pockets, in order to report assets at cost instead of reporting losses. This practice would artificially inflate performance and the associated fees. In addition, the restriction against redeeming shares until a side pocket is sold could cause assets to be locked up beyond an investor's intended investment horizon.

The unique considerations that apply to funds using side pockets should be evaluated on a case-by-case basis. As with any investment, potential investors should conduct proper due diligence to determine whether investing in funds that use side pockets is appropriate for them.

2.4   ARE HEDGE FUNDS BECOMING DECENT?

Concerns have recently been raised about the risks that hedge funds pose to the markets and the protection of investors. Hedge funds are currently restricted to wealthy and presumably sophisticated individuals. However, we are seeing retail investors investing indirectly in hedge funds through funds of funds. The US Securities and Exchange Commission (SEC) recently proposed to raise the minimum net worth requirement for eligibility to invest in hedge funds. The SEC's attempt for a direct regulation of hedge funds in 2006 was overturned by the courts.

In its June 2006 *Review*, the European Central Bank (ECB) stated outright, for the first time, that hedge funds represented a major risk to financial stability. A year earlier, Franz Müntefering, chairman of Germany's Social Democratic Party (SPD), had compared hedge funds to locusts falling on companies and stripping them bare, following Deutsche Borse's failed bid to buy the London Stock Exchange. These events have heightened existing suspicions regarding hedge funds. Is there anyone who has not heard of LTCM and its 2.1 billion dollar loss in August 1998? And what about the headline-grabbing frauds at hedge funds such as Manhattan? Given examples like these, it is easy to brand hedge funds as the black sheep of the market economy and deduce that institutional investors should stay away from investing in alternative funds. But that would be forgetting too fast the contribution that this special type of investment vehicle makes to both stock market mechanisms and other channels of corporate financing.

2.4.1   Improved Market Efficiency

One of the main sources of distrust of hedge funds is short selling, the transaction most widely associated with alternative strategies. Admittedly, at first glance, the idea of making a profit on the decline in the share price of a distressed company hardly seems compatible with playing a beneficial role in the market. And yet, it is.

A number of university studies[3] reveal that companies that had succeeded in restricting short selling of their stock underperformed the index by an average of 24% in the following year. By rapidly factoring in all the information available, short selling helps to determine the right price. Setting a fair price for overpriced stocks undoubtedly leads to higher volatility in the short term. But stability in itself is not an aim if it comes from market incompleteness, which, at its worst, could hide fraud or financial manipulation. Such was the case for a significant number of the companies opposed to short selling that were included in the studies.

Furthermore, short selling is not confined to a single speculative bet that a given stock will fall, but is part of a more subtle investment strategy. Relative-value strategies based on buying underpriced products and short selling others that are overpriced provide the means of correcting valuation errors between financial assets. A rapid reduction in market anomalies is one of the characteristics of efficient markets. This explains why Professor Owen Lamont concluded his hearing by the Senate Committee on the Judiciary on June 2006 with the following recommendations:

> My opinion, therefore, is that we need to change the current lopsided system that discourages short selling. First, in the narrow technical arena, we should consider ways to make the equity lending system work better. [. . .] Second, in the broader arena, we should continue to encourage the development of institutions that channel capital into short selling. [. . .] Third, it would be useful to consider ways of protecting independent analysts from lawsuits. [. . .] Congress and the SEC will continue to hear complaints from companies about short sellers. [. . . , but] when you hear companies complain, keep in mind that short sellers are often the good guys.

In fact, modern portfolio theory is only valid if short selling is allowed,[4] which seems hard to reconcile with the ECB's claim that short selling increases instability over the medium and long terms.

---

[3] See, for example, Lamont (2003) and Ofek et al. (2003).

[4] The separation theorem and the creation of a synthetic beta-neutral asset as a substitute for the risk-free asset are only possible with short selling. The latter is thus a great help in the financial asset valuation model. More intuitively, one can understand that an optimum with a constraint (no short selling allowed) cannot be more efficient than an optimum without a constraint. It is therefore amazing that the keenest supporters of the index-linked approach are sometimes against short selling, even though the market portfolio might thus be suboptimal.

2.4.2 Transfer of Risk

Another way of perceiving hedge funds' contribution to the financial markets is to break down their performance into risk premiums (a typical risk management approach). Ironically, for vehicles named for their ability to reduce and control risk, hedge funds use strategies that can be heavily exposed to risks other than the direction of equity/bond markets (alternative beta).

For example, in bond arbitrage, hedge funds accept to buy the least liquid bonds of international institutions and then hedge against risk by short-selling derivatives based on more liquid bonds. In traditional mergers and acquisitions, hedge funds assumed the risk of the transaction's falling through, whereas many institutional investors were bound by internal or external regulations to sell their position as soon as a transaction was announced. In some currency-based macro strategies, the managers invest in currencies with a high interest rate, while financing this purchase by borrowing in a currency with a low interest rate. This approach implies an exposure to devaluation risk, and the higher the interest-rate differential, the higher the risk. Long/short equity strategies take a global liquidity premium, due to the scarcity of small and medium capitalization equities available for short selling. Lastly, the value-versus-growth bias of some long/short equity funds and statistical arbitrage funds entails a recession-risk premium, as Fama and Fench (1992) have shown.

It thus becomes apparent that, by virtue of their alternative strategies, hedge funds shoulder the risk that certain institutional or private investors wish to transfer. For that very reason, many market players see hedge funds as insurers. Furthermore, for the investors lending the shares all short selling can be viewed as partial insurance against an exponential slump in the price. The reason being, that following a sharp price decline, demand for return of the shares that were loaned prompts hedge funds to buy them on the market, which lessens or stops the decline. This mechanism benefits the lender even more by sparing him the cost of specific protection such as buying a put option on the loaned security.

By favouring risk transfer, hedge funds help to improve the market's ability to answer the economy's needs. That could be seen to imply the danger of systemic market risk if a major 'insurer' were to default, with LTCM's being the most striking example. Fortunately, risk-management techniques and the regulations governing suppliers of leverage have come a long way since August 1998. The ECB and former Fed chairman, Alan Greenspan, agree that even when hedge funds are major players in a market, the leverage and concentration are very different from the environment in which LTCM operated.[5] Therefore, there is little likelihood that one or even several hedge funds could cause a system-wide tremor.

2.4.3 Liquidity Suppliers

By correcting valuation discrepancies and enabling the transfer of risks that others may wish to avoid, hedge funds bring liquidity to the financial markets. They also play an active role in the economy, by offering companies direct financing: some of them have taken over from banks, who can be a bit stingy when it comes to granting credit to medium-size businesses. More recently, hedge funds have increased their exposure to private equity, particularly to US start-ups working in the life sciences. For example, Microbia Inc., Merrimack Pharmaceuticals Inc. and Fibrogen Inc. are said to have raised more than 120 million dollars from hedge funds in 2006.

In the US, many hedge funds invest in companies that have been authorized to suspend their debt servicing by filing for Chapter 11 bankruptcy protection while reorganizing under court supervision. Indeed, thanks to their great flexibility and the absence of regulation, hedge funds are often the last recourse of businesses on the brink of bankruptcy. In actual fact, they play the key role in the recycling of distressed companies, by enabling them to restructure and take on a new lease of life.

Improved liquidity can jeopardize the economy if it comes from a concentrated source: if the source withdraws, it can trigger a major liquidity crisis. That set-up is exactly what we are seeing today, since 70% of global liquidity is coming from the emerging countries, due to the accumulation of foreign currency reserves by Asia and the commodity-producing countries. Whether we worry about this or see it as the sign of a major real shift in the global economy, there is no way we can attribute it to hedge funds.

---

[5] Readers interested should refer to Lowenstein (2000), a fascinating account of the fund and its two Nobel Prize winners. The book describes LTCM as a fabulous money machine: before 1998, brokers and bankers would have done anything to have hedge funds as borrowers. It is hard to imagine the players who had to pay for the LTCM collapse repeating the same errors.

Furthermore, the increase in illiquid financial assets held has been accompanied by a decline in the average redemption frequency that hedge funds offer their investors. From that viewpoint, risk has not risen, contrary to what the ECB might think.

2.4.4 Captive Capital?

In reality, hedge funds have not only realigned the liquidity offered to their shareholders with that of their investments, but have often imposed more restrictive redemption conditions than their portfolio would seem to require. For example, some long/short equity managers who deal only in large capitalizations have introduced lock-up periods (minimum length of participation in the fund) of 1 to 3 years.

Most investors understand when redemption restrictions serve to ensure that the fund's liquidity corresponds to that of the underlying,[6] but they have trouble accepting restrictions that favour the hedge fund manager, as in the preceding case. Furthermore, initially, the notion of captive capital hardly seems to tally with the idea that hedge funds are beneficial to the market. Here too, intuition proves wrong.

In reality, the deterioration in the investment conditions offered by hedge funds is completely in line with the current situation in the industry, even without the effects related to SEC registration. Although it is impossible to conduct an in-depth survey covering all hedge fund positions, various partial analyses and examination of the portfolios of funds in 2006 reveal increasing similarity between hedge funds' positions. The ECB has come to the same conclusion, albeit not by the most appropriate means.[7] It fears that there is a systemic risk: that of massive redemption by hedge funds. However, this scenario of massive redemption at the worst possible moment is incompatible with the preservation measures taken by hedge fund managers in restricting liquidity. In other words, the deterioration in the liquidity conditions offered by hedge

---

[6] Some hedge funds offer more favourable liquidity than the underlying portfolio. If, in that case, for whatever reason, a majority of investors wish to exit at the same time, the manager finds himself forced to sell the positions at prices significantly lower than the true value and thus prejudices the interests of all the shareholders (those that exit and those that stay). Nevertheless, some investors prefer to assume high exposure to this kind of liquidity risk and subscribe, for example, for shares in arbitrage funds offering monthly redemption. Similarly, investors in illiquid strategies through managed accounts have only the illusion of liquidity.

[7] The European Central Bank bases itself on the increase in correlation, using methodology that EDHEC criticizes strongly in a note entitled 'Disorderly exits from crowded trades' – a reply to the ECB's statement on hedge funds'. However, contrary to what the note says, there is a significant increase in short-term correlations, which stems not only from similar exposure to the same risk factors or from increasing correlation between risk factors, but from increasing similarity between hedge fund positions, mainly in directional and event-driven strategies.

funds not only protects the funds' shareholders, but reduces systemic risk.[8]

In truth, only the best managers have the clout needed to impose significant lock-ups on their clients. And thus, like the old adage that 'Only the rich get richer', the best managers are also the most likely to be the best tomorrow: thanks to their restricted liquidity, they will be best placed to profit from a market reversal after a shock. This has been recognized by the funds of funds that have had to restrict their products' liquidity conditions to maintain portfolio quality. Some have even launched products with hedge funds with a lock-up of at least three years.

2.4.5　The Black Sheep of Capitalism?

And yet hedge funds still suffer from a bad reputation; this is clear from the strong reactions to activists. However, as with the other strategies, the distrust is not to do with fears for the economy. What was found shocking about the scotched merger between the German and UK bourses was the failure to take any account of either the European political project or the German process of agreement between trade unions and management. By contrast, the hedge fund minority holders in Deutsche Borse clearly succeeded in rallying a majority of shareholders, who, in their interest, refused the merger.

Questioning the wisdom of a shareholder decision goes beyond economic considerations. Whether one adopts the perspective (distinction of levels) of Comte-Sponville (2004) or that of Talcott Parson, the answer is the same. The aim of capitalism is to reward the shareholders as effectively as possible. Political, moral and social issues are limitations that can only come from outside the system.

Viewed in that light, hedge funds are not the black sheep of capitalism, but one of its pillars. For the markets – that prime source of corporate financing – their contribution is clear: they improve efficiency, provide better liquidity and ease risk transfer. For the hedge fund investor, they have already proved their appeal, whether as diversification in a traditional portfolio or as a substitute. And there is no reason to stop the ongoing institutionalization of the alternative industry.

---

[8] But other factors explain why increasing participation by hedge funds in a market segment is not synonymous with increasing systemic risk. First, as mentioned earlier, the conditions are not in place for another LTCM debacle. Second, the similarity between positions does not signify similarity between strategies, which are often uncoordinated.

However, while some politicians continue to shift the blame of the major financial crises to hedge funds, displaying their poor understanding of the financial markets,[9] concerns have been raised about the risks that hedge funds pose to the protection of retail investors as they are investing indirectly in hedge funds through funds of funds. While the future regulation of the hedge funds industry is uncertain,[10] we may point out that the European regulators concerns with this indirect access to hedge funds is inconsistent with the decision of the Committee of European Securities Regulators in July 2007 to include a particular type of funds of funds (so-called investable indices[11]) in the list of UCITS III eligible assets.

2.5 FUNDS OF HEDGE FUNDS PERSISTENCE

Because of the massive institutional money inflows, hedge funds have, since 2000, adopted increasingly restrictive risk management procedures and have standardized their multi-strategy fund of funds mandates. These two signs of a more institutional approach are seen most clearly in the shift in some of the funds of funds' persistence characteristics. Persistence may be defined as the ability of those managers who delivered the highest returns in the past to continue doing so in the future.[12]

---

[9] On 16 August 2007, in comments on the subprime crisis, Nicolas Sarkozy said, 'We cannot go on like this, with a few hedge funds borrowing from anyone, whoever it may be, at any price, not knowing who takes the final risk, under any conditions'. One month later, N. Amenc, Professor of Finance and Director of the EDHEC Risk and Asset Management Research Centre provided a response to the political leader's blame. As stated in the press release announcing the issue of Amenc (2007):

Hedge funds are clearly not to blame for the subprime crisis and the contagion that has spread to all segments of the credit market. The crisis is ultimately more a crisis of confidence in financial information and the market's capacity to evaluate the solvency of credit institutions. It was not the losses on the subprime or credit markets that forced the central banks to intervene, but an interbank liquidity crisis that had nothing to do with hedge funds. By placing the blame on the wrong parties, European leaders and regulators may very well fail to take on board the true dimension of the subprime crisis, which is above all a regulatory crisis.

[10] Nevertheless, some public officials have made statements suggesting that they do not favour direct legislative regulation after the SEC's attempt for a direct regulation of hedge funds in 2006 was overturned by the courts.

[11] See Chapter 4.

[12] Performance persistence in finance has been the topic of an impressive bulk of papers. In the case of traditional funds, while there is no unanimous agreement, most studies reveal that only the worst-performing managers have shown a tendency in the past to remain the worst (Carhart, 1997; Porter and Trifts, 1998). In bond funds, there may be a slight tendency for the best managers to remain the best (Kahn and Rudd, 1995). As for hedge funds, the results depend upon the model used and can be contradictory. Argawal and Naik (2000a) highlight the fact that in hedge funds, as in traditional funds, the worst performers display persistence. On the other hand, Capoccii and Hubner (2004) demonstrate that the most mediocre performers remain the most consistent, and Kat and Manexe (2003) prove that it is the risk level and the correlation with the markets, and not the return, that is persistent.

The funds of funds example used below is taken from the *Invest Hedge* database, because this base classifies the investment vehicles by strategy, reflecting the types of hedge fund accessible through the funds of funds. One can thus extract for study 382 funds of funds investing in all the strategies from 2000 to 2006. Surprisingly, while this is akin to a portfolio built up from allocations to hedge funds following different strategies, the funds of funds are often studied *en bloc* or with one classification per profile (low/medium/high). And yet, as early as 2000, 42% of funds of funds specialized in just a few strategies. While the hedge fund strategy classifications currently available contain inherent weaknesses, they are the only means of comparing the issues between funds of funds.

2.5.1 Conditional Persistence

Statistically, long-term persistence can be tested by separating the seven years between 2000 and 2006 into two periods and separating the funds of funds sample into either two subgroups (50% constitutes by best performing hedge funds versus the rest), or four subgroups (4 quartiles). In the first case, the methodology used is the cross-product ratio (Christensen, 1990). Let us consider, for each period, the funds of funds whose returns were above the median (winners, expressed as w) and those whose returns were below the median (losers, expressed as l). ww is then the number of funds that ranked in the first two quartiles over the two periods and wl is the number of winners from the first period that ranked among the worst performers in the second period. The cross-product ratio (cpr) is defined as the ratio of the product of the funds that remain in the same category (the number of those winning in both periods multiplied by the number losing in both periods) and the product of the number of funds changing category:

$$cpr = \frac{ww \cdot ll}{wl \cdot lw}$$

The log ratio is governed by a normal law, i.e.

$$\ln(cpr) \sim N\left(0, \frac{1}{ww} + \frac{1}{ll} + \frac{1}{lw} + \frac{1}{wl}\right) = N\left(0, \sigma^2_{\ln(cpr)}\right)$$

When there is a tendency to remain in the same category over the long term, the *cpr* coefficient should be significantly greater than

1. Statistically, persistence is accepted with a confidence level of 95% if

$$z\text{stat} = \frac{\ln(cpr)}{\sigma^2_{\ln(cpr)}} > 1.96$$

Persistence by quartile is measured by means of a chi-squared test. A 4×4 double-entry table is constructed from the sample under observation. The idea of the test is to calculate a distance, expressed as χ^2_{calc}, between the table derived from the sample and that of a population with no persistence. This second table will be such that the variable for position in terms of quartile during the first period and the variable for position in terms of quartile during the second period are independent. The distance expressed as χ^2_{calc} and governed by a χ^2 law with 9 degrees of freedom[13] (the independance is rejected with a confidence level of 95% if $\chi^2_{\text{calc}} > 16.91$) is defined by the following relationship:

$$\chi^2_{\text{stat}} = \sum_{i=1}^{4} \sum_{j=1}^{4} \frac{\left(n_{ij} - \left(n_{i\cdot} \cdot n_{\cdot j}/n\right)\right)^2}{n_{i\cdot} \cdot n_{\cdot j}/n}$$

where n_{ij} indicates the observed line i and column j frequencies, $n_{i\cdot}$ the line frequencies and $n_{\cdot j}$ the column frequencies.[14]

Table 2.3 provides the results of the various statistical tests when one considers two periods of equal length (January 2000 to June 2003, and July 2003 to December 2006). Statistically, there is no long-term unconditional persistence among the multi-strategy funds of funds in terms of those outperforming. For the quartiles, the independence is rejected mainly because of the funds that delivered the lowest returns in the first period and then delivered the highest returns in the following period. This result, which seems surprising at first, is explained by the fact that the period under study spanned a first phase where equities were falling (January 2000 to September 2002) and a second phase where they were rising.

The difference between the bull- and bear-market periods may seem surprising in funds of funds whose allocation to hedge funds supposedly

---

[13] If the number of funds of funds considered for the first period differs from the number for the second period, one must consider the theoretical conditional distribution with a probability of 25% for each quartile of the second period. Such a test has a degree of freedom of 12. The results are similar to those shown here.

[14] An explicit approach (conditional or not) would require a model that took into account the complexity of the dependence of the funds of funds (and thus the hedge funds) upon the equity markets. In that case, the persistence would not be confined to the manager's alpha, but would include his skill in managing his beta. This type of analysis should be based on approaches such as those used by Henriksson and Merton (1981).

Table 2.3   Results of the *cpr* and adjustment tests

	Per half		Per quartile	
	cpr	z_{stat}	χ^2_{stat}	Conclusions
Equal periods: Jan-00 to Jun-03 vs Jul-03 to Dec-06	0.78	−0.73	14.50	The independence is not rejected but the bottom quartile displays a high frequency of funds returning to the top quartile and a very low frequency of those remaining in the bottom quartile.
Bear vs Bull Market: Jan-00 to Jun-03 vs Jul-03 to Dec-06	0.45	−2.34	22.47	The independence is rejected mainly because of the bottom quartile, where the frequency of funds returning to the top quartile is too high and that of funds remaining in the bottom quartile is too low.
Bear Market: Jan-00 to Apr-01 vs May-01 to Sep-02	2.57	2.82	35.81	The independence is rejected mainly owing to the bottom quartile, where the frequency of funds remaining there is too high and that of funds returning to the top quartile is too low.
Bull Market: Oct-02 to Oct-04 vs Nov-04 to Dec-06	2.86	4.01	46.18	The independence is rejected mainly because of the top quartile, where the frequency of funds remaining there is too high and that of funds returning to the bottom quartile is too low.

have an absolute-return target. But bear in mind, first, that we are concerned here with ranking and not performance. This conditional persistence does not reduce the diversification of the hedge funds compared with a traditional portfolio, since the decorrelation comes from the dynamic management of exposures to the global markets, together with the ability to isolate stocks (rising or falling) and specific exposures (the hedge funds' renowned beta).

The second point is that the link between the equity market and the persistence of funds of funds reflects the composition of the hedge funds universe. As a reminder, the long/short funds, which represented 50% of hedge funds in 2000 and 30% in 2007, invest solely in equities. Similarly, the event-driven strategies, which accounted for 23% of hedge funds in 2007, focus predominantly on the equity markets, and some of the substrategies, such as merger arbitrage, have seen their directional exposure soaring. Furthermore, in the CS/Tremont index, where 22%

of the hedge fund strategies are classified as arbitrage, this common designation implies that they will offer complete neutrality. In reality, arbitrage portfolio's exposures are rarely perfectly hedged, for three reasons. First, absolute neutrality proves to be restrictive across a broad range of factors[15] and only strategies based on quantitative models or pair trading can comply simultaneously with all these constraints.[16] Moreover, some arbitrage strategies exploit opportunities where a market segment's risk premium is relatively high compared with the premium available in another, similar segment. This type of comparative advantage can be used to set up a relative value position. Nevertheless, the exposure is not totally neutral, since the segments differ. Furthermore, other strategies under the arbitrage label are not aimed at maintaining a purely neutral exposure. The objective of the two pillars of the portfolio is not to cancel each other out, but to obtain exposure to factors that would be inaccessible using traditional strategies. These specific exposures are sometimes called 'alternative exposures'. The transaction provides access to a financial asset formerly included in another asset. In this case, there is no longer any real notion of arbitrage, but rather, true directional exposure to rises and falls in synthetic financial assets. Finally, the hedging can sometimes prove unintentionally imperfect because the underlying risks have not been correctly perceived.[17]

The hedge fund strategies are thus not exempt from the influence of the equity market, whether that influence be direct (dynamic, non-linear directional exposure to the equity market), indirect (exposure to alternative risk factors with more or less complex links to the equity market) or even temporary. A fund of funds manager thus has only two ways of eliminating the effects of the equity markets when comparing his performance with that of the competition.

The first way is to find a large enough number of niche strategy hedge funds that are more profitable than the equity markets even when the latter are rising, and to construct a portfolio solely with this type of investment vehicles, reviewing the selection continuously. Concurrently, the manager must avoid high exposure to liquidity risks, and, more generally, keep the portfolio well diversified. One can seriously question

---

[15] Absolute neutrality can prove too restrictive. A total absence of directional exposure would require, among other things, neutrality in terms of geographic regions, sectors, style and credit, and also durations, in the case of bonds, statistical sensitivity to market data, in the case of equities, changes in volatility regimes, and so on.

[16] Historically, these strategies have always played a fairly marginal role in the hedge funds universe.

[17] That was what really happened to the funds with positions in collateralized debt obligations (CDOs) in May 2005 – the hedging in place did not work.

whether such an approach is really feasible, since the above conditions smack of the text in certain funds of funds' marketing presentations to inexperienced investors. Furthermore, this kind of mandate scarcely seems compatible with a hedge funds industry where the money flows from institutional investors have radically reduced the duration of the niche strategies' profitability and made questions of capacity central to manager selection. Clearly, while this type of multi-strategy funds of funds mandate is now possible, it applies to a limited number of investment vehicles with limited assets under management. Thus, it cannot be expected to have a significant impact on persistence analyses covering a very broad sample.

Second, one could also obtain unconditional persistence with multi-strategy funds of funds capable of managing their strategic exposures very aggressively; for example, by going from an allocation of 100% long/short funds during bull markets to 100% macro when the markets are restructuring. However, this type of vehicle is fading out, since institutions prefer funds of funds that are well diversified across all the strategies, while overweighing specific allocations according to market cycles. This type of multi-strategy funds of funds is easier to assess and compare, and avoids the risk of major losses entailed in high strategic concentrations.

The conditional persistence of multi-strategy funds of funds compared with the equity markets has thus been strengthened by the conventionalization of the hedge funds industry. Nowadays, institutional investors' mandates are fairly homogeneous and they apply somehow benchmarking methodology to hedge funds. But the declining heterogeneity of hedge fund mandates has also led to a reduction of the interquartile spreads between yearly returns.

2.5.2 Interquartile Spreads

For veteran players, the arrival of the institutional investor on the hedge fund scene signalled the 'pasteurisation of hedge funds'. As far as we know, Georges Karlweis, one of the founders of the fund of hedge funds industry, was also one of the first to coin this term, in an interview published in the July 2002 issue of *InvestHedge*:

> The way the modern-day hedge fund manager manages a portfolio has become a bit pasteurised. There can be benefits of pasteurisation. One is that you sleep better at night. Years ago I remember a journalist asked a manager how he managed to sleep at night with the amount of risk he was taking. He replied: 'Don't ask

Table 2.4   Annual spread between the first 25% multi-strategy funds of funds and the last 25% funds of funds

	1998	1999	2000	2001	2002	2003	2004	2005	2006
Interquartile spread	9.03%	15.64%	9.81%	5.36%	5.10%	4.54%	3.83%	4.34%	4.19%

> me. Ask my investors.' But there are also costs associated with the pasteurisation process, most notably in returns (. . .). Now few people take the amount of risk they took in the past. Their positions rarely exceed 5% of the fund. In the past, people had positions that accounted for 60% of the portfolio. (. . .) Investors had a far higher risk tolerance.

This interview led *EuroHedge* editor Neil Wilson to conclude:

> Risk control is working, but is it working too well.

The pasteurization of hedge funds leads to less heterogeneous annual returns: the use of risk management policies reduces both risk-taking – with a corresponding decline in the frequency of extraordinary gains – and significant aggregate losses. The hedge funds industry's annual return distribution tails have flattened out.

Naturally, this shift in the hedge funds' approach indirectly impacts the multi-strategy funds of funds. Table 2.4 gives the annual return spreads in basis points (bps) between the best fund in the bottom quartile and the worst fund in the top quartile.[18] This interquartile spread has clearly narrowed over time, since it contracted from 903 bps in 1998 and 1 564 bps in 1999 to 417 bps in 2006. In relative terms, this corresponds to a contraction of 54% and 73% compared with 1998 and 1999 respectively. No doubt part of the absolute difference between 1999 and 2006 reflects the general level of hedge fund performance (and thus the performance of multi-strategy funds of funds), but the effect on relative performance is still more striking. The interquartile spread represented 77% of the average returns of funds of funds in 1999 (548% in 1998) but only 42% in 2006, i.e. a relative contraction of 45% (92% in 1998).

Nevertheless, while interquartile spreads are contracting as a result of the institutionalization of hedge funds, 2007 should prove the exception to the rule[19]: the reason being the congruence of two extraordinary

---

[18] This type of approach should not hide that within the last quartile, heterogeneity of returns is particularly high.

[19] First estimates indicate that the interquartile spread may raise to 6.40%.

events. First, the inter-sectoral heterogeneity of equity returns was exceptionally high in 2007; second, the collapse of the US subprime market was a free lunch for many hedge funds. In 2007, those funds of funds investing in managers with short subprime bets delivered substantially higher returns. But again, the performance differential created by the mortgage market crisis was an extraordinary event that should not contribute to the heterogeneity of multi-strategy funds of funds in the future.

Consequently, for the managers of multi-strategy funds of funds, the contraction in the interquartile spreads is set to last; and given the increasingly tough competitive environment, this parameter is becoming a key consideration in portfolio management. Lhabitant and Learned (2003) show that theoretically a portfolio of 10 managers applying different strategies could obtain optimum diversification. But then, 400 bp represent the contribution of two managers suffering a drawdown of 10% to 20% (taking into account the opportunity cost). In reality, there are very few multi-strategy portfolios investing in less than 20 managers,[20] as this type of theoretical result is subject to a strong survivorship bias and does not consider operational and structural risk. Nevertheless, one often sees multi-strategy funds of funds that are composed partly of a highly diversified portfolio and partly of a few allocations concentrated on very risky hedge funds; in which case, these riskier managers can easily account for the 400 bps.

Today's market environment therefore argues in favour of portfolio management that considers that funds of funds may move from the top to the bottom quartile only because of one or two positions. As return attribution is an ex-post measure, the portfolio's current risk attribution is an ex-ante indicator of this loss potential. Assessing portfolios in terms not of money allocation, but rather of risk allocation is the keystone of risk budgeting. But taking this type of approach requires a preliminary step: an efficient synthetic measure the portfolio's risk. The aim of Style and Implicit Value-at-Risk is clearly to fulfil to that need.

---

[20] Generally these investment vehicles have the special mandate to take some concentration risk: it may be quite profitable as long as a mistake is not made. We see also these types of multi-manager portfolios when the selection of the hedge funds and the portfolio management is performed by the same person, as denying the benefit of diversification requires a lot of (self-)confidence.

3
Heterogeneity of Hedge Funds

It is a well-known fact that hedge funds do not constitute a homogeneous group: alternative investment strategies are varied and managers have a large degree of flexibility in the investment processes as well as in the financial instruments employed. In addition, whichever strategy is followed, the manager's ability contributes to generate profits.

The high level of heterogeneity between hedge funds is obvious when trying to find a common definition. While investment in alternative funds is nowadays widely accepted in institutional portfolios, many different definitions co-exist and none benefits from a consensus. Further evidence of the heterogeneity between hedge funds is the difficulty to find a common classification of investment styles. In 2003, the AIMA (the Alternative Investment Management Association Ltd) set up a think tank to tackle the standard classification of hedge funds. The members comprised five highly regarded researchers and 72 hedge fund professionals. A survey revealed that over 50% of investors used their own classification system and that there was no strong consensus among the others regarding external classification. The situation has barely changed since.

For a long time, it was believed that each manager had its own style and there was as many strategies as managers. Obviously, in 2007, with over 10 000 hedge funds available, identifying each manager as having a specific style can no longer be justified. On the other hand, believing that a classification with 10 styles encompasses all the alternative strategies may appear a bit naive. Who would believe that 10 indicators are enough to represent the diversity of the worldwide traditional investment styles? Why should we impose such a restrictive classification to managers that benefit from a high level of freedom in their mandates, in the financial instrument they use and in the way they manage their portfolio? This explains why the MSCI group, when launching their family of alternative style investments in 2002, provided a stratification that could account for more than 120 classes.

The high level of heterogeneity between hedge funds has many implications in the statistical approach for hedge funds as we will see in the later chapters: absence of representative active indices, failure of passive indices and of any explicit modelling of alternative betas. But also, the heterogeneity manifests itself through the absence of a good restrictive classification.

3.1 TESTING SAMPLE

Consider the classification used for the CS/Tremont alternative investment styles indices and a sample composed by 1962 hedge funds with a three-year track at the end of 2006. This data is extracted from the testing sample that is used throughout this book and built from three hedge funds commercial databases (Altvest, HedgeFundIntelligence, Tass – including Tass Graveyards) gathering data from January 1994 to December 2006. The simple union of the three databases covers 15 909 investment vehicles. Two filters are applied to this large set of data. First, all funds of funds are removed from the sample. Second, all the redundant information is erased: when funds are reporting to more than one database, only one occurrence is kept. Finally, only the relevant information is kept: when several currency classes are available, only the US$ class is maintained. Classes that differ only in terms of fees are removed. Moreover, when a fund has an LP version and an Ltd version, the onshore vehicle is excluded unless the track is significantly longer. Finally, hedge funds belonging to the UBP Approved List that do not report to any database are added. Overall, the sample reduces to 5675 fundamentally different hedge funds. Investment vehicles with a short track record within the sample are not excluded; this implies that the number of returns available each month varies not only because of new funds but also because of exiting funds. Table 3.1 tells the story.

On average, the hedge funds of the sample exhibit a track of 59.85 monthly returns while this number is 80.83 for hedge funds that provide at least more than 36 monthly returns. Moreover, 987 hedge funds exhibit at least 136 monthly return testing periods while the 238 hedge funds that continuously provided from January 1994 to December 2006 constitute the Platinum sample. As a result, the testing sample enables 170 108 regressions on a three-year time window.

Each hedge fund from the sample is mapped into its category according to its classification from the database.[1] Table 3.2 provides the annual style distribution of the testing period.

---

[1] The authors want to thank Yves Hennard of the UBP Alternative Investment Quantitative Team for providing the automated classification mapping process for each database.

Table 3.1   Number of monthly returns of the testing sample

Date	Number of monthly returns	Average number of funds per month
1994	9626	802
1995	12 132	1011
1996	14 516	1210
1997	17 006	1417
1998	19 800	1650
1999	22 426	1869
2000	25 145	2095
2001	28 138	2345
2002	32 623	2719
2003	37 502	3125
2004	42 662	3555
2005	45 135	3761
2006	38 030	3169
Total	339 649	2177

3.2   SMOOTHING EFFECT OF A RESTRICTIVE CLASSIFICATION

An efficient classification is characterized by a high level of homogeneity within each group and a high level of heterogeneity between groups. For each of the two dimensions of any classification, we can define a specific indicator based on correlations. Remember that the correlation measures the strength of the linear relationship between two variables. It does not depend on the level of volatility or the average of each variable. Consider manager A and manager B performing exactly with the same kind of strategy but with a different level of leverage. The

Table 3.2   Annual style distribution of the testing periods in percent (%)

	1997	1998	1999	2000	2001	2002	2003	2004	2005	2006
Convertible arb.	3.9	4.0	4.0	4.4	4.4	4.2	4.1	4.2	4.0	3.8
Dedicated short bias	1.5	1.4	1.1	1.3	1.1	1.0	1.0	0.8	0.6	0.6
Emerging markets	8.1	8.6	8.3	8.6	7.7	7.3	6.9	6.0	5.3	5.5
Equity market neutral	2.6	3.0	3.4	3.0	3.3	3.6	3.6	3.8	4.3	4.5
Event-driven	10.9	11.2	11.6	11.3	11.2	10.8	10.4	10.4	11.0	11.7
Fixed income	4.1	4.7	4.7	4.7	5.1	5.3	5.1	5.2	5.4	5.7
Global macro	8.8	8.3	7.8	6.7	5.8	6.0	5.9	6.0	6.2	6.2
Long/Short	34.1	34.9	37.4	39.8	42.3	43.8	45.8	47.4	46.7	45.4
Managed futures	21.2	18.4	15.9	14.2	12.8	11.5	10.5	9.7	9.4	9.2
Multi-strategy	4.7	5.4	6.0	6.0	6.2	6.7	6.6	6.4	7.1	7.5

historical track of both managers will exhibit various levels of volatility with a significative correlation (or various levels of 'beta' with respect to the strategy). Moreover, if manager A is able to outperform manager B due to extra skill, when exposed to the same strategy risk factors, the correlation is high while the 'alpha' regarding the strategy of each one strongly differs. So correlation is both intuitive and provides a rather good indicator to track managers exposed to the same risk factors, even though we will later see a more accurate measure.

Let us define the average intra-correlation as the mean correlation between returns of all pairwise combinations of different hedge funds within the same group. The more homogeneous the group, the higher the intra-correlation will be. This indicator also tends to privilege a very large number of groups composed by the two managers exhibiting the higher correlations. The weakness of such a classification may be groups that do not differ significantly from the others. So consider the average of inter-correlations as the mean correlation of all pairwise combinations of hedge funds of one group with hedge funds not belonging to the same group. This measure reflects the proximity between each group and the other groups.[2]

A good classification provides both a high average intra-correlation and a low average silhouette and/or a low inter-correlation.

For each category, Table 3.3 provides the value of the average intra-correlation, the average inter-correlation as well as the percentage of the inter-correlations that are superior to the average correlation within the group.

The average intra-correlation rises to 0.61 with Short Bias managers and to 0.46 for Convertible Arbitrage funds. Both figures are much higher than the average inter-correlation. However, these two investment styles together represent less than 5% of the sample. For the other strategies, the average correlation within a group are below 0.4, with the figures of Equity Market Neutral and Fixed Income Arbitrage (10.5% of the funds) below 0.1. Statistically, the average intra-correlation and the average inter-correlations are significantly different for each strategy.

The overall average intra-correlation (i.e. the average of all the 10 intra-correlation or the average of all pairwise combinations of hedge

---

[2] However, this indicator may be biased. Consider for instance that each group is very similar to another one but different from all the others. The similarity of each pair of similar groups is diluted in the dissimilarity with the other groups. So the indicator that avoids this pitfall would be the average correlation of each group with the closest group. This is exactly the idea of the average silhouette as introduced by Kaufman and Rousseeuw (1990) and used later.

Table 3.3 Average intra-correlations, average inter-correlations for the CS/Tremont classification on 1962 hedge funds

Alternative style	% of hedge funds	Average intra-correlation	Average inter correlation	% of inter-correlations larger than the average intra-correlation
Convertible arb.	3.9%	0.46	0.19	12
Dedicated short Bias	0.7%	0.61	−0.27	0
Emerging markets	5.6%	0.37	0.24	32
Market neutral	4.7%	0.08	0.11	54
Event-driven	12.1%	0.32	0.23	38
Fixed income	5.8%	0.08	0.11	54
Global macro	5.4%	0.16	0.17	51
Long/Short	45.4%	0.30	0.21	38
Managed futures	8.4%	0.31	0.18	30
Multi-strategy	8.1%	0.29	0.24	43

funds within the same group) is 0.29. While this number is significantly different from the average correlation of 0.22 between returns of all pairwise combination of different hedge funds,[3] we may be a bit disappointed that a stratification of the sample into 10 categories used by one of the most important families of indices improved the average correlation only by 0.07 in absolute terms and still remains below 0.30.

This low homogeneity within the groups is accompanied with a low heterogeneity between groups: for 8 out of 10 strategies, 30% to 54% of the inter-correlations are superior to the average intra-correlation. These combined disappointing results may be explained by three elements:

- Some hedge funds managers did not classify their funds correctly or have changed styles without warning the database promoters: most database providers tend to accept hedge fund managers' self-proclaimed strategy with no check for consistency or historical changes.
- The classification process performed by the database as well as the filter used to consolidate the different databases contain some mistakes.
- Groups are not well specified because the classification is unable to reflect the high level of heterogeneity of hedge funds.

In fact, only the third element really matters. Indeed, consider the following statistical supervised classification: each hedge fund is attributed

---

[3] Whatever the group, i.e. the average of 1 923 741 correlations.

to the strategy whose CS/Tremont index exhibits the highest correlation. Applied to the CS/Tremont classification and to our sample, it appears that 54% of the hedge funds are more correlated with the indices of other groups than with the indicator of the group to which they qualitatively belong. This proportion is too high to be considered as process noise[4] and can be attributed to a non-relevant classification (i.e. the third element).

In reality, this classification gathers funds that exhibit a particularly high level of heterogeneity. The more heterogeneous a group is, the more the computation of an average on it smoothes the differences. This is the principle of the diversification. But for the diversification, ending with a global portfolio that significantly differs from each of its constituents is desirable. While an average/index that differs significantly from its constituent cannot aim to represent its elements, there is a difference between a desired homogenization that should dampen idiosyncrasies and a homogenization that simply hides differences. This process of smoothing differences through the average ends up with a large number of hedge funds that enter into the computation of a given alternative investment style index and are more correlated with an index representing another strategy. This can be easily checked considering a sample of 356 hedge funds with a 36-month track as at December 2006 that are constituents of the CS/Tremont alternative investment style indices. For this in-the-sample analysis, 47.5% of the hedge funds are more correlated with another CS/Tremont alternative investment style index than the one they participate to the valuation.

3.3 HETEROGENEITY REVEALED THROUGH MODERN CLUSTER ANALYSIS

The high level of heterogeneity between hedge funds combined with the impossibility of knowing the total inventory of hedge funds, and also using a poor sampling process, ends up with a non-homogeneous set of alternative investment style indices. As we will see in the next chapter, indices that are supposed to represent the same investment strategy are sometimes non-correlated. The heterogeneity between hedge funds indices has been studied quite comprehensively by Amenc and Martellini

---

[4] If we considered that the data collection, maintenance and the consolidation of classification was so badly performed that more than 50% of the information was not correct, we would conclude that those kinds of databases were in no way reliable. Despite the fact that many investors agree on the disappointing quality of hedge fund databases, we would throw the baby out with the bath water.

(2003), and a great deal of effort has been expended by these academics to find a way to decrease this diversity. Amenc and Martellini (2003) proposed an indices of indices approach, while Goltz et al. (2007) and Huber and Victoria-Feser (2007) built common factors within the hedge funds databases using Factor Analysis. Although these approaches make a lot of sense and are real improvements in our understanding and monitoring of the alternative industry, trying to find out the best restrictive classification does not reflect the complexity of the hedge funds universe and the information contained in the heterogeneity of hedge funds indices is simply lost. Simplification is always desirable, particularly to erase noises and stick to what really matters. But too much complexity reduction may either end up with a biased representation or may require a lot of sophisticated manipulations for a result that can be reached easily with a simple process.

This is the case for the classification problem. For instance, Huber and Victoria-Feser (2007) proposed a classification based on five common factors estimated through the Laplace Approximated Maximum Likelihood Estimator on a filtered version of the TASS database and using 30 monthly returns for each eligible hedge fund. This approach is based on the methodology developed by Huber et al. (2004) that belongs to the more innovative cluster analysis approach, but is quite difficult to implement. However, as we will see below, a very simple process that exploits the heterogeneity of hedge fund indices ends up with a classification that is just as good, or even better, in terms of inter-class heterogeneity – and significantly better in terms of intra-class homogeneity.

3.3.1   Modern Cluster Analysis Measures of a Classification

The homogeneity within each group, as well as the heterogeneity between groups, may be measured with the specific indicators developed by the modern cluster analysis theory. In that effect, data is standardized using the median and the median absolute deviation for the localization and the deviation indicator. Let $x_{s,t}$ be the return of a hedge fund s over period t, with $t = 1, \ldots, T$, then the standardized return $x_{s,t}^*$ is defined as

$$x_{s,t}^* = \frac{x_{s,t} - \mathrm{median}_t(x_{s,t})}{\mathrm{median}_t |x_{s,t} - \mathrm{median}_t(x_{s,t})|}$$

The median monthly returns $\tilde{I}_{j,t}$ of all the funds belonging to the alternative style j for period t are standardized in a similar way and denoted by $\tilde{I}_{j,t}^*$.

The Manhattan distance (the recommended distance for modern cluster analysis[5] between the hedge fund s and the index j) is defined as

$$D_M(x_s^*, I_j^*) = \frac{1}{T} \sum_{t=1}^{T} \mid x_{s,t}^* - I_{j,t}^* \mid$$

The algorithm of supervised classification is as follows. First, start with a family of investment style indices or latent variables and classify hedge fund s to group i if the Manhattan distance is the lowest compared to the one with other indices ($\forall j \neq i$). Then compute the median of each group and repeat the classification of all the hedge funds according to distances with the newly computed median of each group. The algorithm ends when the set of previously computed medians of each group is the same as the set of newly computed medians, or in other words when no hedge funds reclassification is required.[6]

Then, the measure of homogeneity within groups (i.e. the equivalent of the average intra-correlation in the Manhattan metrics) is the average intra-Manhattan distance D_{IF} defined as the mean Manhattan distance between returns of all pairwise combinations of hedge funds within a same group. The lower the distance, the more homogeneous are the groups. For the second measure Huber and Victoria-Feser (2007) propose to follow Kaufman and Rousseeuw (1990) using the average silhouette – an indicator based on the Manhattan distance that captures the heterogeneity between groups. So consider the mapping function $f(s) = i$ that associates to any hedge fund s the index i of the strategy to which the fund belongs. Then the average silhouette D_S of a set of N hedge funds is given by

$$D_S = \frac{1}{N} \sum_{s=1}^{N} \frac{D_M(x_s^*, \tilde{I}_{f(s)}^*)}{\min_{i \neq f(s)} \left(D_M(x_s^*, \tilde{I}_i^*) \right)}$$

A good classification is thus one with both a low intra-Manhattan distance and a low average silhouette.

---

[5] See Kaufman and Rousseeuw (1990).

[6] This algorithm is necessary taking into account both the kind of median indicator used and the fact that the first step is based on 'out of the sample' indicators. As a result, the homogeneity of the group as well as the heterogeneity between groups is improved.

3.3.2 Empirical Comparison

Let's now consider 1959 hedge funds extracted from our testing sample with a 30 monthly returns track as of June 2005. The first classification starts with the five latent factors obtained through the Laplace Approximated Maximum Likelihood Estimator computed on the TASS database, as proposed in Huber and Victoria-Feser (2007).

This pure statistical approach is then compared with 30 classifications of 30 groups each. These sets of alternative stratifications are obtained starting with 194 alternative investment style indices.[7] As the target is a subset of indices as heterogeneous as possible, the opposite of a single hierarchical clustering is performed. First detect the pair of different indices that are highly correlated, i.e. the highest non-diagonal element of the correlation matrix. Then for each index determine its highest correlation with all the other indices. Delete the index that exhibits the pair with the strongest linear link. Repeat the operations until a set of 30 indices is obtained. This can be done with 30 correlation matrices (one for each month from January 2003 to July 2005) computed on the previous 30 data. As correlations are computed on 30 monthly data, 30 classes are the maximum number of styles in order to ensure that the correlation matrix between groups remains, for any data set, a positive semi-definite matrix.

Moreover, the supervised classification algorithm is also applied to the 10 CS/Tremont indices. Figure 3.1 illustrates the 33 classifications in the space of the intra-Manhattan distance and the average silhouette. As expected, the intra-group homogeneity of the classification involving the largest number of groups is the best one, with an intra-Manhattan distance of 1.65 for the five groups obtained through the five factors estimated through the Laplace Approximated Maximum Likelihood Estimator,[8] 1.56 for the one deduced from the 10 CS/Tremont indices, and 1.41 on average[9] with 30 groups.

More interestingly, 8 classifications (i.e. 27%) with 30 groups exhibit an average silhouette below 0.856, i.e. the level of classification with 5 groups.[10] So despite the underlying process, the classification with 30 groups tries only to extract a set of heterogeneous variables

---

[7] See Appendix A for a detailed description of this index sample.

[8] If the algorithm of the supervised classification is not repeated until no reclassification occurs, the distance rises to 1.68.

[9] The maximum intra-Manhattan distance rises to 1.45 while the minimum distance is 1.37.

[10] If the algorithm of the supervised classification is not repeated until no reclassification occurs, the silhouette rises to 0.871.

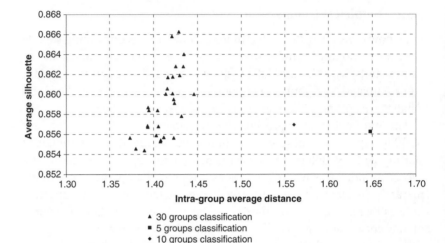

Figure 3.1   Average intra-Manhattan distance versus average silhouette

while the implicit analysis provides a set of orthogonal latent variables that account for most of the variance of the original set,[11] i.e. the first outperforms the second. Moreover, the maximum spread between the silhouette of the 5-group classification and a silhouette of a 30-group classification is 0.01, which is clearly low compared to the 0.15 maximum spread computed by Huber and Victoria-Feser (2007). So, the heterogeneity between classes do not significantly decrease going from an optimal 5-group classification to a suboptimal maximum number of group classification. As the intra-class homogeneity increases with the number of groups, this clearly pleads for a large number of classes and confirms the high level of heterogeneity between hedge funds.

3.3.3   Consequence For Value-at-Risk

The innovation of the original Style Model proposed by Lhabitant (2001) relies on the choice of alternative investment style indices to represent factors influencing the performance of hedge funds. This was a clear pragmatic way to circumvent all the difficulties related with modelling hedge fund returns with respect to traditional risk factors. This difficulty has been recently confirmed by the debate around hedge

---

[11] Obviously, this second dimension is not taken into account in the approach with 30 groups.

fund clones, as described in the next chapter. Moreover, because of the non-representativeness of the hedge fund indices (see also next chapter), the style model for hedge funds is not a style drift model. On the contrary, the model focuses on the information that is really contained in the hedge fund indices: some dynamically managed non-linear exposure to traditional risk factors. Mixing these indices through a style analysis model enables us to build an excellent basket of dynamic non-linear exposures that matches those of any hedge fund.

However, the original model fails to fully take into account the heterogeneity of alternative strategies style investment. Changing the set of possible factors for the model can be performed in two ways. The first consists of adding to the original a selection process of hedge fund active indices. These will be the modifications proposed in the second part of this book. The second way consists of using a non-constraint model, maintaining a simple selection process overlay and exploiting the implicit aspect of hedge funds active indices. This will be done in the last part.

3.4   APPENDIX A: INDICES SAMPLE

The following is a list of the hedge funds non-investable indices:

- ALTVEST: Capital Structure Arbitrage, Currency Trading, Distressed Securities, Emerging Markets, Event-Driven, Health Care, Long/Short Equity, Macro, Merger Arbitrage, Relative Value, Short Selling, Technology.
- BARCLAY: Agricultural Traders, BTOP 50, CTA, Currency Traders, Discretionary Traders, Diversified Traders, Financial and Metal Traders, Systematic Traders.
- BARCLAY/GLOBAL HEDGESOURCE: Convertible Arbitrage, Distressed Securities, Emerging Markets, Equity Market Neutral, Equity Long Bias, Equity Long/Short, Equity Short Bias, European Equities, Event-Driven, Fixed Income Arbitrage, Global Macro, Health and Biotechnology, Merger Arbitrage, Multi Strategy, Pacific Rim Equity, Technology.
- CISDM: CTA Diversified, CTA Equity, CTA Discretionary, CTA Systematic, CPO Asset Weighted, Convertible Arbitrage, Distressed, Emerging Markets, Long/Short Equity, Equity Market Neutral, Global Macro, Merger Arbitrage, Mortgage Backed.

- CS/TREMONT: Convertible Arbitrage, Dedicated Short Bias, Emerging Markets, Equity Market Neutral, Event Driven Distressed, Event-Driven, Event-Driven Multi-Strategy, Event-Driven Risk Arbitrage, Fixed Income Arbitrage, Global Macro, Hedge Fund, Long/Short Equity, Managed Futures, Multi-Strategy.
- EDHEC: Convertible Arbitrage, CTA Global, Distressed Securities, Emerging Markets, Equity Market Neutral, Event-Driven, Fixed Income Arbitrage, Global Macro, Long/Short Equity, Merger Arbitrage, Relative Value, Short Selling.
- GREENWICH GLOBAL: Equity Market Neutral, Event-Driven, Distressed Securities, Merger Arbitrage, Special Situations, Market Neutral Arbitrage, Convertible Arbitrage, Fixed Income Arbitrage, Aggressive Growth, Opportunistic, Short Selling, Value, Futures, Macro, Market Timing, Emerging Markets, Income, Multi-Strategy.
- HEDGEFUNDINTELLIGENCE: Asiahedge Japan Long/Short, EuroHedge Emerging Markets Debt, EuroHedge Emerging Markets Equity.
- HENNESSEE: Arbitrage/Event-Driven Non-Correlated, Asia-Pacific, Convertible Arbitrage, Distressed, Emerging Markets, Event-Driven, Financial Equities, Fixed Income, Global, Growth, Healthcare/Biotech, Hedge Fund, High Yield, International, Latin America, Long/Short Equity Correlated, Macro, Market Neutral, Merger Arbitrage, Multiple Arbitrage, Opportunistic, Pipes/Private Financing, Short Bias, Technology, Value.
- HFRI: Convertible Arbitrage, Distressed Securities, Emerging Markets Asia, Emerging Markets Eastern Europe/Cis, Emerging Markets Global Index, Emerging Markets Latin America, Emerging Markets Total, Equity Hedge, Equity Market Neutral, Equity Market Neutral Statistical Arb., Equity Non-Hedge, Event-Driven, Fixed Income Arbitrage, Fixed Income Convertible Bonds Index, Fixed Income Diversified, Fixed Income High Yield, Fixed Income Mortgage-Backed, Fixed Income Total, Macro Index Market Timing, Merger Arbitrage, Regulation D, Relative Value Arbitrage, Sector Energy, Sector Financial Index, Sector Healthcare/Biotechnology, Sector Miscellaneous, Sector Real Estate, Sector Technology, Sector Total, Short Selling.
- HEDGEFUND.NET: Asia, Latin America, Fixed Income Arbitrage, Fixed Income (Non-Arbitrage), Finance Sector Average, Event-Driven, Energy Sector, Emerging Markets, Distressed, CTA/Managed Futures, Country Specific, Convertible Arbitrage, Asset-Based

Lending, Statistical Arbitrage, Special Situations, Small/Micro Cap, Short-Term Trading, Short Bias, Regulation D, Other Arbitrage, Options Strategies, Multi-Strategy, Mortgages, Merger/Risk Arbitrage, Market Timer, Market Neutral Equity, Macro, Long/Short Equity, Healthcare Sector, Value.

- MSCI: Directional Traders, Relative Value, Security Selection, Specialist Credit, Multi-Process, Equity, Fixed Income, Diversified, Developed Markets, Emerging Markets, Global Market and North America.

4
Active and Passive Hedge Fund Indices

Up until the mid-1980s, only a handful of wealthy private clients invested in hedge funds. Such investments took the form of a discretionary mandate whose target was formulated in absolute terms, i.e. with no reference to the market's average return or the peer group's performance. Therefore, there was no demand for a statistical indicator of the performance of the hedge funds universe.

The mid-1980s onwards saw spectacular growth in the number of hedge funds and investors, and the emergence of private databases charging for their services, to compensate for the lack of official data. In most instances, their promoters calculated an average indicator of returns on the hedge funds in their database. They thus gave birth to the first hedge fund indices, whose purpose was mainly indicative.

The academic researchers who set themselves to investigating the validity of these indices immediately pointed out that compiling a sample aimed at representing the total universe was scarcely compatible with the manner in which hedge fund databases were built, i.e. based on voluntary participation, fairly small relative to a highly heterogeneous population, and with heavily biased computations. In view of the extent of the biases, Fung and Hsieh (2000) suggested using fund of funds indices as a more efficient proxy of the hedge funds universe. This search for greater representativeness by indirect means speaks volumes about the value of a direct approach.

In the early years of the new millennium, the massive influx of institutional investors created a real demand for efficient hedge fund indices. Amenc and Martellini (2003) studied the heterogeneity resulting from the hedge fund indices' lack of representativeness, and compiled indices of indices (the EDHEC indices) to reduce the bias inherent in each database. This approach, while imperfect, represented the optimal solution taking into account the information available, and was favourably received by researchers and industry professionals. As a consequence, Duc (2004a) proposed to combine the advantages of the Fung and Hsieh

(2000) approach with that of Amenc and Martellini (2003) and to use the EDHEC funds of funds index as a proxy for the alternative industry.

However, in 2004–2005, the debate broadened to include the investable indices, as a result of the marketing campaigns conducted by the promoters of these investment vehicles. Géhin and Vaissié (2004) studied the heterogeneity of non-investable indices and those that can be replicated, while Duc (2004a, 2004b, 2004c) demonstrated that this type of product amounts to nothing more than a 'pseudo' passively managed fund of funds.

In January 2006, the consulting procedure employed by the Committee of European Securities Regulators (CESR) relaunched the debate surrounding investable indices, following postponement of the decision on the eligibility of hedge fund indices for inclusion in UCITS III funds. Given how much is at stake for the promoters of these indices, the response showed mounting support for an index-based approach to alternative funds. For example, Amenc and Goltz (2006) make a distinction between index and benchmark and justify the eligibility of investable indices by pointing out the transparency contributed by platforms of managed accounts. By contrast, other articles referred back to the results of a number of previous academic papers on the subject (see below) and applied them to investable indices. Thus, Lhabitant (2006b), having first dissected the biases and underlying heterogeneity and demonstrated the indices' lack of representativeness, listed a minimum 15 quality criteria required for hedge fund indices and three for index products. Clearly, the products available to date did not satisfy these criteria. Moreover, accepting investable active indices as eligible for UCITS III funds is tantamount to admitting the eligibility of any fund of funds with systematic rules of portfolio management.

The polemic surrounding investable indices in 2006 was less heated than that of 2004–2005. However, it raised a new point of contention regarding the indices' heterogeneity that was often used in the past to illustrate the lack of representativeness common to hedge fund indices: that lack was now said to be comparable with that of traditional indices. Empirically, it was difficult to credit such a similarity. Furthermore, the comparison disregarded a fundamental difference: the hedge fund indices available at that time were composed of managers, whereas the traditional indicators are made up of financial assets. The former are active indicators while the latter are passive. Within the framework of traditional investment, the indices represent passive application of the purchasing strategy. In other words, the manager buys the market or a given sector and keeps the positions over the long term. This approach contrasts with that of non-indexed traditional managers who select the market assets or sectors that they find most promising and maintain their positions for a variable period of time.

Denial of this difference also largely explained the success[1] of the active investable indices in terms of assets under management and posed the question of whether this type of product was really eligible for the mass market. Granted, there was a real, overwhelming demand for hedge fund indices that resemble the traditional indices. But the idea of applying the criteria for passive indices to existing hedge fund indices was an illusion that consisted mainly of believing that the active indices could represent their passive counterparts.

At the end of 2006, the debate surrounding indices of alternative funds began to take a different turn, following the launch of the hedge fund clones. The clones position themselves as a response to the demand for a passive approach to hedge funds, able to capture the systematic part of the strategies while eliminating what may be derived from the skill with which they are used. In other words, the hedge fund clones are passive indices of alternative strategies that model a global approach to the strategies in their purest form, without being exposed to selection. They remain passive even when the strategy is active.

Prior to the clones' arrival, passive representation of alternative strategies was confined to academic research, and the rare funds that proposed this approach were not perceived as indices. That changed completely in the space of just a few months. Two renowned professors of hedge funds (Harry M. Kat and Helder P. Palaro) announced the creation of a software program enabling users to replicate synthetically any alternative strategy. Thereafter, major financial institutions and certain fund of funds managers created investment vehicles replicating hedge funds' exposure to various risk factors or offering a comprehensive mechanical approach to a specific strategy. In the middle of 2007, more than 20 investment vehicles of this type were on the market and obviously not all are born equal.

Unfortunately, all the methodologies underlying these products continue to suffer from a number of unresolved theoretical problems. The models prove very disappointing for duplication at the hedge funds level or when tested on samples other than those on which they were built. Without the support of academic consensus, non-representative

---

[1] In addition to various factors relating to delegation of responsibility and marketing.

and sometimes inefficient, the clones are soon seen to be nothing more than specific systematic hedge funds.

This chapter takes a closer look at the illusions conveyed by both active and passive investable hedge fund indices.

4.1 ILLUSIONS FOSTERED BY ACTIVE HEDGE FUND INDICES

The vast majority of hedge fund indices (investable and non-investable) consist of the averages of the yields of a sample of hedge fund managers and not passive modelling of the strategy in its purest form. Any attempt to transpose the rationale for traditional indices to hedge fund indices is based on the illusion that the managers' averages offer a fair approximation of the passive indices or an efficient representation of the hedge funds universe.

4.1.1 The Illusion of Achieving Purity

The first illusion fostered by the active indices is that they can serve as a proxy for a passive index, i.e. provide an efficient approximation of the strategy in its purest form. This is like believing that one can create a proxy of the S&P 500 on the basis of the average of a few non-indexed traditional funds.

Furthermore, in the case of investable hedge fund indices, the way they are constructed and managed in practice proves that they do not claim to represent pure strategies. Close examination of the hedge funds comprising them makes it patently clear that there is little likelihood of their offering effective representation of the pure strategy.

For example, the Dow Jones Convertible Bond investable index has experienced a fair amount of long equity exposure and short convertible bond exposure. These exposures are exactly the reverse of those entailed in pure convertible arbitrage as modelled by a passive index. In addition, despite the fact that hedge funds with a virtually passive approach to merger arbitrage or convertible arbitrage already existed when the investable indices were launched, none of these strategies was included in the new indices, probably because their profitability had already declined significantly.

Lastly, when it comes to replacing the components of the investable indices, the choice is more a matter of the managers' quality than their implementation of the strategy (i.e. pure or complementary to that of other hedge funds). For example, at the end of February 2003, the S&P index replaced the Jemmco fund with the GLC Gestalt Europe fund. Both managers follow the statistical arbitrage strategy, but the former used several statistical models (including a pair-trading model) on mainly US equities, while the latter conducted pair trades on European stocks. It is hard to see how the two hedge funds could represent the same mean approach to the pure strategy or produce the same diversification effects.

The construction and management of investable indices shows, therefore, that the need to replicate a pure strategy counts for little compared with the need to select the hedge funds that are deemed to be the most profitable. One must bear in mind that most of the investable indices are commercial products seeking the best returns and not the best representativeness. In 2005, an advertising campaign actually suggested that the CS investable was the best index in the field because it had posted higher returns than its competitors during the year. In other words, the main point was not to buy the market of pure alternative strategies, but to choose the best managers.

4.1.2 The Illusion of Representativeness

The second illusion is that the hedge fund indices currently available, whether investable or not, estimate the average of the total hedge funds universe.[2] Based on this assumption, hedge fund indices would be passive, not because they represented the pure strategy, but because they provided access to the whole hedge fund market, without being exposed to the selection of specific managers.

Unfortunately, the total inventory of hedge funds remains unknown, and the universe is estimated using information compiled by the commercial databases. But can samples composed on the principle of voluntary input and the indices derived from them offer a correct picture of the hedge funds universe? The non-investable indices' lack of representativeness has been studied in detail by academic research and obtained broad consensus following the work done by Amenc and Martellini (2003). While the indices derive from heavily biased, fairly small samples, the population (unknown) is highly heterogeneous. This lack of representativeness is reflected in a total lack of homogeneity between

---

[2] The point is no longer to capture solely the beta but also the average alpha and the average management of the dynamic betas compared with the pure strategies.

the many indices in terms of construction and returns. For example, the monthly returns may vary by more than 17% and the correlation between indices supposedly representing the same strategy can be negative.

The investable indices inherit this lack of representativeness, since they are merely non-investable indices subject to constraints. The situation has actually worsened, as a global investable index comprises between 20 and 120 hedge funds, whereas the non-investable version has between 400 and 2600 hedge funds. Furthermore, as Lhabitant (2006b) points out, the database bias is accompanied by other shortcomings particular to the investable indices, such as biases in terms of under-representativeness, due diligence, managed accounts and pro forma data.

It is tempting to reason that the investable indices are of better quality than their non-investable counterparts, first, because their track records since inception[3] are not exposed to survivorship bias and instant history bias as a result of their construction. But this advantage is fully dampened by the particularly large exposure to idiosyncratic risk. For instance, from February to March 2008, the CS/Tremont Blue Chip Convertible Arbitrage Index posted a −15% loss because one of the 6 constituents of the investable index suffered a 40% drawdown. In the mean time, the DJ Convertible Arbitrage Index recorded a −4.6% return and the EDHEC Convertible Arbitrage Index returned a 3.98% loss.

Next, one could reason that the investable indices must be more adequate because greater care is taken in composing a hedge fund portfolio of 'live' investments than in the intellectual construction of an index that cannot be replicated. Accordingly, the classification of the hedge funds is bound to be less biased. And indeed, the promoters of investable indices will, at the very least, check the validity of the managers' claims and may also carry out extensive due diligence work on each of the hedge funds.[4] Similarly, the information supplied by each of the underlying funds is checked continuously, since six of the eight investable indices use managed accounts. Furthermore, the launch of these products demands considerable work from the promoter, not only on the funds selected, but on cleaning up part of the databases. For example, when HFR launched the investable versions of these indices, it created a

---

[3] Prior to the launch, there was obviously a pro forma effect.

[4] However, there is a fine line between improved information and due diligence bias. According to Lhabitant (2006b): 'Could one imagine Standard and Poor's refusing to introduce a large listed US company in the S&P 500 on the claim that its operations are not state of the art, or that the quality of its management is insufficient to run the company? Not really.'

subset of its own database, comprising around 200 funds that had been analysed in depth. This subset provided the means of determining the strategic allocation by capitalization of the HFRX index and of building an index serving as reference for the process of allocation optimization[5] per hedge fund within the HFRX. The use of a sub-index rather than the non-investable HFR index could be perceived as an admission of weakness in the non-replicable hedge fund index.

However, despite these improvements, the fact that the investable indices have less components and more constraints as well as biases (both their own and others inherited from the databases), means that they fail to provide better representation than the non-investable indices. Their heterogeneity is higher, on average, than that of the non-investable indices. The opposite impression is given by the changes in volatility trends between the period studied by Amenc and Martellini (2003) and recent years, which saw the launch of the investable indices. For example, the volatilities of the 12 EDHEC indices average out at 1.9 times higher than those measured between October 2002 and September 2006 (3.2 times higher for the fixed income index).

In reality, the difference registered in February 2000 between the real return on the Zurich Long/Short investable index (+20%) and the pro forma return[6] on the FTSE Long/Short (+6.81%) is 14.67%. This difference is similar to that between the non-investable indices. Furthermore, for the period from April 2004 to September/October 2006, the differences in the returns of investable indices following the same strategy are often greater (and the correlations lower) than those between the non-investable versions, as Table 4.1 shows.[7] Clearly, the two families of indices display an almost identical lack of homogeneity. Now, as we stated earlier, it is generally accepted that the non-investable indices are so highly heterogeneous that one must adopt an index of indices approach – despite the cost in terms of transparency and complexity. Similarly, to the survivorship and instant history biases, it would be very surprising here if what condemned one family of indices did not do the same to the other.

---

[5] However, one must have some reservations about the results of optimizations performed on samples that are still heavily biased.

[6] As it is highly likely that the monthly return of the lower bound has been overestimated, the difference in performance is probably underestimated.

[7] Comparison carried out on the non-investable indices Altvest, CS/Tremont, CISDM, EACM, Hedge-fund.net, HFR, Hennesse, MSCI, vanHedge) and the investable indices CS/Tremont, DJ, FTSE, HFRX, MSCI, S&P. The inception date of the most recent family of investable indices determines the size of the sample.

Table 4.1 Comparison of the heterogeneity of 53 investable indices and 45 non-investable indices

	Non-investable		Investable	
Index	Maximum difference	Minimum correlation	Maximum difference	Minimum correlation
Convertible Arbitrage	1.07%	0.96	1.95%	0.81
Equity Market Neutral	2.48%	0.07	1.56%	0.18
Event-Driven	2.51%	0.91	1.78%	0.81
Fixed Income Arbitrage	2.19%	0.07	2.73%	0.56
Global Macro	3.04%	0.69	4.68%	0.19
Long/Short Equity	1.41%	0.94	2.94%	0.7
Merger Arbitrage	1.87%	0.87	1.74%	0.69
Distressed Securities	1.55%	0.82	2.93%	0.49
Managed Futures	10.05%	0.65	5.39%	0.85

The maximum difference between the two long/short indices in February 2000 is greater than that between the traditional-style indices (such as the European equity value and growth indices). This is particularly true given that when comparing investment strategies, one must adjust the differences in return to the average volatility level of each of the styles. That being the case, the homogeneity of the investable alternative indices is significantly lower than that of the traditional indices, so that the correlations between the European equity growth indices[8] are much higher than those between the hedge funds: from April 2004 to October 2006, the minimum correlation is 0.85 (0.95 for the value style) whereas for the investable indices, and depending upon the strategy, the correlations can be in the region of 0.2 (see Table 4.1).

Whether investable or not, the hedge fund indices are subject to a far greater lack of representativeness than the traditional indices. This is because, in the case of the alternative funds, the problem goes well beyond poor classification of financial assets. Rather, it concerns the averages of managers (active indices) with considerable freedom in their mandates, drawn from biased, heterogeneous samples with weak intersections. In reality, by their construction, the investable hedge fund indices can represent neither the hedge funds universe nor open funds nor funds available for investment.

In fact, if the indices attempted to represent the complete hedge funds universe by means of open funds, they would actually suffer from an

---

[8] For the S&P/Citigroup, MSCI, FTSE Style and Dow Jones Euro Stoxx TMI indices.

Table 4.2 Comparison of returns on global investable and non-investable indices

	Inception	Total return on the non-investable	Total return on the investable
CS/Tremont	August 2003	38.11%	20.69%
HFR	March 2003	54.06%	23.69%
MSCI	July 2003	33.23%	18.57%

additional selection bias: that of using open funds to capture the performance of closed funds. This additional shortcoming may not apply in two cases: if there is no difference between the closed and open managers, or if these differences are smoothed out by a methodology particular to each of these indices. Where one of these assumptions applies, there should be very little difference between two indices (one investable, the other not), drawn from the same database, and the creation of two versions of the same index would be justifiable only on commercial grounds. However, there are substantial differences between the investable and non-replicable versions of the same family of indices (see Table 4.2 for the global indices).

Investable hedge fund indices cannot represent the open funds universe, because they are not composed solely of funds belonging to this universe. They contain many partially closed hedge funds, i.e. funds that accept new investments only from investors that have reserved capacity. For example, several hedge funds in the S&P index were selectively open. The weak intersection between the investable indices derives also from the fact that only some of the promoters were capable of reserving sufficient capacity in these funds. Furthermore, certain investable indices plan on maintaining exposure to funds that actually close after being included in the index. In other words, the replicable indices are replicable only for their promoters and do not reflect the universe of open funds. For the indices to be consistent with the open funds universe, they should exclude any hedge fund that refuses the capital of an ordinary investor that complies with the laws governing investment.

The investable indices are also inadequate to represent the universe of hedge funds accessible to the ordinary investor, because the universe in question is made up of open funds and of all the closed hedge funds whose investors include funds of funds. An investor can gain access to a closed fund by investing in a fund of funds that, in its turn, is invested in the closed hedge fund. By their construction, neither the funds closed before the launch of the investable index nor the funds of funds may participate in a replicable index. And as the closed funds induce a discriminatory effect, the investable indices fail to represent the universe of accessible funds.

Since the investable funds fail to represent hedge funds in their entirety (open or not), the investable indices can claim only to describe the sample from which they are drawn. And this sample depends ultimately upon the selections made by the promoters of the investable indices. From that viewpoint, the investable funds are almost indistinguishable from funds of funds.

Thus, the investable indices do not offer passive exposure to the average of managers in the universe. Instead, they expose the investor, in real terms, to the selection of the hedge funds included, in the same way as funds of funds, but over a smaller group of alternative funds, i.e. those that are willing to reserve capacity for the index and/or adhere to a platform of managed accounts. Indeed it is not surprising that one of the most perverse effects of the strong contribution from manager selection, in the case of both investable indices and funds of funds, is pro forma outperformance. Since inception, the MSCI, HRFX and CSFB investable indices have underperformed their non-investable versions, whereas they were all more profitable during the periods of simulation.

4.1.3   The Illusion of Optimality

While true representativeness of the total universe thus proves impossible, it is also far from optimal, and is therefore not really desired.

The reason is that the hedge funds universe contains managers of varying quality. Seeking to invest in the average portfolio of the universe amounts to seeking exposure to these mediocre hedge funds. As demonstrated by Liew (2003), for a given universe of hedge funds, selection quickly becomes profitable. Furthermore, the opinion held by some financial players that fund of funds selection is not efficient arises from comparing the returns on non-investable indices with those of funds of funds. The latter tend to underperform the average indicators, owing not only to all the biases and methodological problems, but also to the fact that they are not operating in the same universe. Many funds of funds tend to avoid funds that have a high exposure to certain risks, such as fraud or liquidity risks (Reg. D) or catastrophe risk. This is also the type of exposure that hedge fund investors seek to avoid.

Moreover, if the hedge fund indices were truly representative, they would reveal substantial turnover. Today, an estimated 12% of funds in the hedge funds universe cease to exist after a year. The hedge fund indices should thus reflect this aspect of the universe and offer at least the same degree of rotation.

Similarly, contrary to the case for traditional funds, there is no fundamental justification for the allocation by capitalization, since hedge funds are not a class of financial assets. Their capitalization does not reflect a company's performance and its financing needs, but rather, the capital flows into the strategy and the fund[9]; and these flows are destined primarily for the recent winners. For example, in a study of arbitrage strategies, Agarwal et al. (2003) show a strong relation between flows in one year and average returns in the previous year. In other words, flows into the strategies reveal that, on average, investors are chasing returns. This allocation process is clearly suboptimal, as it runs counter to the lack of an average persistency in hedge fund returns and to the existence of cycles between strategies.[10]

The investable indices, albeit only funds of funds in disguise, indirectly inherit these various shortcomings. For example, the components of the CS/Tremont index are weighted by capitalization. Similarly, the FTSE, HFR and MSCI products, among others, use platforms of managed accounts and restrict determination of an average selection through their various biases. In fact, even if the investable indices' track record is not sufficient to demonstrate the lack of optimality, it is nevertheless revealing that, to date, none of the investable indices has offered, since inception,[11] higher profitability[12] than the average for funds of funds, as measured by the EDHEC index (Table 4.3).

---

[9] On this basis, weighting by capitalization does not correspond to a buy-and-hold strategy, since the weighting is not only adjusted passively by the returns, but must be modified based on new capital inflows. Furthermore, the weighting by capitalization is inadequate by the terms of alternative strategies. On the one hand, the hedge funds can make use of the leverage effect by borrowing capital, so that two hedge funds of the same size may have very different exposures to the strategy. On the other hand, hedge funds do not have the monopoly of the alternative strategies. For example, banks' trading desks make extensive use of alternative strategies (indeed, they are the prime source of hedge fund managers).

[10] See, for example, Amenc, et al. (2002).

[11] Since the investable indices are funds of funds, using data from prior to the index's launch is equivalent to using the simulated returns on a fund of funds, an error that any sophisticated investor is reluctant to commit. The pro forma data either is the result of an optimization process (and thus always highly favourable) or has influenced hedge fund selection. Although all selectors are aware that past performance is no guarantee of future results, there remains a natural tendency to prefer hedge funds that have delivered attractive returns in the past.

[12] And yet, the comparison of the indices' returns as provided by their promoters on the Web and by Bloomberg would seem to favour the investable indices. Indeed, the investor is only informed of the returns on the indexed funds; and these may include tracking fees, management fees, entry and exit fees and differences due to tracking error.

Table 4.3　Comparison of returns on global investable indices and the funds of funds

	Inception	Total return on the investable intex	Return on the EDHEC fund of funds index
CS/Tremont	August 2003	20.69%	26.67%
FR	April 2004	6.52%	17.08%
HFR	March 2003	23.69%	33.20%
MSCI	July 2003	18.57%	26.67%

4.2　PASSIVE INDICES AND THE ILLUSION OF BEING CLONES

There are three methods for creating a passive index. The first is to apply a strategy defined by certain rules to the market as a whole. The second is to provide access to the strategy's betas after having calculated these using a factorial model. The third method is to reproduce the return distribution over a long period. Unfortunately, the technical knowledge required to set up these three approaches is not yet available.

4.2.1　Mechanical Replication

Mechanical replication is the approach most closely resembling the traditional passive indices, because it applies the strategy explicitly to the whole market. For some alternative strategies, this kind of modelling is fairly easy, at least temporarily. For example, in the case of merger arbitrage, the strategy's passive index is defined by the returns generated by investing in all the mergers/acquisitions announced. A passive index of this kind is the equivalent of a traditional index, since there is no selection from amongs the various investment opportunities. The index is thus distinct from the managers who implement this strategy actively by selecting only those mergers/acquisitions that they believe have the greatest chance of success.

Other alternative strategies may easily be replicated. For example, a passive convertible arbitrage strategy – in its classic form – is a portfolio comprising all the issues of delta-hedged convertible bonds. Obviously, the passive approach by replication is easily applicable in the case of systematic strategies. For example, Spurgin (1999) suggests a simple and ingenious method of replicating a diversified CTA. Similarly, the strategies dependent upon a specific catalyst, those where the risk premiums can be automatically extracted or the arbitrage between derivatives and the underlying products can be reproduced mechanically.

To obtain a global index, one could simply draw up a complete inventory of the alternative strategies and then define the rules for replicating each of the investment styles. The aggregate of the cloned strategies would represent the hedge funds universe. In that respect, mechanical replication is a way of overcoming the absence of a representative hedge fund sample.[13]

Unfortunately, setting up passive indices for all the alternative indices entails several problems that have not yet been resolved, despite the efforts of numerous researchers and industry professionals. First of all, the strategies evolve: some that were once quite easy to model can become more complex and give rise to several very different passive approaches. Such is the case with merger arbitrage.

Up until the mid-1990s, any financial assets issued by a company targeted for a merger or an acquisition were considered highly risky and out of bounds for the management mandates of certain institutional portfolios. Indeed, when a deal was announced, the assets concerned were systematically sold by the institutional investors, whereas they were bought by arbitrageurs. The post-announcement risk premium therefore reflected not only the currency's time value and the transaction risk premium, but an inefficiency: namely certain institutional investors' barrier to entry. This barrier disappeared in 2000, when all the brokers and other players in the institutional segment set up a portfolio devoted to securities affected by restructuring. The annualized global risk premium after announcement, which had exceeded 13% between 1992 and 1999, declined to 5% at the beginning of the consolidation cycle in 2003 and rose only moderately during the interest-rate hikes. In Europe, by contrast, for more than 52% of the offers, the market price not only reached the bid price soon after announcement, but went on to exceed it, so that the premium turned negative (as seen with Arcelor and Elior).

And yet, hedge funds can take advantage of the current consolidation in the manufacturing sector by focusing on mergers and acquisitions that show a strong chance of closing – especially on the basis of an upwardly

---

[13] In reality, this too is an illusion, since the vicious circle of representativeness (cloning an average hedge fund by a passive index when there is no representative sample of the hedge funds universe) is merely transferred from funds to strategies. It is impossible to be sure that the definition by extension of the investment styles that is used for the mechanical replication is the one used by all hedge funds. Similarly, for a global index of alternative strategies, a weighting by capitalization seems more appropriate than equal weights. However, the weights per cloned strategy require a representative sample and knowledge of the different levels of leverage.

revised offer. In the case of a hostile bid, the target itself might make a counter-offer or negotiate a higher bid by the acquirer or another suitor (white knight). If the offer is friendly, the high likelihood of the deal's being closed reflects a win–win situation for both parties: the feasibility and profitability of the transaction for the acquirer should inspire the envy of its competitors, who will make higher, hostile bids. Under these conditions, the transactions that are the most profitable and contain the highest chance of escalating bids are those concerning small/medium capitalizations. It is therefore hardly surprising to see more and more merger arbitrageurs fishing in these particular waters.

This new way of applying the strategy is similar to that consisting of betting on restructuring before it is announced. In 2005, mergers funded entirely with cash represented over 75% of total transactions (stock-for-stock mergers having declined from 41% in 1998 to 9% in 2005). The strategy boils down to purchasing the assets of the target company. Since then, many portfolio managers have increased their exposure to unannounced transactions.

As a result of this trend, merger arbitrage, like many other relative-value strategies, is shoring up its profitability by increasing its exposure to market direction and/or liquidity risk. Strictly speaking, this is no longer arbitrage, and the passive approach outlined above thus ceases to be at all representative of the investment strategy.

In the same way, since the sharp decline in implied volatility in 2003, very few hedge funds have engaged in convertible arbitrage simply by means of long volatility positions. Instead, some managers play on the credit component of the convertible bond while others bet on the spread between credit premiums and implied volatility. Similarly, in the past, bonds with a BB credit rating have had a very attractive risk–return profile compared with those rated B and BBB. This relative excess premium was explained by the conjunction of two phenomena. On the one hand, many investors did not want or were contractually unable to purchase bonds rated less than BBB. On the other hand, investors in bonds from low-quality issuers tended to prefer the highest-yielding paper, i.e. the Bs. Going long BB and simultaneously short B and BBB enabled the investor to capture the excess premium. The development of CDOs has severely eroded this premium, but has also generated other types of arbitrage between and within the tranches. Even though the managers are still invested in the same asset class, they are applying a very different investment style. Today, mechanical replication of how managers capture the relative value of BB bonds would no longer be profitable; nor would it accurately reflect what the hedge funds are achieving.

A basic characteristic of hedge funds is their ability to profit from the new market structures. How can one adapt the mechanical rules of a niche strategy that by its very nature, evolves over time, as inefficiencies disappear? What is the point of cloning a strategy that no one has been using in this particular way for years? That is the first challenge for mechanical replication.

Second, passive indices assume that the various strategies are clearly defined. Classification remains a key point for hedge funds, given the freedom accorded by the mandates and the heterogeneity with which they are carried out. In 2003, AIMA set up a think tank to tackle the standard classification of hedge funds. The members comprised five highly regarded researchers and 72 hedge fund professionals. A survey of them revealed that over 50% of investors used their own classification system and that there was no strong consensus among the others regarding external classification. The situation has barely changed since. In a universe as heterogeneous and opportunistic as that of hedge funds, can there exist any such thing as an exhaustive inventory of styles?

Lastly, even supposing agreement were reached on efficient classification of the various strategies and that classification were updated continuously, the complexity of some of the strategies and the contribution of the discretionary aspect are becoming so significant that, for the time being, they make efficient modelling virtually impossible.[14]

Changing approaches to the strategies and the absence of an efficient classification mean that an investment vehicle that sets out to replicate a strategy mechanically could soon cease to reflect the strategy in its current, pure form, and end up being nothing more than a specific systematic hedge fund.

4.2.2 Exposure Replication

The second way to create a passive index is seen in the products launched recently by large financial institutions using factor models. A strategy's returns are broken down into, on one hand, exposure to a subset of financial factors, and, on the other, a residual supposed to represent the

---

[14] But is this really a problem of classification? Or, more likely, a sign of the limits of a passive approach to funds that, philosophically, are the antithesis of indexation.

manager's skill. A portfolio composed solely of the financial factors (accessible through derivatives or ETFs) and whose weights are the sensitivities calculated previously, constitutes the passive index.

To our knowledge, the first published indices by exposure replication were the CISDM passive indices, which were based on the methodology developed by Kazemi et al. (2001), but academic literature abounds with factorial hedge fund models. None of them has won general acceptance for prediction, because the underlying active management of alternative strategies and the use of risk management tools enabling action to be taken if market conditions deteriorate (e.g. reduce the positions) induce both absence of linearity and non-stationarity in returns.

For instance, let us consider a simple strategy of investing in the S&P 500 index. At the beginning of each month, exposure is increased by 40% if stocks posted a gain the previous month, or reduced by 40% in the event of a loss. The level of exposure must, however, be held at between −40% and 120%. If the strategy starts in March 2002, the statistical sensitivity of returns versus the S&P 500, after two years, shows an exposure of 7% and a correlation of less than 0.2, though the average exposure is 43%, and for 11 months, the portfolio is over 80% invested. This result is not unusual. Let us consider, for example, all the strategies possible with either a 40% reduction in exposure or a 10% increase in exposure each month, while keeping the constraints of an upper limit of 120% and a lower limit of −40%. This corresponds to more than 1.2 million simulations for a period covering 25 months. In 98% of cases, the application of a regression model to the S&P 500 index would explain less than 25% of the information.

Furthermore, some factorial models currently used by the clones assume that the hedge funds have fairly stable market exposures. What else could explain the predominance of equity factors in the choice of explanatory variables, reflecting the hedge funds' current timely but temporary exposure to this type of market? The other factors, those that can be of most interest to investors in an environment less propitious for equities, are often neglected. Unsurprisingly, the simulations of those very same clones are lower in profitability and higher in tracking error in falling markets.

A natural step consists of incorporating non-linearity through options pay off as in Fung and Hsieh (2001, 2002) or Agarwal and Naik (2000a). These papers are based on the idea that alternative investment strategies either have a convergence component that can be modelled as a short position in a (lookback) straddle or a trend following component that can be duplicated by a long position in a (lookback) straddle. Theoretically, if these approaches were applied to a large set of absolute and spread risk factors, all alternative investment strategies could be modelled. If the market timing of the different strategies could be captured, the different pattern of sensitivity to the asset-based style factors would enable to cluster hedge funds and find an efficient classification.

In reality, only a restrictive set of factors have been used until now[15] and if the methodology proposes to duplicate some alternative or exotic beta, it fails to clone efficiently individual hedge funds and adjusted R-square are particularly low.[16]

This is why some argue that the incorporation of non-linearity and time varying exposure through options are probably not sufficient to reflect the particularities of hedge fund returns: efficient modelling would require complex methodologies that may not be nearly robust enough, given the size of the samples available. In a ground-breaking paper, Diez de los Rios and Garcia (2006) use an innovative statistical methodology to determine the portfolio of option strategies with a statistically determined strike price that best approximates the return of any hedge fund and tests if the estimated non-linearities are significant. As pointed out by the authors

> Given the limited information available on hedge fund returns, the statistical evidence is not as overwhelming as previous studies tended to conclude. [...] Our findings indicate that using a proper statistical methodology matters. Not all categories exhibit significant nonlinearities even though casual evidence from a scatter plot may be suggestive of an option-like pattern of return [...] The appearance of nonlinear features in hedge funds is supported statistically for only one third of the individual funds.

Obviously, to date, the factorial models, linear or not, can at best reproduce indices or portfolios where the high heterogeneity between hedge funds (as documented in Chapter 3) led to over-diversification. As observed by Harry M. Kat: 'The hedge funds features have been

---

[15] Beside the practical problems linked with the selection and the creation of a comprehensive set of factors (including all the relevant straddles), this status of the research may simply reflect the opinion that hedge funds benefit from a restrictive set of opportunities.

[16] One may argue that the level is similar to the one obtained by factor models for individual stocks. But, as a matter of fact, the comparison with traditional investment should not be conducted at the stock level (a long/short equity portfolio is a portfolio of stocks not only one stock) but at the mutual fund level, where the quality of the adjustment is quite important.

diversified away and that's why they can replicate it.' This explains why some of the out-of-sample results of the various models are frankly disappointing, as illustrated by Amenc and Meyfredi (2007). That is also why the early CISDM passive indices are no longer published on the website – the non-simulated returns soon moved away from the benchmark indicators. This also explains why the RiskMetrics Group, one of the most important promoters of the factor models for traditional assets, proposed in Daul and Finger (2007) the use of an auto-regressive approach for hedge funds. While replicating the past is easy, predicting the future in terms of exposure appears to be a far more complex affair.

Some promoters of clones position their products as replicas of diversified funds of funds. This approach has several advantages. First, as mentioned earlier, it remedies the factor models' inability to replicate efficiently strategies more complex than those dependent upon the equity markets. Second, this positioning enables the clones to be sold as passive indices and to compete head-on with the investable indices. Third, it makes the clones more attractive in terms of cost, since the hedge funds are replicated based on their net, rather than gross, returns. As a result, the only reduction in fees occurs in relation to investment vehicles with two layers of fees, i.e. funds of funds. Fourth, and final, advantage: considering the clones as replicas of funds of funds enables their promoters to get around the absence of active management during market shocks. As one promoter pointed out at the EDHEC Asset Management Day 2007 held in Geneva on 13 March, the liquidity restrictions mean that the funds of funds managers, too, are prevented from taking action in market reversals. However, this argument fails to convince, owing to a basic difference: funds of funds are composed of hedge funds that are themselves managing actively.

Moreover, all the investment vehicles that claim to replicate the hedge funds' exposures no doubt rely on recent academic findings – sometimes as yet unpublished – but it seems strange to be proposing financial instruments whose underlying mechanisms have never been proved valid. All the more so since the industry has already, in the past, succumbed to the lure of creating passive non-investable indices with a factor model before having any sound validation (CISDM passive indices). In all likelihood, this haste is motivated by the desire to stimulate academic research.

Lastly, replication by exposure raises two fundamental questions. First, modelling a strategy assumes the existence of a representative sample of managers following this strategy.[17] As previously demonstrated, such a sample does not exist. We can thus expect the level of heterogeneity between clones to be even higher, owing to the diversity of the models employed. Second, one could question the value to an investment vehicle of having short-term positions with a lag of two years; after all, the regressions performed on the monthly returns determine the average positions over the past 24 months (at least for the adjustment quality). There can be no better way to end up systematically lagging the field on all past opportunities.

In the absence of representativeness, any passive index is thus nothing more than a systematic hedge fund. Not surprisingly, promoters of clones are aware of this feature[18] and try to take advantage of the real nature of a so-called hedge funds clone. Indeed, we may, for instance, regret that many Commodity-Trend-Following managers have somehow perverted the CTA strategy initiating in the early 2000s important exposure to equity market. During the first quarter of 2005, a large number of long-term trend followers allocated more than 60% of their risk budgets to a long position in the equity market. With such exposure, it becomes difficult to see the kind of protection against sudden equity market turmoil that these CTAs are supposed to offer. This explains why some clones of Managed Futures Strategy do not attempt to duplicate the current trend-following betas, but propose to offer exposure to the alternative betas that are similar to these of Fung and Hsieh (2000), computed for the period from 1989 to 1997. These so-called CTA clones can no longer claim to be representative, even though it makes a lot of sense to include them within a multi-manager portfolio because of their specific exposure.

4.2.3   Replication of Distributions

Another type of passive index results from a cloning methodology aimed not at reproducing the exposures to risk factors, but at supplying a return distribution similar to that of any hedge fund over the long term. Taken month by month, the returns may differ significantly and thus contain a substantial tracking error; but the two distributions should enable the

---

[17] To circumvent this issue, some clones propose to duplicate the alternative and exotic betas of some selected managers. But in the absence of representativeness, clones can only claim to be specific, actively managed investment vehicles.

[18] As a consequence, for the portable alpha issue, clones can be used only for a small part of the core portfolio.

same levels of return, of risk (volatility, asymmetry and thickness of the distribution tails) and of correlation with a given traditional portfolio. The synthetic returns are obtained by setting up a systematic strategy on a selection of forward contracts. When applied to a series supposed to represent an alternative strategy, this methodology produces a passive index.

In the same way as the model replicating exposures, the model cloning the distributions depends for its validity upon its predictive power. And this type of model too is far from having achieved consensus as regards the out-of-sample results. Amenc and Meyfredi (2007) applied the methodology to indices of hedge fund indices and found, over a period of eight years, that while the real and synthetic distributions were fairly similar in terms of risk measurements, their averages differed. Furthermore, over three years, the distributions may not correspond at all.

This type of product will therefore interest only those investors who do not feel the need to check the returns regularly and who can concentrate solely on the long term, ignoring the levels of return. For the others – and there are many – this type of passive index is no more than a specific hedge fund that, in the short term, may even be de-correlated from the strategy that it purports to duplicate.

4.3 CONCLUSION

The early 2000s also brought the first investable indices, followed more recently by others from the major providers of traditional indices, such as MSCI, S&P, Dow Jones and FTSE, as well as from high-profile names in finance (CS and Royal Bank of Canada) and alternative investments (HFR). Despite these vehicles being funds of funds in disguise,[19] it is estimated that in 2006 over 12 billion US dollars were invested in index products for alternative funds.

This boom stems above all from the sheer force of marketing. After all, for the promoters, and also their investors, the investable indices are the ideal tool for delegating responsibility. For hedge fund analysts, the pseudo-representativeness offers a ready-made excuse for selection errors. For the managers of the index-linked vehicles, the task consists

---

[19] The inclusion of hedge fund indices among the assets eligible for UCITS III vehicles tends to signify in practice that any fund of funds or fund of managed accounts could be distributed to retail investors. The fund of funds managers would only have to disseminate a few arbitrary systematic rules describing the way they manage their hedge fund portfolio, with no need for representativeness, and proclaim themselves indices.

of managing a fund whose benchmark is its own performance. For the sellers of the indexed products, the confusion created by the various levels of return and the assumed representativeness enable the use of either pro forma data, or gross data or even those of another product. Finally, for the managers of institutional portfolios, allocating funds to a product reputed to be an index provides a means of avoiding all responsibility for selection. Nevertheless, the advantages to institutional investors of delegating responsibility for index selection were contradicted recently by the Refco bankruptcy, which hurt investors in the Standard and Poor's hedge fund index.

But the success of the investable indices also relates to the strong demand for two types of product that are missing from the market, a fact from which they benefit.

First, a portion of the shareholders in the investable indices wishes to obtain exposure to the alternative strategies without being dependent upon the choice of managers. They could thus create a core portfolio geared to the beta of the alternative strategies and add a portfolio of a few hedge funds carefully picked to capture their alpha. The selectors of hedge funds could limit their exposure solely to the managers' talents by short-selling the strategic indices and investing in the strategy's best hedge funds. These viable approaches require the creation of so-called passive indices, i.e. indices that represent only the strategy without the added value of the manager. Clearly, these indices cannot be obtained by grouping the allocations to a large number of hedge funds. Instead one must replicate the strategies by means of derivative products and systematic management. The hedge fund clones, of which the first were launched at the end of 2006, strive to reply to that demand. Unfortunately, while those on offer are fairly efficient at replicating the past upon which they are built of overdiversified portfolio, they have trouble predicting the future or duplicating individual hedge funds.

Launching hedge fund clones before the underlying models have been validated by academic consensus smacks of commercial interests. At the very most, one could also see a desire to stimulate academic research, as the first investors are indirectly financing such studies; and while, for the investable indices, the future lies in eliminating the legal restrictions, for the clones, everything is open. One day, someone may well discover a means of replicating the returns of a vast majority of hedge funds. In that case, the gains generated by a method that is efficient across all strategies will throw new light on the opportunity for a passive approach to funds whose philosophy is the antithesis of indexation. But so far, the clones, which are neither representative nor able to replicate the returns of individual alternative funds, duplicate only themselves and are nothing more than specific systematic hedge funds.

The second type of product sought after through the investable indices is not a type of index, since representation of the hedge funds universe is not really the point. On the contrary, the investor is mainly seeking portfolios that reflect the selection.

The indexing revolution that began for traditional assets in the early 1970s also ushered in a new trend: the diminishing role of the arbitrary element in financial management. Nothing could be more fundamentally opposed to indexing than hedge funds, in view of the freedom of their mandates: the manager's renowned skill, his 'alpha', is a monument to all that is arbitrary. To this must be added a second layer of discretionary influence, induced by the active management of a hedge fund portfolio. For many years, allocation by strategy was determined in the early stages of portfolio construction according to the portfolio's aims and constraints, and any subsequent adjustments were minor. There were two main justifications for this approach: first, the different strategies and styles displayed a certain degree of stability in their risk–reward profiles over a 24-month horizon; second, the hefty returns on hedge funds at the time did not justify tactical allocation, which was rendered difficult by the subscription and redemption restrictions imposed by the hedge funds. As of the beginning of this century, the situation changed profoundly. Empirically, the relations between the risk–reward profiles of the various strategies/styles were no longer as robust in the medium term, and the decline in returns was accompanied by changes in the cyclical behaviour of the styles' performances. Today, within a fund of funds, the tactical re-allocations, particularly for the various arbitrage styles, are a significant source of upside potential, as demonstrated by Amenc, et al. (2002).

For institutional investors accustomed to benchmarks, this increase of the arbitrary element in fund of funds management was a spur to seeking a more objective approach, such as that proposed by the investable indices. However, in reality, the demand focused on highly diversified portfolios, managed passively and composed of hedge funds that, on the one hand, satisfied the stringent due diligence requirements of institutions, and, on the other, were used in various funds of funds or portfolios with special mandates seeking something other than pseudo-representativeness. In fact, investors were hoping to gain access to a portfolio of the list of approved funds, i.e. the raw material of the fund of funds managers.[20]

Unfortunately, the investable indices do not really answer this demand. Six out of the eight index families use platforms of managed accounts and expose their investors to an additional bias: that of managers that agree to offer managed accounts or whose strategy is not incompatible with the liquidity requirements of this type of platform. As a result, only three of the 20 largest hedge funds are found on these platforms. In addition, the two families of indices composed of funds and not of managed accounts seek to represent the universe by weights that reflect either the capitalization or the strategy allocation. Finally, the index products are generally the core business these promoters and the hedge funds selected are not used primarily for differentiated mandates.

Very few investment vehicles to date reply to this specific demand. Rare indeed are the fund of funds managers with a list of approved funds and a sufficiently large range of products to offer their clients access to a portfolio of at least 150 open hedge funds. Furthermore, these hedge funds must be allocated to one of their funds of funds or to managed accounts. In reality, when the managers meet these two conditions, they prefer to reserve the hedge funds' capacity for the products whose alpha will be less diluted and fees are higher. Moreover, as the alternative industry largely benefited from the benchmark bubble bursting, promoters of funds of funds tend to disregard any approach linked with benchmarking investment.

The real conflict raging around the indices is neither the attack of the clones nor a battle between active and passive. It is simply a race for access to hedge funds of good quality – a capacity war. The surge in hedge fund assets since the start of this century has, at one and the same time, attracted managers of inferior quality and led hedge funds to refuse new investors very soon after being created. All the more reason why the banks, funds of funds and consultants that are the usual providers of access to alternative funds must rush to track down the Bacons, Moores and Medallions of tomorrow in a constantly expanding universe. Some players have preferred to withdraw from the competition, in view of the cost of the research involved, but have found other side routes into this lucrative market. The first solution is to package their funds of

---

[20] The optimal approach in terms of representativeness is to invest in a portfolio of portfolios of the approved list of the 10 largest alternative fund investors. Here too, the use of an index of investable indices currently available would be an unsatisfactory approach, due to the biases of under-representativeness and managed accounts.

funds differently by calling them investable indices, to manage them pseudo-passively, and to select the more easily available hedge funds of mediocre quality. The second solution is to create their own systematic hedge funds (a model is always cheaper than a team of managers in the medium term) and call them clones. In both cases, the products' ability to represent the hedge funds universe is of little importance.

5

The Four Dimensions of Risk Management for Hedge Funds

What is a good risk management approach for hedge funds? This question has been confusing for at least two reasons. First, the concept of risk gathers a large set of factors. Rahl (2003) relates a 'galaxy of risks' whose partial listening counts about 59 risks. Second, this question is actually addressed to two different financial agents whose needs are different. As a matter of fact, the hedge fund manager is the first person to wonder about the risk management process he or she should put in place. Answering this question requires a clear vision of what a hedge fund really is, which is slightly tricky as reflected by the non-existence of a standard definition. However, Schneeweis (1998) significantly improved the understanding of the notion of hedge funds by the following definition[1]:

> Some hedge funds can be viewed as the privatisation of the trading of the investment banks. New technology has permitted investment professionals to invest-ment banks and trade externally what formerly was conducted only internally.

As a consequence, the risk management to be performed by the hedge fund manager is very similar to that of any financial services company, but unlike strongly capitalized asset managers, hedge funds are mainly very entrepreneurial firms tending to put their main resources on the investment aspects. The second aspect concerns the hedge fund investors. Here, the above definition also helps. Considering the hedge funds as a company will lead investors to perform a due diligence work analysing the operational risk, the market risk and the credit risk. As noted by Ineichen (2003):

> 'By viewing hedge funds as a separate asset class or as alternative investment strategies, one might have a tendency to underestimate operational risk.'

Indeed, a study carried out by Feffer and Kundro (2003) indicates that about 50% of hedge fund failures can be attributed to poor operational

---

[1] Moreover, this definition provides the fundamental reason why hedge fund growth is not a bubble and announces the consolidation of the traditional and alternative investment management.

risk controls. By adopting sound practices in the areas of operational risk, funds can mitigate investors' concerns. This constitutes the first dimension of risk management for hedge fund investors. The basics should include adequate segregation of duties, frequent cash and position reconciliations, satisfactory systems, and sufficient and capable staff. This is especially important when investing with hedge fund managers, who may operate in an environment of limited regulatory oversight and may provide investors minimal transparency.

The second dimension of risk management for hedge fund investors relies on the fact that when investing in alternative funds, both portfolio management and risk management of this portfolio is delegated to a third party. This delegation of risk requires a clear understanding of both the investment policy and the market risk management policy. For this second dimension, the Schneeweis (1998) definition reminds us that when the credit analysts have conducted bottom-up due diligence work on quoted companies, traditional investors in financial services company do not continuously attempt to obtain trading desk positions in order to do their own risk measurement.[2] Delegating requires not only the ability to overlook, monitor, and recuperate the mandate if it is no longer in line with the initial agreement, but also to restrict oneself to redo the job. If one is not able to do so, one should not delegate as it is simply not optimal and, in the case of hedge funds, fees are simply not justified.

As a consequence, deep due diligence conducted through exhaustive interviews and cross-checking is required from the investors on the background and integrity of the fund's key people, on the process and the philosophy of investment decision, on the construction (including the trading practice) of the portfolio, on the economic source of the returns and the edge of the manager, and on the capacity of the strategy.

Moreover, studying fund managers' approach to risk management – such as the systems and procedures in place to monitor and effectively control their own risk – is a key part of qualitative analysis. The path rate of financial innovation accelerated significantly during the 2000s. The broad range of products now being traded and created in the market for equity investments and credit markets include vanilla cliquet products, swing and reverse swing cliquet products, multi-asset structures, and dispersion products involving models based on the vol-gamma, the

---

[2] In that sense, the transparency argument against hedge funds seems completely unjustified. As mentioned, by Professor Amenc during the EDHEC Alternative Investment Days 2007 in London: 'Does the total lack of transparency on oil reserves prevent people from investing in oil companies?'

skew-gamma and cross-gamma effects. The belief that one single software or one standard process would be able to handle the risk measures and the risk control of all the financial products has turned out to be an illusion. This new environment requires special expertise within a qualitative research analyst team.

However, there is one part of risk management that an investor in hedge funds cannot delegate to the managers: the measure of the risks embedded in the mix of hedge funds and the management of his multi-managers' portfolio. This is the third dimension of the risk for the investors in alternative funds. While the interquartile spread between multi-strategy funds of funds is tightening, risk budgeting through a global risk measure and risk attributions at the basket of hedge funds level becomes a crucial issue.

But as evidenced by the debate surrounding hedge funds, the level of technical knowledge required for efficient and robust passive indices is currently not available. So, the risk-budgeting approach could be performed through two types of indicators: one related to the risk of the underlying position of the managers and the other based on the risk attached to the strategy.

Finally, the portfolios of many multi-managers are not managed by the final investor: a third party receives a mandate whose guidelines and targets should be internally monitored by an independent entity. Banks and large financial institutions have set up, for their other investments, a risk management desk that operates the financial control. This risk control at the multi-managers' portfolio constitutes the last dimension of risk management for the investors in hedge funds, and will not be discussed further is this text.

5.1 OPERATIONAL AND STRUCTURAL RISK

Structural risk is defined as consisting of all non-investment related risks associated with hedge fund investing. It is the risk of loss caused by deficiencies in internal controls, business processes, or information systems and may be the result of either internal or external events. These risks may range from minor operational issues to highly significant and pervasive structural deficiencies, and may be present at any level of an organization. Examples of structural risks in hedge funds include: deficiencies in internal controls in a hedge fund manager's back-office; deficiencies in controls in the administrator's organization; legal and/or regulatory non-compliance; fraud and criminal acts; business interruption, including systems failures and ineffective disaster recovery plans; and weak corporate culture and/or lack of ethics within the hedge fund firm.

Since nearly half of all hedge fund failures are attributable to issues other than performance, operational due diligence should be performed by someone who is not only knowledgeable in the underlying investment strategy but is also familiar with hedge fund managers and their operations. A thorough due diligence evaluation will involve questions about the trading strategy and implementation as well as questions about the overall business aspects of the hedge fund.

Even the most effective system of internal controls and procedures cannot provide absolute assurance that a fund will not suffer a loss for structural reasons since there remains a possibility that even robust controls can be over-ridden. However, an effective control environment can dramatically reduce the risk of loss, illustrating the value of sound operating practices for any hedge fund. Any process to assess structural risk should have at least two stages. First, assess the level of structural risk present in any hedge fund, then examine the adequacy of risk controls implemented by each manager to reduce the operational risks to an acceptable level.

5.1.1   Sources of Structural Risk

There are three primary factors that significantly influence the level of structural risk in any hedge fund: the fund's investment strategy, the size of the organization, and the length of time the management company has been in business.

Investment Strategy and Pricing Issue

The types of securities traded influence the degree of operational risk in any fund. For example, investments in derivatives, private placements, or distressed securities require a higher degree of operational sophistication than that required to support a long/short equity strategy. Similarly, securities pricing may introduce valuation risk into the portfolio, as we already witnessed with the side pocket issue.

Valuation methodology is critical because hedge funds offer periodic liquidity (i.e. monthly or quarterly redemptions). Therefore, management and incentive fees are paid, and redemptions are made on actual realized gains as well as on unrealized gains. Pricing (i.e. unrealized gains) is often determined by the manager, which puts the responsibility on the client to conduct thorough due diligence.

Investment fund portfolios are priced in accordance with generally accepted accounting principles (GAAP), and therefore investments should be reported on the fund's books at 'fair value'. Fair value, defined by the Financial Accounting Standards Board (FASB), is the price at which an asset or liability could be exchanged in a current transaction between knowledgeable and unrelated parties.

The fair value for exchange-traded instruments is typically the exchange closing price. Operational risk is increased when a fund holds non-listed securities or over-the-counter derivatives. Non-listed investments may include distressed and convertible debt, bank debt, swaps, or private investments. These investments inherently have a higher risk profile.

Non-listed securities trade in negotiated markets; therefore, shareholders cannot rely on an exchange to provide pricing. These securities have inherent pricing risk due to the subjectivity applied in determining valuation. Liquidity also affects pricing as these securities could have significant bid/offer spreads making it difficult to determine the true price for the investment. Non-listed securities are generally marked manually by the manager, and every manager performs his pricing process differently. A variety of pricing practices can be used to determine the fair value of non-listed instruments. However, dependent on the source of the data, the amount of data used, and the liquidity of the instrument, pricing of the same security by various managers could be materially different.

Over-the-counter derivatives are also generally priced manually by the manager using sophisticated models and broker quotes. Model input errors and a lack of knowledge regarding the models increase the risk of misvaluation. Relying solely on the counter-party's mark also creates a conflict of interest.

Private investments may include private equity or direct lending positions. Private equity is typically kept at cost; however, in accordance with GAAP, market data should be incorporated into the fair valuation process. Securities therefore can be marked up or down if there is an economic event that supports a change in the valuation of the company. While private investments are often segregated into side pockets where incentive fees are not charged until the investment is realized, this is not always the case. For lending funds, the valuation is based on a combination of the accounting for interest payments, the credit worthiness of the creditor, and the value and existence of the underlying collateral. Private loans are a specialized business and therefore are subject to various subjective elements.

Restricted securities, such as PIPEs (private investments in public equity), also present pricing subjectivity. Accounting guidance calls for these securities to be valued using a discount to market price. Many managers price their PIPE investments differently: some managers do not use a discount and some apply their discounts in a subjective manner. Over the years, pricing for less liquid securities has become easier due to the addition of data providers in markets such as secondary bank loans and credit derivatives, and a knowledge of the industry standard practice for each asset class is critical when determining whether a hedge fund has an acceptable amount of valuation risk.

Obviously, in most circumstances, structural risk increases with the complexity of the investment strategy.

Organization Size

The size of a management company influences the degree of inherent structural risk in any fund. Management companies can be classified among three categories: small, medium to large and institutional. Structural risk is assessed to be higher for smaller organizations that may have less-developed operational infrastructures. Among other things, smaller organizations may have a lesser degree of segregation of duties; the investment manager may have significant influence over the valuation of the portfolio; portfolio/trade management and accounting systems may not be adequately sophisticated; compliance policies may not be well defined or monitored; and the quality of back office personnel may be lower.

Length of Operating History

Moreover, a start-up company, even of large size, may expose investors to increased operational risks as new operating policies and procedures are implemented and employees become acquainted with each other and with their new roles and responsibilities. A portfolio manager that has always been part of a larger operation will go through a learning curve as the new firm learns to handle not only portfolio management but also payroll, personnel, legal, accounting, and other administrative distractions. At the opposite end of the spectrum, succession planning and motivation for the portfolio manager to remain in business must be evaluated for mature organizations.

Considering investment strategy and management company size together with the time the manager has been in business, determines the level of structural risk present in any hedge fund. The highest levels of structural risk are present in start-up funds which implement a complex or intermediate strategy yet are of a small size, suggesting that their operational resources may not be sufficient, given the operational demands of the investment strategy.

5.2   RISK CONTROL

Structural risk should also identify and evaluate the quality of controls and procedures implemented by a hedge fund manager using a comprehensive approach to address all areas of a fund's operations. Information is obtained through a corporate documentation review coupled with on-site visits to the manager and the fund's administrator. A particular focus is to identify sound practices in key operational areas, and assess the extent to which a manager matches the controls and procedures implemented by industry leaders within its peer group.

5.3   DELEGATION RISK

For hedge fund investors, the delegation risk regroups both the market and credit risk exposure taken through the investment performed by the manager and the risk control put in place by the hedge fund. Analogically to the operation risk, the sources of the delegation risk are the market, the credit and the liquidity risk, while the risk control is the risk management process on these three operational aspects.

5.3.1   Market Risk

Selecting hedge fund managers is similar to choosing a potential exposure to the risk factors attached to dynamic investment strategies with alternative betas, high level of alpha and a risk management overlay (at the hedge fund level). This is why the hedge fund selection is generally performed through qualitative analysis that target to provide deep insights on the motivations and on the construction of the portfolio.

Even though each manager may implement an alternative strategy in a very different way and there does not exist a standard strategy classification, some general risk exposures can be extracted by a large set of alternative investment styles. Table 5.1 shows the theoretical risk matrix adapted from Sidani and Soueissy (2003) for the CS/Tremont classification and provides a global view of the main risk exposures.

As a simple illustration, Appendices B and C describe the risk exposure embedded with some classical alternative investment styles as well as some common risk to several styles. Deeper analysis can be found in Reynolds Parker (2000), Rahl (2003) or Jaeger (2002).

5.3.2   Risk Controls

Selecting a manager also involves choosing a risk manager. The key issue is the match between the investment process and the investment risk management.

Obviously, as a first step one must check whether the investment risk management is an intimate part of the portfolio construction process and whether it complies with existing external regulations if any. While most managers apply very strict rules and have hired complete teams to take care of this activity, some make it a very loose guideline. Moreover, the investment risk control may be conducted independently, be imbedded in the investment approach in the case of systematic traders or may be taken care of by the investment officer at his own discretion. Another important aspect is to know whether the current risk management process is a new add-on to the firm or whether it has existed since the inception of the fund.

Moreover, hedge fund investors should first identify the internal risk procedures and guidelines a given hedge fund uses to manage and control the various risks inherent to its investment style. An examination of the history of stop-losses, hits and of the frequency of consecutive trading up is a crucial element in understanding the actual contribution of risk management in the investment process. In the same way, the leverage policy may be crucial. For instance, dynamic trading strategies could be adjusted to reflect the amount of leverage employed, or if the leverage is not aligned with the level of risk embedded to the strategy, creditors may impose additional costs on the manager that could dampen returns and, in a snowball effect, end up in an even higher level of leverage. More generally, the existence and the level of hard limits on leverage, concentration in positions in both explicit and implicit exposures, as well as on risk budgets, should be clearly understood.

Table 5.1 Theoretical Risk Matrix with respect to Short Term Interest Rate Risk (STIR), Long Term Interest Rate Risk (LTIR), Yield Curve Interest Rate Risk (YCIR), Business Cyclical Risk (YCIR), Business Cyclical Risk (BUS), Volatility Risk (VOL), Correlation Risk (COR), Credit Risk (CRT), Liquidity Risk (LIQ), Event Risk (ER)

	STIR	LTIR	YCIR	BUS	VOL	COR	CRT	LIQ	ER
Convert	LO(−)	HI(−)	HI(−)	HI(+)	HI(++)	LO(−)	HI(−)	MED(−)	LO(−)
Short	HI(−)	LO(−)	HI(−)	NDR	NDR	HI(−)	NDR	HI(−)	HI(−)
Emerging	NDR	NDR	NDR	MED(−)	MED(−)	NDR	HI(−)	HI(−)	HI(−)
M. Neut.	NDR	NDR	NDR	NDR	NDR	HI(++)	NDR	LO(−)	NDR
Event-D.	MED(−)	LO(−)	NDR	HI(+)	NDR	NDR	MED(−)	LO(−)	NDR
Fixed I.	HI(++)	HI(++)	HI(++)	NDR	HI(++)	LO(−)	HI(−)	HI(−)	NDR
Macro	HI(−)	HI(−)	HI(−)	NDR	NDR	NDR	HI(−)	HI(−)	NDR
L/S	NDR	NDR	NDR	NDR	NDR	HI(+)	NDR	LO(−)	LO(−)
CTA	NDR	NDR	NDR	NDR	HI(++)	HI*	HI(−)	MED(−)	MED(−)

When a risk management system is used, the hedge funds managers should be aware of any weaknesses in the risk software chosen. Furthermore, the manager should have developed a particular policy to complement the signal provided for the financial products that are incorrectly valuated by the system.

5.4   DIRECT INVESTMENT RISK

A structural and qualitative analysis, although vital, is not sufficient: the financial market instability of recent years and the complexity of hedge fund strategies demand regular risk monitoring after the investment has been made, and the quantitative measurement of hedge fund risks is an essential part of this monitoring process since it is systematic, continuous and can be automated – unlike qualitative monitoring, which requires frequent, meticulous analysis and on-site assessments. Moreover, institutional clients consolidate the market of their total portfolio which requires a simple and synthetic risk indicator such as Value-at-Risk. Finally, an efficient portfolio management assumes an understanding of the risk attached to each position and how they really diversify each other. This has become particularly crucial for multi-strategy funds of funds managers, since the spread between the best investment vehicles and the worst has significantly tightened.

The alternative funds industry is characterized by the lack of a standard risk measurement and reporting format. This lack of uniformity makes risk consolidation a difficult task at multi-manager portfolio level. For example, not only are there different ways of calculating Value-at-Risk, but the measurement of the latter also depends, among other things, on the time horizon, the frequency of data and the likelihood of any expected loss. Adding up the Value-at-Risk supplied by the managers is therefore the equivalent of adding up apples and pears. Furthermore, it does not include the diversification effects among different asset classes.

To understand precisely the risks in a fund of funds, the risk factors in each alternative fund should be captured in standardized ways conducted by the investors. However, an efficient explicit modelling of all the alternative strategies with respect to the traditional risk factors does not currently exists as the debate around hedge fund clones has proved. Therefore, a combination of two approaches can represent the risk, the first one focusing on the underlying allocation of each hedge fund's portfolio and the other focusing on the implicit risk embedded in the hedge fund's strategy.

5.4.1 Underlying Approach

The underlying approach consists in the fund of funds manager adding up the investment positions of each manager. According to the degree of transparency provided by the hedge funds, consolidation of exposure to asset classes (macro), or of individual positions (micro), takes place.

In the case of macro consolidation, the investor acts as risk manager for the entire portfolio by consolidating the major positions. First, market risk exposure and credit risk exposure are evaluated taking into account the manager's strategy. The measurement process is then refined. For example, for long/short funds that have exposure to a specific sector, an appropriate measurement tool will be the adjusted exposure to the relevant sector index. With a multi-manager portfolio, the process of consolidating the sensitivity to the market sector under consideration tends to underestimate the total coefficient. Indeed, within the same sector, managers make optimal use of diversification effects. The sector subportfolio that results from the combination of the different funds' positions does not provide an optimal diversification. A conservative approach therefore consists in systematically increasing the adjusted exposure.

Macro consolidation, even if it only offers an approximation to financial risk measurement, avoids the duplication of exposure and an excessive sensitivity to certain risk factors within a portfolio, following periods of market dislocation. Thus, it is a realistic compromise between the simple addition of total risk data supplied by each manager and a micro approach that requires scrutiny.

Micro consolidation assumes the total transparency of alternative funds. All the individual portfolio positions of different managers are gathered together in one unique portfolio that contains all the shares, bonds and derivative products in which the fund of funds is invested through the managers.

Micro consolidation is only possible in three cases: when the portfolio is made up of managed accounts, when managers supply all the positions taken by the funds to investors, and when information is provided to a third person in charge of measuring the portfolio's risk. Managed accounts offer not only total transparency but also control of the investment process. However, most performing and desirable managers only offer the option of a fund as an investment vehicle. Indeed, investable indices giving the average performance of managers on managed account platforms clearly underperform the average funds of funds. Furthermore, managed accounts imply a greater responsibility by the investor (reimbursement of losses exceeding the initial invested capital). Investment in this type of vehicle is therefore sometimes neither possible nor desirable. The remaining funds, as a general rule, offer a limited level of transparency.

Managers justify their lack of transparency with three arguments. First, although it is admitted that transparency is of great value when managing risk, the benefits from it are low because of the liquidity of the funds and the lack of involvement by investors in the hedge fund investment process. Second, the disclosure of a number of managers' positions (especially short-selling positions), can work against the fund's interest. Finally, managers fear losing their competitive advantage if they fully reveal their strategy and how it is applied.

For all these reasons, the use of a third person that can assure confidentiality may lower managers' reluctance about divulging their positions. The intermediary can collect the information and use its own platform to calculate the total risk in the portfolio. As a further solution, the hedge fund manager may buy specific risk management software to disclose the consolidated output to the third party who will perform the aggregation of the individual standardized reports for the funds of funds.

Although, some years ago, the use of a third party risk transparency provider was theoretically possible, it was difficult to apply in practice. On the one hand, many managers refused either to disclose all their positions even to a third party or to buy other risk management software only for the purpose of client relationship as the various bodies offering their services as intermediaries between alternative funds and their investors did not offer a sufficiently large hedge funds universe. On the other hand, many of these risk transparency third parties tried to capture the risk attached to the strategy. Given the underlying position, this required each hedge fund to model the strategy. As already mentioned about the hedge funds clones debate, no one has currently the knowledge to do so and the information provided was a mix between strategy risk exposure and underlying risk sensitivity due to the mis-modelling of investment styles.

The situation has recently improved. First, some intermediaries gave up the idea of measuring the risk of the strategy and decided to stick to measuring the risk of the portfolio allocation. Second, some of the third party risk transparency providers have increased the list of managers that agree to report to them. This, of course, reflects the ongoing institutionalization of the hedge funds industry, as well as the fact that some third parties gave up the idea of selling their programs to hedge fund managers or of imposing any constraint (financial or not). However, as at the end of 2007, much work remains to convince managers to report to a third party provider. A lot of hedge funds still fear that micro consolidation would provide a completely wrong view on the risk of the portfolio, as based on an approach that denies both the fact that they have put in place dynamic trading strategies with risk management policies and that no single software (and particularly those used by some third party risk transparency providers) can correctly measure the risk of their portfolios. They are particularly aware that despite the fact that micro consolidation is only one small part of a multi-dimensional approach to risk, investors will tend to focus on this measure of market risk, and will later do the same for their traditional portfolios. The success of the underlying approach will depend on the ability of investors to convince hedge fund managers that micro consolidation is only one part of a multi-dimension approach to risk management, and that the information provided by risk transparency intermediaries should be interpreted according to a clear vision of the strategy risk. Otherwise the universe of managers agreeing to report to this kind of risk platform will never grow without depreciating its average quality.

5.4.2 Strategy Risk Approach

Indeed, even though indirect underlying transparency was possible for the whole hedge funds universe, micro consolidation carries significant weaknesses. First, exposure is not sufficient – it is also necessary to know the exposure limits that the manager has established for each of its investments. For example, even if two long/short funds buy the same stock, their risk exposure will differ according to the stop-loss orders attached to the underlying. The simple adding up of exposure would provide an incorrect risk measurement for the fund of funds. Second, as already mentioned, no single software is able to handle the risk of the whole set of financial assets and derivatives. Till (2007) relates to the LTCM collapse and more recent hedge fund debacles owing to market risk share in common that the potential losses have been underestimated by risk metrics using underlying recent historical data. The risk measure provided through micro consolidation would therefore also be largely

Table 5.2   Simulated monthly position for a particular trading strategy over a six-month period using Lo (2001) weekly data

Month	Price ($)	Position (Shares)	Value ($)	Financing($)
0	40.000	7,057	282,281	−296,974
1	36.875	27,128	1,000,356	−1,024,865
2	39.875	5,621	224,153	−176,479
3	40.625	3,230	131,205	−76,202
4	39.750	4,267	169,609	−117,814
5	39.750	3,510	139,526	−87,917
6	40.000	2,445	97,782	−45,617

misleading. Third, managers that exploit short term imperfections can quickly change the entire composition of their portfolio. Consolidation therefore combines current positions with investments that have ceased to exist in the portfolio.

Finally, the underlying position reflects neither the dynamic aspects of the alternative investment styles nor the different ways to implement it. Positions may be fully transparent, while strategies may not. For instance, Lo (2001) gives an example of a strategy that can appear through static micro consolidation to be simply long a stock. Analysing the position of Table 5.2, month by month, excluding the second one, may suggest that the manager is implementing a contrarian strategy, increasing position when price declines and reducing exposure after price advances. The second month reveals that when prices drastically drop, the leverage is highly increased. Actually, Table 5.2 reveals that the manager trades a delta hedging strategy that synthetically replicates a short position in a two-year deep out-of-the-money (strike price is USD 40) European put option on 10 million shares. As a consequence, the strategy may lead to extreme losses that are completely undervalued by the initial positions. Obviously if the full position disclosure may be completely misleading for a simple portfolio composed of one stock, one can imagine the low level of relevancy of micro consolidation on portfolios composed of many assets or derivatives without strategy risk transparency.

In order to capture the risk of the strategy, one could try to model the alternative strategy returns with respect to traditional risk factors. Obviously, this is completely related to the problem of passive indices that we discussed in the previous chapter. As a consequence of the current state of knowledge, the pragmatic solution for a quantitative measure of hedge funds' market risk means giving up the explicit side of the model and focusing on an efficient measure. The model should not try to explain explicitly the kind and the level of exposure to traditional risk factors, but simply measure the sensitivity to risk factors that contains implicitly various types of exposures to traditional assets. This is what the Style and Implicit Value-at-Risk models develop in Parts II and III.

5.4.3 Overlapping Approaches

Beside these two risk measures, which constitute the third dimension of any risk management process for investors in hedge funds, two other types of quantitative indicators may be implemented: pure quantitative measures and hybrid indicators. These approaches are important in any investment process, however they do not constitute one additional dimension as they fall in between two existing ones.

Pure Quantitative Analysis

The first family of these risk measures is only quantitatively oriented, focusing mainly on the historical track of the hedge funds. No factor models are used, the historical track being the only single input. Indicators from this type of approach mix information related to the strategy risk and to the underlying risk. As no efficient explicit model exists to explain the alternative investment returns with respect the traditional risk factors, the model used by the hedge fund clones currently available also belongs to this type of approach.

These purely quantitative risk indicators constitute a set of useful tools to challenge qualitative assessment and to check that nothing is forgotten in the qualitative due diligence. Examples of pure quantitative methodology can be found in Lhabitant (2004).

Hybrid Approach – Between Qualitative and Quantitative Analysis

The second family of indicators can be seen as the quantitative expression of the due diligence work performed on the delegation risk and thus locates itself between the measurements of delegation risk and strategy risk.

The track record's lack of validity can be supplemented by information gathered from qualitative analysis. This involves the creation of a data type that is more predictive than historical returns. Singer et al. (2002) propose the establishment of a historical returns database, which uses both quantitative and qualitative data for all funds regardless of their age. This new type of data can be used as endogenous variables in factorization models and leads to different estimates.

Even though qualitative analysis is at the heart of hedge fund selection, the creation of a historical returns database demands a high level of effectiveness in its qualitative assumptions. The effects of fundamentals on the fund should be correctly understood for each month. It seems more advisable not to establish a track record, but to restrict oneself to situations where non-linearities may occur. In other words, it is not necessary to calculate the full distribution in order to measure strategic risk but one can focus with a limited number of expectations (performances relating to certain situations) for each fund. This approach is termed hybrid since it carries out quantitative operations on information derived from a qualitative process. It allows for the measurement of risks when applying a strategy despite the absence of stationarity. The relevance of the result depends on the quality of analytical work on the hedge funds and on the regular updating of information.

The hybrid approach presents the advantage of being forward and not backward looking. Then, the treatment of the information is quantitative and performed only on part of the qualitative process that can be perfectly duplicated by a quantitative process. In term of efficiency, the risk of a quantitative mistake performed within a qualitative process is minimized. Furthermore, the process systematically demonstrates a part of the information used to formulate arguments for approval. This obviously clarifies the qualitative decision process, enables the information flow between the selection and the portfolio management to be optimized, and prevents it from drifting away from its initial perception of the hedge funds to a more complaisant approach once approved. In other words, formulating qualitative information also enables the use of this information for the rest of the investment process: monitoring, portfolio construction in terms of return and, of course, risk budgeting.

5.5 CONCLUSION

Parts II and III of this book provide some Value-at-Risk indicators that are limited to the strategy risk of the investment delegated to the hedge fund managers. Indeed, no model can claim to detect the total risk, including the risks related to fraud, liquidity, investor concentration and redemption suspension, together with operational and legal risks. Questions pertaining to the structure of hedge funds may be so complex that it would be sheer folly to invest in one without first having the structure thoroughly audited by a team of specialists in that field. Some hedge fund allocators have been pushed by clients demands to put in place a selection based only on quantitative criteria. This often ends up compensating for the deficiencies of such a hedge fund selection process by inflating Value-at-Risk and other risk indicators in various manners. Doing so assumes at least that the knowledge to have both risk measures based on efficient passive indices and robust Value-at-Operation Risk for hedge funds, is available. If not, then the notion of Value-at-Risk is simply deformed through the introduction of an error that is totally arbitrary and devoid of all theoretical or empirical basis. The due diligence work remains an essential first step in any investment in hedge funds, and no prudent investor can skip it. And as for traditional investments, the quantitative tools are all the more pertinent when the universe has been carefully cleaned of all irregular data.

5.6 APPENDIX B: RISKS EMBEDDED WITH SOME CLASSICAL ALTERNATIVE STRATEGIES

5.6.1 Pure Short Selling

Short sellers are exposed to the same risks as those linked to the buying process, but in a reverse manner and with additional risks. Among the different types of exposure, market risk is by far the most significant. Indeed, the potential losses of a short position are unlimited, as opposed to those involving a purchase. For example, by short selling a share that triples in price the investor loses three times the value of the original share.

The exposure of funds to this risk of unlimited losses varies according to the use of diversification, stop-loss orders and size limits. However, in certain cases, the last two parameters can increase the risk of losses. A systematic policy of stop-loss orders carried out in a set manner (e.g. +10% increase in sale price for all assets), or relative to the recent historical performance of the market, exposes the fund to significant losses during a period of increased market volatility. The losses arising from successive short selling are systematically realized, whereas limit violations arise only due to the increase in market instability and not because of a rising trend.

Short selling also generates risks linked to the stock lending process. Indeed, the short seller can be forced to return the borrowed shares upon demand, either because the owner wishes to protect the asset (despite their interest in lending the shares), or because this is related to their own portfolio management. While the owner of the shares would make a profit following an increase in share price, the short seller will register losses. The degree of risk depends on the quality of the relationship between the alternative fund and its prime broker. While, in theory, brokers require the return of the shares lent most recently (LIFO), in reality the most important clients in terms of their size are often the last to be called upon to return their shares. To a lesser degree, a decreased borrowing capacity as well as certain regulations regarding operational execution, also affect the management of a portfolio, as well as the increase in positions following profitable short selling.

Finally, this strategy is exposed to company-specific risk. After short selling the shares of a company, the announcement of a credible bid for that company will lead to an increase in the share price.

With strategies where short selling is used in order to protect certain positions or to exploit market inefficiencies, a lack of availability to borrow certain shares will considerably restrict investment opportunities. Merger and acquisition arbitrageurs see their participation in certain share deals restricted by the availability of borrowing shares in the companies involved in a transaction.

5.6.2   Long/Short Equity

By combining opposite types of exposure, long/short managers reduce their general risk profile compared with traditional equity managers and compared with pure short sellers. A fairly rough indicator of the exposure to systematic market risk is the difference between the value of purchases and sales, divided by the capitalization of the fund (net exposure). This measurement is refined, taking into account the sensitivity to market movements of long positions and short sales. In this way, two hedge funds A and B that have the same net exposure may have a market risk exposure that is completely different. For example, A may only invest in defensive stocks and B may only invest in growth stocks hedged by defensive stocks.

Technically speaking, net exposure is beta-adjusted, i.e. adjusted to regression coefficients against the market index. But the complementarity between long positions and short sales is never totally perfect. As a result, the specific risks attached to short selling and to long positions remain and the criteria employed for risk management of single strategies must be used. When the complementarity between long positions and short selling positions does not exist, net exposure (adjusted or otherwise) is replaced by gross exposure. Indeed, the difference between long positions and sales allows the measurement not only of the amount of leverage in the fund but also a rough calculation of the exposure to an unfavourable market for each of the positions.

Risk exposure from company-specific characteristics in which a manager has invested depends on the manager's selection capacity, the size of the fund and the number of positions. Finally, long/short hedge funds can be exposed to liquidity risks if they invest in small capitalization companies as well as to model risks, in the case of a quantitative approach.

Some long/short strategies are conducted with a neutrality constraint between purchases and short sales, whether this is in terms of size of the positions or of adjusted exposure. The neutrality can be maintained within sectors, within industries, within market capitalization ranges, or within traditional risk factors. Because of the difficulty of short selling certain sectors or at certain levels of market capitalization, funds that have a total neutrality constraint cannot invest in certain sectors or in relatively illiquid markets.

Obviously, compared to other long/short hedge funds, alternative funds with a neutral exposure therefore have a low level of exposure to systematic risk. In addition, the risk related to asset selection should be measured in relative terms. The strategy does not require price growth in all its long positions and a price fall in those stocks which are sold short. It will be sufficient if the former outperform the latter in a rising market (and inversely in terms of losses in a declining market).

A number of managers use statistical models in this strategy. Model risks are therefore important, because they relate not only to errors in formula calculation or model construction, but also to the hypotheses underlining the majority of statistical models (even if the refinement can be developed to model the non-stationary data). As a general rule, there is a positive relationship between a model's specification and a model's risk. The most extreme case is a specification that seeks to quantitatively replicate historical data in the most exact possible manner, without statistical links being able to be justified from a fundamental point of view. Its predictive power is therefore inversely proportional to the quality of its quantitative description. Over the course of time and with the smoothing out period becoming more distant, the model tends to become less and less useful. In less extreme cases, the existence of a significant technical and theoretical support structure allowing the inclusion of new parameters to the model will reduce exposure to this type of risk. Finally, exceptional events (such as the terrorist attacks of 11 September 2001) or the deleveraging effect on market segments where the strategy is over-invested (August 2007), produce sudden and brutal changes in the historical relations on which these models are built.

5.6.3 Convertible Arbitrage

Convertible bond arbitrage, in its most simple and classical form, benefits from inefficiencies in the valuation of convertible bonds by buying the convertible bond and short selling the underlying equity. A convertible bond, a hybrid instrument made up of a bond and equity, is subjected to the risks arising from its two components: the equity is sensitive to financial market fluctuations whereas the bond, an interest rate instrument, is affected by interest rate levels and credit quality.

In order to hedge against changes in the underlying equity of the convertible bond, the arbitrageur short sells a defined number of shares: exposure to the equity markets is therefore low. However, in a sharply falling market in which the price of the underlying equity decreases in an abnormal manner, the conversion options go too deeply out of the money and the value of the convertible falls significantly.

Bonds are also sensitive to the company's credit quality. After an in-depth study of the credit quality, the manager determines the capacity of the issuer to repay its debt. Sharp movements and fluctuations in bond prices reflect market expectations about potential default. Excluding a company's fundamentals, a company's market capitalization and market liquidity have a determining effect on the credit's characteristics: the weaker the capitalization, the higher the risk of credit spreads widening.

To hedge themselves against credit risk, managers diversify their portfolios with a mixture of different quality debt: debt from a variety of sectors and debt from various geographic regions. For example, a manager can invest its assets in US, European and Japanese convertible bond arbitrage with different credit risk qualities. Fluctuations in interest rates can give rise to movements in credit spreads. In the short term, an increase in interest rates is positive since it indicates a healthy state of the economy. On the other hand, a sustained increase in interest rates makes debt repayments more difficult for companies. The greater the deterioration in credit quality, the lower the capitalization of companies becomes and the closer the conversion option value approaches zero. To counteract interest rate risk, managers use swaps that allow exchanging a floating rate for a fixed rate or they may engage in the short selling of treasury bonds or futures.

5.6.4   Fixed Income Arbitrage

Fixed income arbitrage strategies make their gains from price differentials between interest rate instruments, by simultaneously buying a bond and short selling another bond or an interest rate swap (or any other interest rate derivative). Profits are realized from the elimination of temporary anomalies among the returns of what are broadly similar instruments: T-bills against Euro-Dollars, treasury bonds with the same maturity but different issue dates, different positions on the yield curve or bonds for which the manager has identified strong historical links.

In simple terms, the more similar the instruments, the lower the probability that anomalies will remain, and the more the manager must employ leverage to achieve an attractive rate of return. The degree of similarity between the amount of purchases and sales, as well as the amount of leverage employed, allows us to classify the risks inherent in the strategies of different managers. The degree of similarity can be measured in terms of interest rate risk, credit risk, liquidity risk and of risk linked to exceptional events.

The value of nearly all bond instruments is determined by, among other factors, interest rates: when the latter decrease, the value of bonds increase. The exposure to interest rate risk depends on the equilibrium between the sensitivities of the long and short portfolios to interest rate changes. Three types of changes in interest rates affect the strategy: the direct effect of the change, a parallel shift in the yield curve and changes in the shape of the curve. Duration measures the marginal impact of a change in interest rates. A fund with the same duration in its long and short positions is an indicator of a low linear exposure to interest rate risk (convexity measurements allow the incorporation of non-linear effects). Analysing the sensitivity of the portfolio to parallel shifts in the yield curve, as well as to changes in the shape of the curve, allows us to complete the picture with regards to measuring risk exposure to interest rates.

Certain arbitrage strategies focus on the ability of different qualities of bonds to honour their interest and principal repayments. The fund's credit risk exposure then depends on the quality of positions in the long and short portfolio.

Other arbitrage strategies are the equivalent of receiving a risk premium by financing the purchase of a bond with low liquidity through the sale of a very liquid bond. During financial crises or periods of flight to quality, the prices of the less liquid bonds can fall significantly. In addition, during these periods it becomes difficult to trade certain instruments, which may otherwise be deemed liquid under normal conditions. Exposure to liquidity risk is just as important when leverage levels are high: funds may receive margin calls, thereby forcing sales at lower prices.

This strategy can also be applied to anomalies between bonds with different fundamental characteristics (liquidity, quality, region, etc.), but which have shown strong links historically. These links allow a high degree of confidence when analysing these opportunities. And yet, unexpected events may take place and have an important impact. Funds with this type of approach have a high degree of exposure to exceptional event risk.

Finally, many managers that follow this strategy make heavy use of valuation models that analyse prices or other parameters in order to identify historical trends. As a result they have a significant exposure to model risk.

5.6.5 Risk Arbitrage

Merger and acquisition arbitrage produces its returns from the price differential between the shares of the company making a bid and the target company. In order to be accepted, any acquisition offer must be profitable for the seller. The offer is therefore made at a premium to the market price. This strategy seeks to capture that premium.

The main risk of this strategy lies in the acquisition or merger falling through. A portfolio that holds positions in a number of different transactions with size limits for each individual transaction will reduce the impact of a deal falling through. Portfolio diversification in this strategy however is a highly variable parameter that depends greatly upon merger and acquisition deal flow. During the third quarter of 1998 and after the fourth quarter of 2001, investment opportunities for funds in this strategy significantly decreased: a manager that in normal circumstances would be considered as diversified, during such a period, may see a concentration in its portfolio and an increase in risk exposure to transactions falling through. The exposure to this type of risk decreases not only in relation to the quantity of positions within a portfolio, but also in relation to an active management of the portfolio and to the quality of the transactions. The manager conducts fundamental analysis at the company level in order to determine the probability of a transaction falling through. These criteria are the bidder's ability to finance a transaction as well as its reputation, the probability of the transaction being approved by regulatory authorities, the nature of the agreement between the two parties (agreement in principle, letter of intent, etc.), the degree of confidence in growth expectations of the target company, etc. Exposure to transactions falling through is low for a manager that undertakes an in-depth fundamental analysis and that only invests in those transactions that are most likely to succeed, adjusting weights in proportion to the likelihood of the transaction going through. At the other end of the scale, exposure is extremely high when conducting arbitrage on a transaction that has not been confirmed and is based on rumours.

The risk of losses is linked to financing being available and to stock market risk. Mergers and acquisitions can take different guises and there is a fairly strong relationship between market risk and the risk of a transaction falling through. If the acquisition is done at a set price per share, the arbitrage consists in buying the shares (or a call in the money) of the target company. If the transaction involves an announced share exchange, in the best case scenario strong movements in share prices will lead to parties negotiating the transaction and in the worst case scenario, to its abandonment. A transaction in which the target company's share price is subject to a minimum threshold represents the extreme case combining both risks.

Finally, certain hedge funds can carry liquidity risk if they are involved in transactions between small capitalization companies. The risk profile of different managers must then be assessed with regard to the level of leverage employed. To obtain the same return objective, a portfolio invested in a large number of high-quality transactions carrying a low degree of uncertainty makes greater use of capital borrowing than a portfolio invested in several transactions that carry high premiums. The leverage effect increases returns but it also increases the impact that different risks may have, in particular for transactions with low liquidity or with a high degree of market exposure.

5.7   APPENDIX C: OTHER COMMON HEDGE FUNDS RISKS

5.7.1   Leverage Risk

Hedge fund managers can borrow in order to increase their performance. In the case of unwise investments, losses are amplified in a symmetrical manner and the costs of borrowing increase. The two most widely used measurements of leverage are gross exposure and net exposure. Although these indicators have little meaning for funds following different strategies, they provide a relative and reliable measurement when applied to the same strategy.

Leverage reflects both volatility risk and the risk of financing being available. For strategies with a low level of non-systematic risk, statistical indicators such as Value-at-Risk are better measurements of volatility risk. For strategies with a high level of non-systematic risks, such as arbitrage on companies undergoing restructuring, the different quantitative approaches are supplemented by qualitative methodologies. The latter focus on strategy diversification, positions, allocation control, use of stop-loss orders, etc.

A manager that uses leverage is exposed to the risk of having to return upon demand any borrowing to the brokers. The availability of financing is measured by the quality of the relationship between the manager and its main broker. This is generally positively correlated to the size of the funds. The impact of requirements by the main broker to return borrowing is clearly linked to the liquidity of the investments undertaken by the fund.

5.7.2   Liquidity Risk

With financial assets, liquidity is reflected in circulation potential, i.e. the equilibrium level between the number of buyers and sellers. Treasury bond futures are the most liquid instruments, whereas products linked to emerging market equities offer less liquidity. With hedge funds it refers to the time limits imposed upon investors before they can exit from a fund. A realistic compromise should exist between the liquidity in a portfolio's positions and the liquidity offered by the fund. As an example, let us suppose that for whatever reason the great majority of investors wish to exit a fund at the same time. If the liquidity of the investments is much lower than that offered to the investors in the fund, the manager might see itself forced to sell positions at prices significantly lower than their real value and in this way prejudice the interests of its shareholders. It can also suspend its redemptions if it is incapable of selling (or hedging) its positions. To come to a compromise, the effects on the portfolio have to be thoroughly assessed. Even if a fund is invested in extremely liquid assets, its ability to turn its portfolio around can be reduced by the potential impact this may have on the market.

Finally, because alternative funds can make significant use of leverage, their prime brokers can force managers to sell positions at particularly unfavourable moments.

5.7.3 Counter-Party Risk

The liquidity of an alternative fund must also be analysed through counter-party risk. Indeed, if 50% of capital comes from only one investor, it is likely that redeeming this investor will affect performance. In more general terms, there should be a diversification in terms of types of investors, since investment flows tend to be very similar according to investor types. The investor base, however, is less important if the fund has established limits on the amount of capital that can be repaid during a cash-rich period in its offering memorandum. Counter-party risk can also be seen in the balance between the liquidity levels of the financial instruments and the notice period which the prime broker must respect before changing its lending and margin calls policy. An analysis of the historical frequency of margin calls and of various sources of borrowing allows risk to be evaluated.

5.7.4 Specific Event Risk

The performance of certain strategies can be attributed to the cashing in of risk premiums, whether these premiums are real or synthetic, the latter as a result of different positions taken by the manager. In both cases the returns are characterized by long periods of great stability followed by several months of significant losses. Like an insurance agent, the manager cashes in on the premiums as long as the event for which it is undertaking the risk does not occur.

The most extreme case is a fund that sells volatility. For example, from May 1995 to May 2000, the FTSE 100 index increased 92% in sterling terms, with an average monthly volatility of 3.71%. All things being equal, there is one chance in a hundred, i.e. one month in every eight years, that the index will produce a monthly return below −8.12% or above 10%. When carrying out a simultaneous out-of-the-money sale of a call and a put (a strangle) with a strike price that relates to an event that should not happen more than once in a hundred times, the manager receives the premiums for the two options. The initial capital and the risk premium are invested in a risk-free asset. The number of put and call options (i.e. the leverage) depends on the premium amount for each 'strangle', on the returns produced by the risk-free asset and on the performance that the manager hopes to attain if no option is exercised. The strategy cashes in on the premiums on a regular basis during stable periods, but can lose everything if the market is volatile.

The manager can undertake to hedge a certain amount of volatility risk by simultaneously buying put and call options that reflect extremely volatile events (beyond four standard deviations) at the same time as carrying out a strangle. This operation, which is known as a condor (mainly because of the form of the pay-off diagram), reduces the value of the premium cashed in by the purchase premiums.

In order to achieve the same returns that a non-hedged strategy offers, leverage is increased. As a result, the partial protection of the extreme risk component is obtained by increasing the impact of non-hedged events. In June 2000, a London-based manager launched a fund with a similar strategy. After 15 months, the hedge fund had posted a return of 50%. Following September 11th 2001 and the sharp increase in market volatility, the total performance of the fund since inception fell drastically to 3%.

Other strategies show an asymmetrical distribution of returns by in-cluding a risk premium even if the exposure is significantly smaller than in the previous case. In the case of fixed income arbitrage, hedge funds agree to purchase less liquid bonds from international institutions and hedge themselves by short selling more liquid bonds. They therefore assume the exposure to liquidity risk that belonged to the institutions. If a merger takes place, the arbitrageur assumes the risk of the trans-action falling through. The historical analysis of this strategy shows a return profile similar to that of an options seller. With foreign exchange investments, managers buy the currencies with a high interest rate and finance the purchase by selling the currencies with a low interest rate. If the difference in rates is significant, the strategy carries with it a high degree of exposure to devaluation risk. The latter tends to increase during periods of financial panic and the distribution of returns of this strategy is similar to that found in systematic options selling.

Part II
Style Value-at-Risk

6

The Original Style VaR Revisited

The Value-at-Risk of an asset is aimed at measuring the magnitude of the likely maximum loss that an asset could experience over a finite time horizon with a given probability. Following the standards, the confidence level that is considered here is 99%.[1]

It is a well known fact that Value-at-Risk is not a coherent risk indicator whereas this is the case for conditional Value-at-Risk or Expected Shortfall. The target of the latter consists of measuring the average loss that can be expected when the threshold is exceeded. Expected Shortfall can be simply considered as a composite of Value-at-Risk for different levels of probability and the quality of the Expected Shortfall depends somehow on the efficiency of the Value-at-Risk methodology on which it is based. Moreover, the computation of the Expected Shortfall within the Extreme Value Theory does not raise additional difficulties, as it will be shown in section 7.1.4.

For hedge funds, two types of market risk can be measured: the first is the risk that is inherent to the underlying positions of the hedge fund's portfolio, while the second is the risk explained by both investment strategy and the risk management implemented by the hedge fund manager. If both approaches are complementary, in reality, the first is conducted within the hedge fund (see previous chapter). Moreover, the second is clearly more adapted for investors in hedge funds who benefit from restrictive liquidity conditions from the hedge funds and who finally are exposed to funds using dynamic investment styles with their own risk management. As the risk embedded with the manager's implementation of a dynamic investment style can be captured only through his past performance, the Value-at-Risk for hedge funds should be computed on a monthly Net Asset Value variation. This raises the questions of the scarcity of data due to the low frequency of observations and makes non-parametric estimation unreliable. On the other hand, the parametric estimation for the whole distribution does not rely on any particular

---

[1] Regulators typically insist on a 10-day period and a 99% confidence level.

economic intuition and more particularly hedge fund returns typically exhibit skewness and fat tails.

When facing such a problem, the usual solution is to explain the returns through a factor model whose essence is that the risk embedded in any hedge fund can be split into two components: the first is a function of the systematic factors to which the manager is exposed; the second is the risk that remains unexplained by these factors and as such can be referred to as specifically identified with a certain manager. Three types of models are generally identified: implicit factor models, explicit factor models and the multi-index approach. The weakness of the first approach assumes that real risk factors are not directly observable and change over time. Moreover, the approach relies on the sample from which the implicit factors are extracted, requires heavy computations and faces an important level of model risk. The second approach integrates either macro-economic or micro-economic factors. However, the lack of robust passive indices for hedge funds prove the difficulty of this approach for alternative investments. The last approach was popularized by Sharpe (1988, 1992) in the context of style analysis for mutual fund managers. It is calculated by replacing risk factors with representative indices of all the risks.

The hedge fund multi-index model was originally applied in Lhabitant (2001) and Lhabitant (2002a). For the Value-at-Risk, a methodology that combines the style analysis approach and the factor push approach on each index[2] is proposed. This chapter presents the model and the results obtained in the two seminal papers as well as updates of the backtest.

6.1 THE MULTI-INDEX MODEL

6.1.1 The Sharpe (1988) Model

The return-based style analysis originally suggested by Sharpe (1988) explains the returns of an investment vehicle s as a weighted average of reference portfolios or strategy indices that represent a particular asset class or investment style

$$r_{s,t} = \sum_{i=1}^{n} \omega_{s,i} I_{i,t}$$

---

[2] Note that the model does not take into account credit risk.

where $r_{s,t}$ is the return of the investment vehicle s over period t, $I_{i,t}$ is the return of the investment style i, and $\omega_{s,i}$ is the weight of the investment style i in the decomposition of the return $r_{s,t}, i = 1, \ldots, n$.

Sharpe imposed two restrictions on the parameters of the equation. First, the portfolio restriction requires that the style weights are interpreted as portfolio holdings

$$\sum_{i=1}^{n} \omega_{s,i} = 1.$$

Second, the short-selling restriction requires that all portfolio holdings are long positions expressed for $i = 1, \ldots, n$ by the following inequality

$$0 \leq \omega_{s,i} \leq 1 \quad \forall s$$

In practice, the approach takes the form of the regression model

$$r_{s,t} = \sum_{i=1}^{n} \omega_{s,i} I_{i,t} + \varepsilon_{s,t}$$

where $\varepsilon_{s,t}$ is a disturbance term that denotes the proportion of $r_{s,t}$ that cannot be explained by the investment styles.

6.1.2 Application to Hedge Funds

Since the seminal work of Sharpe, several extensions of the model have been put forward. Lhabitant (2001) and Lhabitant (2002a) applied the multi-index model to hedge funds. The specifications of the Sharpe model were adapted to accommodate a more flexible way of managing assets. In particular, to allow possible excess returns, a constant term α is added to the set of regressors.[3] In place of traditional investment style indices, the right-hand side variables are hedge fund indices. This stems from the fact that the use of leverage and derivatives results in non-linear exposures to traditional asset classes, which is incorrectly captured by a linear factor model. By using hedge fund indices rather than traditional asset classes, the non-linearity problem disappears. Consequently, the analysed fund can be seen as a portfolio of hedge fund indices that represent alternative strategies, which may be linearly or non-linearly related to traditional asset classes. In this context, the β coefficients can

---

[3] In the original Sharpe's model, it is assumed implicitly that the manager does not generate alpha as the disturbance is supposed to have an expectation of zero.

be interpreted as exposures to hedge fund strategies and the model is generally understood as a style analysis model.

Now the regression of the returns $r_{s,t}$ of hedge fund s takes the form of the factor model

$$r_{s,t} = \alpha_s + \sum_{i=1}^{n} \beta_{s,i} I_{i,t} + \varepsilon_{s,t} \qquad (6.1)$$

where the error $\varepsilon_{s,t}$ is distributed according to a zero mean and a variance denoted σ_ε^2.

As leverage is common practice in hedge fund management, there is no upward restriction on the β's contrarily to the long-only world. However, Lhabitant (2002a) proposes to maintain the non-negativity constraints on the coefficients justifying it with the fact that

> the underlying indices are style indices, not standard asset class indices. There-fore, having a negative exposure to a particular style could be hard to justify economically. For instance, what would mean a negative exposure to the Short Bias Style[4]?

6.1.3   Hedge Funds Indices as Risk Factors

The set of regressors appearing in equation (6.1) is crucial from many different aspects. In particular, the explanatory power of the model depends on the chosen variables. Ideally, the indices should be exhaus-tive and mutually exclusive in terms of alternative strategies. Lhabitant (2001, 2002a) proposed to use the CS/Tremont sub-indices as, among other reasons, they are mutually exclusive.

Thus, the original model is composed by $n = 9$ indices, i.e.:

$I_{1,t} =$ return on the CS/Tremont Convertible Arbitrage index at time t

$I_{2,t} =$ return on the CS/Tremont Short Bias index at time t

$I_{3,t} =$ return on the CS/Tremont Event-Driven index at time t

$I_{4,t} =$ return on the CS/Tremont Global Macro index at time t

$I_{5,t} =$ return on the CS/Tremont Long/Short Equity index at time t

$I_{6,t} =$ return on the CS/Tremont Emerging Markets index at time t

$I_{7,t} =$ return on the CS/Tremont Fixed Income Arbitrage index at time t

$I_{8,t} =$ return on the CS/Tremont Market Neutral index at time t

$I_{9,t} =$ return on the CS/Tremont Managed Futures index at time t

---

[4] As we will explain in the last part of this book, we may disagree with this point of view.

Lhabitant (2001) proposed to use a 36-month historical window to estimate the β_i for $i = 1, \ldots, 9$ of equation (6.1).

6.2   THE STYLE VALUE-AT-RISK

6.2.1   The Value-at-Risk Model

The model decomposes the Value-at-Risk of hedge fund s into two components, the Value-at-Market-Risk or Value-at-Strategy-Risk (denoted by VsR_s) and the Value-at-Specific-Risk or Value-at-Idiosyncratic-Risk (henceforth ViR_s). This stems from the fact that the risk of a hedge fund results partly from the market as the manager is exposed to some common or systematic factors, while the risk that is not related to these factors can be qualified as being specific for the examined hedge fund. Accordingly, the following breakdown that is inspired by the one used in the variance–covariance method suggested by RiskMetrics applies

$$\text{VaR}_s = \sqrt{\text{VsR}_s^2 + \text{ViR}_s^2}$$

The Value-at-Strategy-Risk estimates systematic risk. It is obtained through three steps. First the sensitivity ($\beta_{s,i}$) of hedge fund s to each of the $i = 1, \ldots, 9$ risk factors is measured. Second, each index is pushed to the most disadvantageous situation according to the confidence level (here 99% and so the most important loss for one out of 100 monthly returns). Finally, the impact at the hedge fund s level is estimated by aggregating the estimated sensitivity ($\hat{\beta}_i$) and the percentile moves while taking into account the estimated correlation ($\hat{\rho}_{i,j}$) between factors. Mathematically, the Value-at-Strategy-Risk of hedge fund s is defined as

$$\text{VsR}_s = \sqrt{\sum_{i=1}^{9} \sum_{j=1}^{9} \hat{\rho}_{i,j} \, \hat{\beta}_{s,i} \, F_i \, \hat{\beta}_{s,j} \, F_j} \qquad (6.2)$$

where F_i is the one percentile move of the risk factor i, all indicators being computed over a 36-month time period.

Estimated variance of residuals for hedge fund s, henceforth $\hat{\sigma}_{s,\hat{\varepsilon}}^2$, is the difference between the total estimated variance $\hat{\sigma}_s$ and the estimated variance explained by the multi-indices model over the 36-month period:

$$\hat{\sigma}_{s,\hat{\varepsilon}}^2 = \hat{\sigma}_s^2 - \sum_{i=1}^{9} \sum_{j=1}^{9} \hat{\rho}_{i,j} \, \hat{\beta}_{s,i} \, \hat{\sigma}_i \, \hat{\beta}_{s,j} \, \hat{\sigma}_j \qquad (6.3)$$

where $\hat{\sigma}_i$, and $\hat{\sigma}_j$ denote, respectively the volatility of the risk factor i and j over 36 months.

From then on, the value at idiosyncratic risk is obtained by applying a push factor corresponding to a 99% confidence level for a normal variable

$$\text{ViR}_s = 2.33\,\hat{\sigma}_{s,\hat{\varepsilon}}$$

6.2.2   Original Backtesting

Lhabitant (2001) backtested the original model using a sample of 2934 hedge funds extracted from four databases (MAR, HFR, TASS and EACM) where the funds meet the two following criteria: first, providing returns for at least 37 months between January 1994 and October 2000 and, second, managing more than $5 million. The sample also contains funds of funds as well as hedge funds that stopped to report performance to the database. If a test period is defined as a three-year sample, in total the sample provides 94 549 test periods. Table 6.1 exhibits that the average R-square value is 0.56.

Consider a Value-at-Risk exception as being a situation when, within a month, the return of a fund drops by more than the forecasted Value-at-Risk at the end of the previous month. Then the exception rate of the backtest should tend to 1% for a Value-at-Risk computed for a 99% confidence level. Let us define a test period as the comparison between the return for a given period of hedge fund s and the Value-at-Risk as computed one month before using the previous 36 months. The average exception for 94 549 test periods is 1.06%, a fairly high result considering that the average number of test period per hedge fund is around 29 months. However, the major exceptions occurred in August 1998, a period universally considered as a non-representative event. So the total exception rate reduces to 0.43 if August 1998 is excluded from the exception rate computation (Table 6.2).

Table 6.1   Annual average R-square values and average R-square value for the overall period as computed by Lhabitant (2001)

	1997	1998	1999	2000	Total
Average R-square	0.48	0.53	0.6	0.6	0.56

Table 6.2 Annual proportion rate of exception and average rate for the overall period as computed by Lhabitant (2001)

	1997	1998	1999	2000	Total	1998 (Aug-98 excluded)	Total (Aug-98 excluded)	Aug-98
Average exception rate (%)	0.45	3.34	0.13	0.39	1.06	0.86	0.43	30.13

6.3 BACKTESTING REVISITED

6.3.1 Fundamentals of an Updated Backtesting

Lhabitant (2001) performed a comprehensive backtest. However, a new empirical test on the original model is required for at least four reasons. The first two should lead to minor differences in the backtesting results while one can expect the last two to have a significant impact, as they reveal significant differences between the targets of the original model and those of this book.

First, as already mentioned, no sample can claim to be fully representative of the hedge funds universe as the sampling process used is based on the voluntary principle. In order to assess the impact of the biases on the backtesting results, a simple approach consists of taking another sample into account.

Second, the model tested is not exactly the same. Indeed, the original model was a multi-index model containing the nine CS/Tremont hedge funds sub indices. In 2003, the CS/Tremont Multi-Strategy Index was launched with a backtrack starting in April 1994, and there were some empirical reasons at that time to incorporate this index into the original model.

Indeed, even though the Multi-Strategy Index may be seen at first as a composition of the other strategies, the correlation was very low with the other indices, as shown in Table 6.3. This feature can be explained for at least two reasons: first, the multi-strategy managers were very actively changing their exposures and thus the index contains a timing element within the time windows; second, the way the multi-strategy managers were performing the single strategy was sensibly different in average from the one performed in average by the single strategy

Table 6.3   Three-year correlations between the Multi-Strategy Index and other sub-indices

Index	Jan-95 to Dec-97	Jan-96 to Dec-98	Jan-97 to Dec-99	Jan-98 to Dec-00	Jan-99 to Dec-01	Jan-00 to Dec-02
Convertible Arb.	−0.06	0.51	0.47	0.48	0.42	0.58
Short Bias	0.14	0.26	0.13	−0.07	−0.39	−0.45
Emerging Markets	0.01	0.06	0.05	0.11	0.29	0.3
Eq. Market Neutral	0.05	−0.15	−0.10	−0.11	0.30	0.4
Event-Driven	−0.06	0.06	0.04	0.04	0.21	0.51
Fixed Income	−0.28	0.64	0.56	0.58	0.17	−0.06
Global Macro	−0.11	0.30	0.43	0.41	0.06	−0.14
Long/Short	−0.16	−0.04	0.12	0.21	0.34	0.38
Managed Futures	−0.01	−0.12	−0.07	−0.11	−0.16	−0.23

managers.[5] For these reasons, many risk managers added the Multi-Strategy Index into the original model and this incremented version is tested thereafter.

Third, the target of Lhabitant (2001, 2002a) deeply differs from the one of this book: while we aim to present risk budgeting at the multi-manager portfolio level, the original model is proposed as a tool for global analysis on hedge funds. As a consequence, funds of funds are considered as hedge funds in the original backtest: the Value-at-Risk is computed on the historical track record of the investment vehicle and not on the underlying positions. But if, for a hedge fund, the underlying portfolio consists of exposure to traditional assets, for a fund of funds the portfolio is composed by hedge fund managers. In other words, the original approach was built for investors in funds of funds while we aim to provide a model for a fund of funds manager or any investor that has only direct exposure to hedge funds.

Finally, the time framework differs as the sample in Lhabitant (2001) covered the period from January 1994 to October 2000, and thus the backtest was performed from January 1997 to October 2000. With our sample starting in January 1994 and ending in December 2006, we are

---

[5] Retrospectively, we know that another reason explains the low correlation. We already pointed out that for investable indices the track before the actual launch of the investable indices always contain a significant pro forma bias. Even though the CS/Tremont non-investable indices are capital weighted and more diversified than the investable versions, they are indirectly also exposed to such a bias. When considering only the actual performances of the CS/Tremont non-investable Multi-Strategy Index, the additional information brought by the index is quite poor: for the period from January 2004 to December 2007, correlations between the CS/Tremont Multi-Strategy Index rises to 0.89 with the Long/Short Index, to 0.91 with the Event-Driven Index to 0.81 with the Convertible Arbitrage, to 0.73 with the Emerging Markets Index, and to 0.72 with Global Macro Index.

able to fully assess the nature and the impact of the LTCM and Russian Default Crisis for the alternative industry.

Indeed, it is a well-known fact that August 1998 can be considered as a special event and so should be handled with care, but we cannot yet unambiguously affirm that it was not a 1% event. It will be the case, only if the 298 months following August 1998[6] do not exhibit a similar level of loss. In summer 2023, we will be able to assess, with a 95% confidence level, if the August to October 1998 period was or was not a representative 1% event for the hedge funds industry. But until now, the August 98 loss (-6.16%) of the EDHEC Funds of Funds Index,[7] accounts for 226% of the maximum loss from January 1999 to February 2008 (-2.72% in January 2008 or -2.69% in April 2000).

Remember that Value-at-Risk provides an estimate of the loss threshold for a given time horizon, which could be exceeded with a given probability and stable market conditions. The aim is to capture the risk associated with random features of the markets. Obviously, Value-at-Risk does not indicate the average loss that can be expected when the threshold is exceeded. Moreover, by definition, it does not take into account exogenous shocks or potentially catastrophic scenarios. There are other indicators (stress tests, analysis of scenarios, etc.) that measure this kind of effect. These indicators are particularly appropriate for investment strategies exposed to unlimited losses and, as pointed out by Jorion (2007), Value-at-Risk should always be used in connection with these types of measures. In other words, Value-at-Risk should be calibrated independently of exogenous shocks and be complemented by stress tests or scenario analysis.[8]

Here, one should not be confused: since Balasko (1988) and Balasko and Ghiglino (1995), we know that even in a very simple system of supply and demand, drastic changes in price as well as all the cycle (i.e of any order) may occur without any external inputs, simply because of the internal dynamic. These price moves are the ones that we try to measure when computing a risk indicator on the tail of a distribution. In that sense, the Tech bubble bursting or the more recent subprime crises are endogenous to the system and Value-at-Risk aims to capture

---

[6] Let p be the probability of a 1% event to occur. By definition, $p = 0.01$ and $q = 1 - p = 0.99$ is the probability for this event not to materialize. The probability for the 1% event to show up at least once on n successive trials is given by $1 - q^n$. Starting at 1% for $n = 1$, it goes to 95% when $n = 298$.

[7] EDHEC Funds of Fund Index can be considered as the best indicator of hedge funds universe performance (see Chapter 4 or Duc, 2004a).

[8] A historical stress test and a risk measure based on liquidity crisis are proposed in Chapter 13.

these changes. But including a stress test period in the estimation sample and in the backtesting sample of a Value-at-Risk distorts the results as well as the concept of Value-at-Risk. First, as all correlation coefficients drastically increase during stress periods, the coefficient of determination of any multi-factor/index model is skewed. Then, the inclusion of a stress period in the estimation sample will inflate the Value-at-Risk and decrease the number of exceptions after the stress period.

This distortion in statistics can, in fact, be a pragmatic way to detect a stress period and, contrary to Lhabitant (2001), we benefit from a time window sufficiently important (Jan-04 to Dec-06) to fully assess the effect of the 98 hedge funds crisis on the original results of the model. Indeed, as we will see thereafter, since October 2001, i.e. after the full exclusion of August, September and October 1998 from the estimation sample of the Value-at-Risk, the coefficient of determination and the exception rate are similar (and even worse) to the one before summer 1998. Moreover, the fluctuations of both indicators from October 2001 to December 2006 are much smaller than the one caused by the exclusion of August to October 1998. So, because of its equally weighting underlying structure, the simple percentile approach on a rolling three-year window is exposed to a so-called 'ghost effect': percentiles may be unduly high until a monthly loss falls out of the estimation sample. But the magnitude of the Ghost effect of the LTCM and Russian Crisis is drastically higher than those occurring thereafter. So implementing an age-weighted or a volatility-weighted structure does not constitute a relevant solution. The 1998 hedge funds crisis was simply an extraordinary event for the alternative industry.

In other words, even though 25 years have not passed since August 1998, some empirical evidence on the most recent hedge funds debacles tends to prove that there is little likelihood that one or even several hedge funds could cause a system-wide tremor. The day-to-day behaviour of the overall alternative industry during different market turbulence occurring in 2005, 2007 and the beginning of 2008 confirms that something really different happened in 1998, mainly due to structural reasons. Indeed, the 1998 hedge funds crisis was implied by the sequence of a major country default and the existence of LTCM in an environment where the access to leverage for alternative investment vehicles was characterized by the near absence of efficient barriers or internal rules. For these aspects, the turmoil of August 1998 to October 1998 can be considered as the founding event of the institutionalization of the alternative industry. It was mainly first of all a leverage provider crisis (this explains why these same leverage providers agree to rescue LTCM) and since then, as pointed out in section 2.4, risk-management techniques and the regulations governing suppliers of leverage have come a long way. These measures were the requisite for the development of the hedge funds industry without increasing the exposure to systemic risk.

As we will see in Chapter 13, the 1998 liquidity crisis may be considered as an endogenous shock of the monetary system put in place by Nixon when abrogating the dollar–gold parity, but was structural (and thus exogenous) for the hedge funds industry. This explains why the period from August to October 1998 is excluded from both the estimation sample and the backtesting in what follows. But this period, in its excesses, is quite representative of any sudden and drastic liquidity crisis for hedge funds. Thus, these three months are preserved for stress test analysis and liquidity adjusted Value-at-Risk (see also Chapter 13). However, we may simply disagree with considering the 1998 hedge fund crisis as exogenous shocks. We will first show that, in terms of backtesting, this will not change the result of the original model (but it will have a significant impact for the other specifications proposed thereafter) over a long period of time. Second, excluding these three months from the estimation sample enables us to assess the efficiency of the original model when the estimation sample does not contain the kind of event that is aimed to be forecasted. In some ways, this is a more conservative approach.

6.3.2 Updated Exception Rate

Using the sample of 5675 hedge funds as described in section 3.1, the updated backtesting of the original Style Model is performed from January 1994 to December 2006 on the model with 10 indices. This will be conducted first on the full track, then fully excluding August, September and October 1998 from both the estimation sample and the testing sample.

The average exception rate of the 16 472 testing period is 1.65%, significantly higher than the original backtesting. Indeed, as shown in Table 6.4, when available in the original sample, each annual average exception rate is much higher for the new sample (i.e. the comprehensive testing sample) than in the original one.

Moreover, as 11 years are considered, the exception rate is only slightly impacted by the exclusion of August 1998 (1.43% vs 1.65%) and the difference between the two samples is magnified (1.43% for

Table 6.4 Annual proportion rate of exception as well as the average rate for the overall period as computed by Lhabitant (2001)

Average exception rate (%)	1997	1998	1999	2000	2001	2002	2003	2004	2005	2006	Total
Original sample	0.45	3.34	0.13	0.39							1.06
Testing sample	2.23	6.75	0.82	1.28	1.82	1.84	0.51	0.87	1.73	1.37	1.65

Table 6.5 Impact of August 1998 for the two backtests

Average exception rate (%)	Total	1998 (Aug-98 excluded)	Total (Aug-98 excluded)	Aug-98	Sep-98	Oct-98
Original sample	1.06	0.86	0.43	30.13		
Testing sample	1.65	3.17	1.48	44.98	5.74	6.77

the testing sample excluding August 1998 vs 0.43% for the original model). Applied solely to hedge funds, the methodology thus tends to underestimate the 1% Value-at-Risk (Table 6.5).

Out of the 3643 hedge funds providing a testing period, 1526 experience at least one Value-at-Risk exception, i.e. 42.7%. Among them, about 52.3% had one exception (for 48 median number of testing periods per hedge fund), about 27.4% experienced two exceptions (for a 74 median number of testing periods per hedge fund) and 12.0% three exceptions (median number 77).

Table 6.6 shows the result when August to October 1998 are fully excluded from both the Value-at-Risk and the exception ratio computation.[9] Obviously, the annual exception rate for 1999, 2000 and 2001 significantly increases. The apparent robustness of the original model during the Tech bubble burst were involved by a Value-at-Risk error due to the inclusion of the outlier in the estimation sample. Moreover, the total ratio does not significantly differ from the one obtained when the

---

[9] When computing the exception rate, the Value-at-Risk as at the end of July 1998 should be compared with the November 1998 return.

Table 6.6   Impact of full exclusion of August, September and October

Average exception rate (%)	Total/*Total* (*Aug-98 backtest excluded*)	1998/*1998* (*Aug-98 backtest excluded*)	1999	2000	2001
Original sample	1.06/ *0.43*	3.34/ *0.86*	0.13	0.39	
Testing sample	1.65/ *1.43*	6.75/ *3.17*	0.82	1.28	1.82
Truncated testing sample	**1.66**	**2.80**	**1.72**	**3.24**	**2.40**

Table 6.7   This table shows the confidence interval of monthly exception rate average based on the testing sample excluding August 1998 to October 1998

	Lower bound	Upper bound
Average monthly exception rate	1.42%	2.27%

model with August 1998 (i.e without excluding the backtesting result of this month) is used.

Each exception rate actually is an average of a binary variable taking the value of 1 in the case of an exception and 0 otherwise. As each month provides in between 580 and 2229 testing periods, under the assumption of independently and identically distributed exceptions, the exception rates follows a normal law by the central limit theorem.

As shown in Table 6.7, the confidence intervals do not include 1% and the upper bound is larger than 2%. In other words, under the assumption of independently and identically distributed exceptions, the 1% risk is largely underestimated by the Value-at-Risk and we could not reject that the Value-at-Risk could generate on average a monthly 2.27% rate of exception.[10]

---

[10] However, this conclusion should be handled cautiously because the assumption of identically and independently distributed monthly exception rates is clearly not satisfied. Indeed, assume that each month would provide the same number of testing periods $m = 580$, this figure corresponding to the number of testing periods in January 1997, i.e. the month with the lowest number of testing periods. Then, the monthly exception rate P would be distributed according a Normal law with an average equal to $p = 1\%$ and a variance equal to $p(1 - p)m^{-1} = 1\%; \times 99\% \times 580^{-1}$. Note that choosing the value of m as the smallest monthly sample size is conservative, as the variance is largest. Under this assumption, one should experience an exception rate larger than 1.78% in only 2.5% of the months. Actually, 37 months out of 117 (i.e. 32%) experienced larger exception rates. More accurately, when examining each month with its actual number of exceptions, 41 months (35%) recorded an exception rate significantly larger than 1%. Obviously, the different monthly exceptions rates are not identically distributed and because of some risks aspects that are not correctly captured, some months t have an exception rate $\bar{p}_t$ significantly larger than 1%.

6.3.3   Sources of Risk Underestimation

Once it is determined that some parts of the risk are underestimated, the next question points to an examination of the source of underestimation. In particular, do we observe some specific underestimations for some investment styles? Obviously, a comprehensive answer to this question would require an efficient classification. As shown in Chapter 3, the high level of hedge fund heterogeneity is difficult to capture through such a restrictive stratification as the one proposed by the CS/Tremont Indices. However, it is worth examining the backtesting result of the Style Value-at-Risk for the 10 alternative styles as the model is based on the 10 associated hedge fund indices. This will enable us not to end with a conclusion that is conditional to the classification, but to separate the source of underestimation from those effects that dampen the underestimation.

As shown in Table 6.8, the Value-at-Risk computed on the truncated sample underestimates the risk for all strategies. Under the assumption of identically and independently distribution, Table 6.9 provides the bounds of the confidence interval of the average monthly exception rate for all styles. The confidence interval does not include 1% for all strategies except for Equity Market Neutral. On the other hand, the upper bound is larger than 2% for all strategies except Global Macro, and larger than 3% for Convertible Arbitrage, Dedicated Short Bias and Emerging Markets. In other words, under the assumption of independently and identically distributed exceptions, the 1% risk is significantly underestimated by the

Table 6.8   Annual exception rate in percent (%) by strategy for the truncating testing sample (i.e excluding August 1998 to October 1998 both from the estimation and the backtesting; years whose exception rate are impacted by the reduction of the sample are followed by an asterisk)

	1997	1998*	1999*	2000*	2001*	2002	2003	2004	2005	2006	Total*
Convert.	2.0	1.4	1.2	4.7	2.5	1.1	0.7	1.5	5.7	0.9	2.3
Short	3.5	6.1	5.7	3.2	4.9	0.6	0.5	1.1	0.6	1.9	2.5
Emerging	7.3	10.0	0.7	2.5	1.5	1.3	0.1	0.7	0.7	2.2	2.0
M.Neut.	1.5	0.5	3.6	2.9	1.7	0.8	0.4	0.3	1.0	1.1	1.2
Event-D.	0.2	1.9	1.2	3.6	3.2	5.1	0.2	0.8	2.6	0.9	2.0
Fixed I.	0.6	3.1	2.0	5.7	2.6	2.3	2.2	0.5	1.2	0.9	1.8
Macro	1.9	2.0	1.2	2.4	1.3	2.3	0.6	1.3	1.0	1.6	1.5
L/S	2.2	2.6	1.8	4.1	2.1	1.4	0.3	0.8	1.4	1.5	1.5
CTA	2.1	1.6	2.1	0.8	3.6	1.0	1.1	1.1	1.3	0.9	1.5
MS	1.4	1.3	1.3	2.1	1.9	1.9	0.3	0.9	3.1	1.6	1.6

Table 6.9 Confidence interval of both the monthly and annual exception rate average based on the comprehensive testing sample excluding August 1998 to October 1998

Index	Monthly exception rates average		Percentage significantly larger than 1% monthly exception rates
	Lower bound	Upper bound	
Convertible Arbitrage	1.20%	2.95%	17.95%
Dedicated Short Bias	1.51%	4.02%	18.80%
Emerging Markets	1.11%	3.80%	13.68%
Equity Market Neutral	0.90%	2.05%	89.40%
Event-Driven	1.11%	2.77%	16.24%
Fixed Income Arbitrage	1.51%	3.60%	24.79%
Global Macro	1.19%	1.94%	15.38%
Long/Short Equity	1.33%	2.33%	28.21%
Managed Futures	1.02%	2.12%	15.38%
Multi-Strategy	1.06%	2.08%	14.53%

Value-at-Risk for all the strategies except Market Neutral. Moreover, for all strategies, we cannot reject that the Value-at-Risk is a risk indicator of 1.95% risk. In particular, we cannot refuse that the Value-at-Risk estimates a 3% risk for Convertible Arbitrage and a 3.90% for Dedicated Short Bias and Emerging Markets.

Table 6.9 also shows that as two strategies with two exclusive confidence intervals do not exist, we may not say that two chosen strategies have significant different average monthly exception rates. However, the null hypothesis that all the 10 strategies have a common average exception rate is clearly rejected through an Anova test whose results are given by Table 6.10. Moreover, we find a different classification when investigating if some strategies tend to experience their difficult months at the same time. Indeed, Table 6.11 provides the correlation of the monthly exceptions. For all the bold numbers, we can reject that the correlation is not significantly different from zero. Thus, for all these pairs of strategies, there is some evidence of underestimation of common systematic risks.

This analysis at the strategy level reveals some underestimations of systematic risk with different dependence structure between strategies. This weakness of the model could be explained by the combination of four features at the multi-index level:

• no perfect independence between the indices;
• inefficient classification;

Table 6.10 Comparison between the variance explained by a common average the one that is not explained. If the contribution of the explained variance is important, the null hypothesis of a common average is accepted. This is clearly not the case here (p-value = 36%)

Source of variance	SS	df	MS	F	p-value	F_{crit}
Between groups (i.e. explained by a common average)	0.018858	9	0.0020954	1.094591	36%	1.8879361
Within group (i.e. **not** explained by a common average)	2.220567	1160	0.0019143			
Total	2.299425	1169				

- underestimation of the risk attached for each index;
- proxy error in the consolidation of risk;
- low fitting of the regression.

The first two points are obvious. The last two elements deserve investigation. Table 6.12 provides the number of exceptions per year for each CS/Tremont substyle Index excluding the period August 1998 to October 1998 (both from the computation of the extreme moves and of the exception number). For the 10 indices, the average exception rate is 3.4%, reaching 4.42% for the CS/Tremont Event-Driven Index and 5.31% for the CS/Tremont Short Bias Index. The underestimation of the

Table 6.11 Correlation matrix of the monthly exception rates per style. The correlations in bold fonts are significantly different from zero, i.e. non-independent

	CA	SB	EM	MN	ED	FI	Mac	L/S	CTA	MS
Convert.	1									
Short	−0.1	1								
Emerging	**0.2**	0.0	1							
M.Neut.	−0.0	**0.2**	−0.0	1						
Event-D.	**0.3**	−0.1	**0.2**	0.0	1					
Fixed I.	**0.2**	−0.1	**0.2**	0.0	**0.4**	1				
Macro	**0.2**	**0.2**	**0.5**	0.1	**0.4**	**0.4**	1			
L/S	**0.3**	−0.0	**0.4**	**0.2**	**0.6**	**0.4**	**0.6**	1		
CTA	0.1	0.0	**0.2**	0.1	−0.0	0.1	0.1	0.1	1	
MS	**0.5**	−0.1	**0.3**	0.1	**0.6**	**0.3**	**0.5**	**0.7**	**0.3**	1

Table 6.12 Annual number of exceptions of the CS/Tremont substyle indices for the truncating testing sample (i.e. excluding August 1998 to October 1998 from both the estimation and the backtesting; years whose exception rate are impacted by the reduction of the sample are followed by an asterisk). (%) denotes the exception rates

	97	98*	99*	00*	01*	02	03	04	05	06	Total	(%)
CS Convert.	0	1	0	0	0	1	0	0	2	0	4	3.6%
CS Short	0	2	1	1	0	0	1	1	0	0	6	5.3%
CS Emerging	0	1	0	0	0	0	0	0	0	1	2	1.8%
CS M.Neut.	1	0	0	0	0	0	0	2	1	0	4	3.6%
CS Event-D.	0	1	0	0	1	2	0	0	1	0	5	4.4%
CS Fixed I.	1	0	0	0	0	2	0	1	0	0	3	2.7%
CS Macro	0	0	0	1	0	0	0	0	1	0	4	3.6%
CS L/S	0	0	0	2	0	0	0	0	1	1	4	3.6%
CS CTA	0	0	0	0	2	0	0	0	0	0	3	2.7%
CS MS	0	0	1	1	0	0	0	0	1	0	3	2.7%
Total	2	5	2	5	3	5	1	4	7	2	36	3.4%

1% risk is clear and can be statistically assess through a Kupiec (1995) test. The test is not reliable except with very large sample sizes,[11] the null hypothesis ($H_0 : p = 1\%$) acceptance regions being large for small sample. So, the test has poor power characteristics and there is a high probability of accepting the null hypothesis when it is false. However, this is the standardized backtest prescribed by some regulatory prescriptions as the 1996 Amendment to the 1988 Basel Accord. Moreover, even this deceptively favourable framework, the null hypothesis will often be rejected for the indices.

If we consider the Value-at-Risk model to be perfectly correct (null hypothesis), then theoretically the model should generate a correct exception rate (here 1%) and, in addition, exceptions should be independent of each others. This results in a sequence of identically and independently distributed events (with a probability p of success for each event, the success being a tail loss). Then, the number of tail losses Y follows a binomial distribution whose parameters are m, the number of testing periods and the probability is $p = 1\%$. The probability to have i exceptions can be computed with

$$P(Y = i) = \binom{m}{i} p^i (1 - p)^{(m-i)}$$

---

[11] A Kupiec test is not really relevant for hedge funds as the median number of testing period for the sample is 11.

Given a number of observed exceptions y_s for an index s, a hypothesis test with the null hypothesis $H_0 : p = 1\%$ can be constructed using the likelihood ratio LR (y_s,m):

$$\text{LR}(y_s, m, p) = 2 \ln\left[\left(1 - \frac{y_s}{m}\right)^{m-y_s} \frac{y_s}{m}^{y_s}\right] - 2 \ln[(1 - p)^{m-y_s} p^{y_s}]$$

Under the null hypothesis, the likelihood ratio LR has (asymptotically) a chi-squared distribution with one degree of freedom. This test is the uniformly most powerful test for a given sample size.

With 117 test periods for each sub-style index, the null hypothesis is rejected for four exceptions. So even with a small sample size and thus a high probability to accept the null hypothesis when it is false, the percentile approach on three years is rejected to provide a good estimate of the risk at 1% for 6 out of 10 indices. Three other sub-style indices exhibit three exceptions, and given the poor power of the test, it is prudent to consider that it is highly probable that the risk is also underestimated for these indices.

This result may be surprising. Historical Value-at-Risk is popular with practitioners as it tends to overestimate the risk, as demonstrated by Finger (2006). However, the method depends on the quality of the sample available and more particularly on its size. The temptation to use it for hedge funds was great, but with monthly returns, the size of the samples available for hedge funds is not appropriate to the historical Value-at-Risk approach and approximations are not very robust. The first section of Chapter 7 focuses on an alternative methodology that better fits the characteristics of the hedge funds indices, while section 8.2.4 will propose an adjustment of the percentile methodology that can be a suitable solution for a not too small sample.

At the hedge fund level, the underestimation of the risk by the historical percentile is compensated by the consolidation of the risk exposures. Indeed, the figures of Table 6.12 are much larger than both the 1.73% total exception rate on the truncated sample and the exception rates by the strategies in Table 6.8. This means that the consolidation of risk exposure improves the quality of the measure. In other words, the risk computation on the index level is speculative while the risk consolidation is very much conservative. The next chapter proposes a more accurate way of consolidating the risk at the investment vehicle level.

Furthermore, the Value-at-Risk is composed of two elements, the Value-at-Strategy-Risk and the Value-at-Idiosyncratic-Risk. The poorer

Table 6.13   Average R^2 on the sample cleaned form funds of funds and excluding August to September 1998 data from both the indices and the hedge funds data. Years whose exception rate are impacted by the reduction of the sample are followed by an asterisk

	97	98*	99*	00*	01*	02	03	04	05	06	Total
R^2	0.38	0.39	0.41	0.41	0.42	0.42	0.42	0.4	0.41	0.38	0.41

the fitting of the regression model underlying the Value-at-Strategy-Risk, the higher the contribution of the Value-at-Idiosyncratic-Risk. The latter being proportional to the volatility, the Style Model can be seen as a generalization of a Value-at-Risk based on variance, adding the information provided by the Style Model. In other words, when the model is not able to explain the hedge fund, it reduces it to a simple variance. So the quality of the Value-at-Risk model strongly depends on the quality of the Style Model. The average coefficient of determination of the original backtesting is 0.56. However, this test was performed on a sample mixing funds of funds and hedge funds, while the latter exhibits a higher average R^2. For instance, if we consider a sample extracted from the *InvestHedge* database composed of 319 multi-strategy funds of funds, 109 arbitrage funds of funds, 34 macro currency funds of funds and 120 long/short funds of funds with at least 37 monthly returns from January 2000 to December 2006, the average coefficient of determination rises to 0.73 in total, with 26% above 0.85. Moreover, the inclusion of the stress period in the testing sample unduly raised the coefficient of determination. In the original backtest, the average R square was 0.48 in 1997 and 0.6 in 1999 and 2000. Excluding the 1998 stress period and the funds of funds leads to an average $R^2 = 0.41$ for the period from January 1997 to December 2006 as shown in Table 6.13. The last part of this book is devoted to present an implicit model whose target is to improve the poor fit of the explicit style analysis.

7

The New Style Model

One of the results of the updated backtesting relies on the simultaneous underestimation of the risk embedded with the factors and the overestimation of the global risk through a conservative consolidation. The fact that these two errors somehow dampen each other explains the good overall result of the original backtesting. However, in this chapter we will consider an alternative to the percentile approach to assess more accurately the extreme events by modelling the tail of the return distribution. Moreover, we will propose a consolidation that decreases the estimation error and may preserve a quadratic form that enables us to conduct closed form risk budgeting.

In classical statistics, the main interest generally turns around the average behaviour of a random phenomenon while risk managers tend to focus on the tails of the variable's distribution. As it is non-parametric, the percentile approach presents the advantage of not relying on a specific assumption. However, the percentile methodology has the drawback of requiring a large data set. As shown in the previous chapter, the Value-at-Risk at the 1% confidence level deriving from the percentile approach is severely biased if the sample size is small. Assuming a parametric distribution would be one solution, however it has been well documented in the literature that hedge fund returns are far from being normally distributed. In order to take into account the typical fat tails observed in the distribution of hedge funds, researchers exploit non-Gaussian models such as the Student distribution, the mixture of Normal distributions or the family of stable Pareto distributions. However, these approaches fail to find any economic intuition justifying the choice of a particular probability law for the whole distribution. Moreover, it is worth stressing that simultaneously fitting the average and the tails of the distribution may be very difficult.

The extreme value theory attempts to address these issues. First, it does not rely on particular assumptions concerning the distribution of the returns as, under quite broad conditions, the limit theorem underlying the approach holds no matter what the distribution. Second, it is specifically aimed at extrapolating what happens in the tail of the distribution when there might be no data available for the very extreme of the tail. To the best of our knowledge, very few papers have attempted to evaluate hedge funds risk with the help of the extreme value theory. Fascinating insights are however, given by Blum et al. (2003). In their analysis, the authors focus on the maximum likelihood technique to derive the extreme moves of a bunch of hedge funds indices. Further alternative methods can be exploited to obtain interesting estimators. In particular, it is well known that, to be reliable, the maximum likelihood estimates usually require large samples, but the amount of data available for hedge funds is rather small.

7.1   EXTREME VALUE THEORY

This section offers a comparison of various estimation approaches. Furthermore, the value of the tail index of the generalized Pareto distribution is discussed within its financial interpretation. In this respect, we propose a simple procedure to get sensible parameter estimates of the model. On the empirical side, we apply the methodology to the CS/Tremont hedge fund indices. As hedge fund data typically feature autocorrelation issues, we complement the analysis by comparing the results obtained from the observed return series with the figures derived from the standard unsmoothing technique.

7.1.1   The Generalized Pareto Distribution

Two different approaches have been researched to study the distribution of the largest or smallest values of certain phenomena: the block maxima method and the peaks over threshold approach. As the name suggests, the former is about modelling the series of maxima observed over successive blocks or non-overlapping periods of time. Though this approach is interesting, it is often difficult to implement in practice as there are typically few observations that can be considered as extreme. This issue is particularly acute for hedge fund data as track records are especially short in this area. By contrast, the peaks over threshold method allows us to make more efficient use of the data and this is the route we will focus on.

Consider a sequence of n loss measurements $x_1, \ldots, x_n$.[1] Extreme events can be defined by identifying a high threshold u for which some observations, say x_j, are higher than u

$$x_j \geq u.$$

Label these peaks over threshold by $x_1, \ldots, x_k$, and define the exceedances or threshold excesses by

$$y_j = x_j - u \quad \text{for } j = 1, \ldots, k.$$

Under quite general assumptions,[2] it can be shown that the exceedances over the threshold, as defined in section 7.1.1 follow a generalized Pareto distribution, henceforth GPD, whose cumulative distribution function is

$$\text{GPD}(y; \xi, \sigma) = \begin{cases} 1 - \left(1 + \dfrac{\xi}{\sigma} y\right)^{-1/\xi} & \text{if } \xi \neq 0, \\ 1 - e^{-y/\sigma} & \text{if } \xi = 0, \end{cases}$$

for $y \in [0; +\infty)$ if $\xi \geq 0$ and $y \in [0; -\sigma/\xi]$ if $\xi < 0$.

The parameters ξ and σ ($\sigma > 0$) are the so-called shape and scale parameters respectively. The former reflects the fatness of the tail in the distribution in the sense that higher values of ξ mean fatter tails. As such, this parameter is also known as the tail index in the literature.

Note that when $\xi = 0$, the GPD reduces to the exponential distribution with mean σ. By comparison with the latter, the GPD has a heavier tail for $\xi > 0$ (long-tailed distribution) and a lighter tail for $\xi < 0$ (short-tailed distribution).

In terms of the parent variable X, we have for $x > u$

$$P\left(X > x | X > u\right) = \left[1 + \xi \left(\frac{x - u}{\sigma}\right)\right]^{-1/\xi}. \tag{7.1}$$

As mentioned above, the distribution has no upper limit when $\xi \geq 0$ while there is an upper bound for $\xi < 0$. In that respect, the distribution with a non-negative shape parameter has to be preferred to model hedge fund returns as one cannot fix an upper bound for financial losses.

---

[1] As it is usual practice in risk management, the reasoning is done in terms of losses: a loss of $x\%$ means a return of $-x\%$.

[2] See Pickands (1975), or Balkema and de Haan (1974).

7.1.2   Parameter Estimation

There are several ways to estimate the parameters of the GDP, namely the maximum likelihood approach, the method of moments, the method of probability-weighted moments and the elemental percentile method.[3] Before discussing their pros and cons within the context of hedge fund data, we briefly review how the different estimators are computed. The interested reader may refer to Hosking and Wallis (1987), Grimshaw (1993), Tajvidi (1996a, 1996b) and Castillo and Hadi (1997) for more detailed discussions.

The Method of Maximum Likelihood

The maximum likelihood estimator of the parameters ξ and σ can be defined as

$$(\hat{\xi}, \hat{\sigma}) = \arg \max_{\xi, \sigma} \log L(\xi, \sigma | y)$$

where the log-likelihood function is given by

$$\log L(\xi, \sigma | y) = \begin{cases} -k \log \sigma - \left(\dfrac{1}{\xi} + 1\right) \sum_i^k \log \left(1 + \dfrac{\xi}{\sigma} y_i\right) & \text{if } \xi \neq 0, \\ -k \log \sigma - \dfrac{1}{\sigma} \sum_i^k y_i & \text{if } \xi = 0. \end{cases}$$

As there are no analytical solutions, the maximization is carried out using numerical optimization algorithms. The approximate distribution of the parameters is multivariate normal with a mean (ξ, σ) and variance–covariance matrix equal to the inverse of the observed information matrix evaluated at the maximum likelihood estimate. Note that the maximum likelihood estimators do not exist if ξ is equal to or smaller than -1.

When the shape parameter is taken to be equal to zero, the estimation for σ is particularly simple. In that case indeed, the maximum likelihood estimator has a closed-end form given by

$$\hat{\sigma} = \sum_{i=1}^{k} y_i / k$$

---

[3] Note that the Hill estimator can also be used to get estimates of the parameters (see, for instance, Embrechts et al. 1997). Even though the Hill estimator features interesting properties, it is very sensitive to the value of the threshold. As we have generally little guidance on what u should be, we will not consider this approach.

The Method of Moments

As the name suggests, this approach derives the estimates from the moments of the distribution. In the case of the GPD, it can be shown that

$$E\left(1 + \frac{\xi}{\sigma}Y\right)^r = \frac{1}{1 - r\xi}$$

provided that $1 - r\xi > 0$. In particular, we get for $r = 1$ and $r = 2$ respectively

$$E(Y) = \frac{\sigma}{1 - \xi} \qquad \xi < 1,$$

$$V(Y) = \frac{2\sigma^2}{(1 - 2\xi)(1 - \xi)^2} \qquad \xi < \frac{1}{2}.$$

Rearranging yields

$$\xi = (E(Y) - \sigma)/E(Y)$$

$$\sigma^2 = V(Y)((1 - 2\xi)(1 - \xi))$$

Substituting the theoretical moments for their empirical counterparts, the estimators are defined as

$$\hat{\xi}_{\mathrm{MoM}} = -(\bar{y}^2/s_y^2 - 1)/2$$

$$\hat{\sigma}_{\mathrm{MoM}} = \bar{y}(\bar{y}^2/s_y^2 + 1)/2$$

where $\bar{y}$ and s_y^2 denote the sample mean and the sample variance of the exceedances respectively. Note that these estimators do not exist if ξ is greater than $\frac{1}{2}$. When ξ is equal to zero, the estimator for σ admits the same expression as the one obtained by maximum likelihood.

The Method of Probability Weighted Moments

Estimates based on probability weighted moments are often considered to be superior to standard moment-based estimates. The basic principle is to match the moments of the distribution via the L-moment conditions as described in Hosking and Wallis (1987).

Specifically, the probability weighted moments of the random variable Y are defined by the generic expression

$$M(p, r, s) = E\left[Y^p(F(Y))^r(1 - F(Y))^s\right]$$

Accordingly, two special cases emerge

$$\alpha_s = M(1, 0, s) = E[Y(1 - F(Y))^s]$$

$$\beta_r = M(1, r, 0) = E[Y(F(Y))^r]$$

whose unbiased estimators are given by

$$a_s = \frac{1}{k} \sum_{j=1}^{k} \frac{(k - j)(k - j - 1)\ldots(k - j + 1)}{(k - 1)(k - 2)\ldots(k - s)} y_{(j)}$$

$$b_r = \frac{1}{k} \sum_{j=1}^{k} \frac{(j - 1)(j - 2)\ldots(j - r)}{(k - 1)(k - 2)\ldots(k - r)} y_{(j)}$$

where $y_{(j)}$ is the jth order statistic in the sample.

In the context of the GPD, it can be shown that $M(0, 1, s)$ has the form

$$\int_0^1 \left(-\frac{\sigma}{\xi}[1 - (1 - F(Y))^{-\xi}]\right)(1 - F)^s \, dF = \frac{\sigma}{\xi}\left(\frac{1}{1 + s - \xi} - \frac{1}{s + 1}\right)$$

for $s = 0, 1, 2, \ldots$ The probability weighted moments estimators of ξ and σ are then defined as

$$\hat{\xi}_{\text{PWM}} = -\bar{y}/(\bar{y} - 2M) + 2$$

$$\hat{\sigma}_{\text{PWM}} = 2\bar{y}M/(\bar{y} - 2M)$$

where $M = 1/k \sum_i^k (1 - q_{(i)}) y_{(i)}, q_{(i)} = (i - 0.35)/k$. For the same reason as for the method of moments, the probability weighted moments estimators do not exist if ξ is higher than $\frac{1}{2}$.

The Elemental Percentile Method

The idea of this estimation method is to match the theoretical distribution, in this case the GDP, with the empirical distribution.

Specifically, the postulated distribution evaluated at the observed j-order statistic is

$$\text{GPD}(y_{(j)}; \xi, \sigma) = 1 - \left(1 + \frac{\xi}{\sigma} y_{(j)}\right)^{-1/\xi}$$

while the empirical distribution is given by $p_{(j)} = j/(k+1)$. The goal is to set the unknown parameters of the distribution as such to have equality between the theoretical and the empirical distribution.

Doing so for two distinct order statistics, say $y_{(i)}$ and $y_{(j)}$, we get a system of two equations in two unknowns

$$\begin{cases} 1 - \left(1 + \dfrac{\xi}{\sigma} y_{(i)}\right)^{-1/\xi} = p_{(i)} \\ 1 - \left(1 + \dfrac{\xi}{\sigma} y_{(j)}\right)^{-1/\xi} = p_{(j)} \end{cases}$$

Rearranging and taking the log yields

$$\begin{cases} \log\left(1 + \dfrac{\xi}{\sigma} y_{(i)}\right) = -\xi \log(1 - p_{(i)}) \\ \log\left(1 + \dfrac{\xi}{\sigma} y_{(j)}\right) = -\xi \log(1 - p_{(j)}) \end{cases} \tag{7.2}$$

Eliminating ξ, we obtain

$$\log(1 - p_{(i)}) \log\left(1 + \frac{\xi}{\sigma} y_{(j)}\right) = \log(1 - p_{(j)}) \log\left(1 + \frac{\xi}{\sigma} y_{(i)}\right) \tag{7.3}$$

whereas eliminating σ/ξ, we get

$$y_{(i)}\left(1 - (1 - p_{(j)})^{-\xi}\right) = y_{(j)}\left(1 - (1 - p_{(i)})^{-\xi}\right) \tag{7.4}$$

We can then solve (7.4) for ξ to obtain $\hat{\xi}(i, j)$ and substitute $\hat{\xi}(i, j)$ in (7.2) to obtain $\hat{\sigma}(i, j)$. Note that the case where $\xi = 0$ requires separate treatment.

The resulting estimators are based on two order statistics. Castillo and Hadi (1997) describe an algorithm to get more efficient estimators by exploiting the whole sample. The detailed procedure is reported in Appendix D.

7.1.3 Method Selection

Obviously, the methods described above yield different estimates and the question now is to choose one of them. Without touching upon the issue related to their small and large sample properties, the different methods are not appropriate for all values of the parameters.

When ξ is smaller than -1, the maximum likelihood function is infinite and the maximum likelihood estimator (MLE) does not exist.[4] When ξ is larger than $\frac{1}{2}$, the second and higher moments of the GPD do not exist. Hence, the method of moments and probability-weighted moments cannot be carried out. Furthermore, it has been documented that these estimators can produce nonsensical estimates. Simulation studies have also pointed out that the probability-weighted moments estimator is not reliable if ξ is higher than 0.2.[5]

By contrast, the elemental percentile method (EPM) works for all possible values of the parameters. In that regard, the EPM has a definite advantage over the others. Note, however, that if there are reasons to believe that ξ equals null, the maximum likelihood estimation method – which is also the method of moments in that case – should be favoured as the MLE is easy and efficient.

The selection of the threshold also constitutes a long-standing issue. From a theoretical standpoint, too low a threshold is likely to violate the asymptotic basis of the model, leading to bias; from an empirical point of view, too high a threshold is likely to generate few excesses with which the model can be estimated, leading to high variance. In short, the threshold must be set in order to have a reasonable number of exceedances above the threshold, but there is no definite answer about the number of data points that are required in practice. The standard is to adopt a threshold as low as possible, subject to the limit model providing a reasonable approximation.

In practice, two techniques have been put forward in setting the value of u. The first is an exploratory technique carried out prior to model estimation. This technique refers to the examination of the mean excess plot also known as the mean residual plot in the statistical literature. The idea stems from the fact that the mean of the excesses over the threshold, say $\bar{u}$, should be a linear function of u, that is for $u > \bar{u}$

$$E(X - u | X > u) = \frac{\sigma_{\bar{u}} + \xi u}{1 - \xi}. \tag{7.5}$$

Using the average of the excesses over the threshold, this can be checked visually. In other words, above the value of the threshold at which the

---

[4] Moreover, it has been shown that the MLE has a problem when the tail index is higher than -1, but smaller than $-\frac{1}{2}$. As our interest is about non-negative values for ξ, this is not a concern in the present case.

[5] See Hosking and Wallis (1987).

GPD provides a valid approximation to the excess distribution, the mean residual plot should be approximately linear. The issue, however, is that the higher the value of the threshold, the smaller the number of data. Consequently, the information in the plot for large values of u might be unreliable.

The second method is an assessment of the stability of the parameter estimates based on the fitting of models across a range of different thresholds. It means examining if the estimated scale and shape parameters are constant as a function of u.

Finally, the search for an automatic determination of the threshold has led the practitioners to choose u so that a certain percentage of the data lies above it. For example, Neftçi (2000) considers the 95th percentile for the value of u.

7.1.4   Extreme Quantiles to Value the Risk

In the context of financial modelling, extreme quantiles of returns are generally referred to as Value-at-Risk figures. It follows that the generalized Pareto threshold model provides a direct method for assessing the risk of holding an asset.

Formally, we are interested in the return level, say x_m, that is exceeded on average once every m observations

$$P(X > x_m) = \frac{1}{m}.$$

For instance, the 10-year return level stands as the estimate that should occur once every 10 years. In view of equation (7.1), this is the solution of

$$\zeta_u \left[1 + \xi \left(\frac{x_m - u}{\sigma} \right) \right]^{-1/\xi} = \frac{1}{m}$$

where $\zeta_u = P(X > u)$ provided that m is sufficiently large to ensure that $x_m > u$. Rearranging yields[6]

$$x_m = u + \frac{\sigma}{\xi} \left[(m\,\zeta_u)^\xi - 1 \right]$$

---

[6] Remark that when $\xi = 0$, the expression reduces to $x_m = u + \sigma \log(m\,\zeta_u)$.

The estimation of the Value-at-Risk is obtained by substituting the scale and shape parameters for their estimates resulting from one of the methods described above.

In this respect, an estimate of ζ_u, the probability of an individual observation exceeding the threshold u, is also needed. A natural estimator is given by the sample proportion of points exceeding u

$$\hat{\zeta}_u = \frac{k}{n}$$

where k is the number of observations over the threshold and n is the total number of observations in the sample. Since the number of exceedances follows a binomial distribution, $\hat{\zeta}_u$ is also the maximum likelihood estimate of ζ_u.

Finally, the Value-at-Risk estimate is given by

$$\hat{x}_m = u + \frac{\hat{\sigma}}{\hat{\xi}}\left[\left(m\frac{k}{n}\right)^{\hat{\xi}} - 1\right]$$

where m is interpreted as the confidence level.

Note that the extreme value theory can be exploited to yield estimates of the potential size of the loss exceeding the Value-at-Risk. This alternative measure of risk, known as the expected shortfall, is defined as $E(X \mid X > \text{VaR})$. In the case of the GDP with parameter $\xi < 1$, it can be shown that the estimate of the expected shortfall is of the form $\text{VâR}/(1 - \hat{\xi}) + (\hat{\sigma} - \hat{\xi}u)/(1 - \hat{\xi})$.

7.1.5 Assessing the Risk of Hedge Funds

Hedge fund data have relatively short histories as compared to traditional assets such as stocks or bonds. Furthermore, the returns distribution of alternative investments has been shown to be far from normal. These now well-known properties render the classical Value-at-Risk computations delicate and the extreme value theory is especially appealing to gauge the risk embedded in hedge fund holdings.

We comment below on the results of the peaks over threshold approach applied to the CS/Tremont hedge fund indices. The sample is about the track records up to December 2006, that is from January 1994 to December 2006.[7] As the frequency of the data is monthly, the sample is made up of 156 observations.

---

[7] Note that the Multi-Strategy Index does not provide any data from January to March 1994.

Table 7.1   GPD, parameter estimates for CS/Tremont indices (from January 1994 to December 2006)

Index	$\hat{\xi}_{MoM}$	$\hat{\xi}_{PWM}$	$\hat{\xi}_{ML}$	$\hat{\xi}_{EPM}$	$\hat{\sigma}_{MoM}$	$\hat{\sigma}_{PWM}$	$\hat{\sigma}_{ML}$	$\hat{\sigma}_{EPM}$	$\hat{\sigma}_{ML|\xi=0}$
Convert.	−0.011	0.029	−0.034	0.041	0.013	0.012	0.013	0.012	
Short	−1.780	−1.755	−0.935	−0.968	0.080	0.079	0.080	0.056	0.029
Emerging	0.031	−0.148	0.012	0.276	0.035	0.042	0.036	0.034	
M. Neut.	−0.124	−0.048	−0.281	−0.204	0.005	0.005	0.005	0.005	0.005
Event-D.	0.324	0.312	0.304	0.700	0.008	0.008	0.008	0.007	
Fixed I.	0.195	0.180	0.184	0.485	0.008	0.008	0.008	0.007	
Macro	−0.003	−0.019	−0.017	0.165	0.024	0.024	0.024	0.023	
L/S	0.166	0.150	0.156	0.438	0.014	0.014	0.014	0.012	
CTA	−0.018	0.046	−0.053	0.030	0.021	0.019	0.021	0.020	
MS	0.166	0.304	0.324	0.339	0.008	0.007	0.007	0.007	

As discussed in section 7.1.2, the parameters of the GDP can be estimated by various procedures. By reporting the results of each of them, we compare the different approaches in practice. Following Castillo and Hadi (1997), the elemental percentile method should be favoured in the general case where ξ is not equal to zero.[8] However, when the EPM provides a negative value for $\hat{\xi}$, we have set this parameter to zero and the model has been re-estimated by maximum likelihood. Note that in all cases, the threshold has been set as the third quartile of the sample.

Table 7.1 compares the results of the different estimation methods. It is shown that the estimates for σ are very similar whereas the results can differ substantially for the tail index. Regarding the latter, we can see that the figures are negative in many instances. Specifically, the estimated parameter is negative 5 out of 10 times for the method of moments, 4 for the method of probability-weighted moments, 5 for the maximum likelihood method and 2 for the elemental percentile method. As such, only two figures are displayed in the last column of the table. Note that the condition imposed by the method of moments ($\xi < 0.5$) is satisfied.

Table 7.2 reports the extreme moves resulting from the different approaches. When there is no constraint on ξ, the method of moments, the method of probability-weighted moments and the maximum likelihood approach provide quite similar estimates. By contrast, the elemental percentile method generally yields substantially

---

[8] According to the authors, the elemental percentile approach yields the most attractive estimators when compared to the other methods.

Table 7.2   EVT Value-at-Risk of CS/Tremont indices (from January 1994 to December 2006)

Index	MoM	PWM	ML	EPM	ML with $\xi = 0$
Convertible Arbitrage	3.8	3.9	3.8	4.0	
Dedicated Short Bias	7.6	7.6	8.5	8.6	12.3
Emerging Markets	13.2	12.0	13.1	18.9	
Equity Market Neutral	1.1	1.2	1.0	1.0	1.2
Event-Driven	4.2	4.2	4.1	8.1	
Fixed Income Arbitrage	3.4	3.4	3.4	5.2	
Global Macro	7.7	7.7	7.7	9.7	
Long/Short Equity	6.5	6.4	6.5	8.9	
Managed Futures	8.0	8.2	7.8	8.3	
Multi-Strategy	3.2	3.4	3.6	3.7	

higher figures. In particular, the quantiles for Emerging Markets, Event-Driven and Fixed Income Arbitrage clearly stand out from the other methodologies.

As stated above, the EPM should be preferred when the estimated tail index is greater than zero while when the EPM provides a negative value for ξ, the extreme quantile resulting from maximum likelihood with this parameter set to zero is computed. The last column of the table shows that the move is bigger than the one obtained when $\hat{\xi}$ is negative. Thus the Value-at-Risk for each index is the EPM estimate but CS/Tremont Dedicated Short Bias Index and CS/Tremont Managed Futures Index.[9]

We now investigate the results of the model when excluding August, September and October 1998. The rationale was explained in section 6.3.1: the efficiency of a model should not depend exclusively on the inclusion of a specific period and the Russian crisis and the collapse of *Long Term Capital Management* (LTCM) constitutes an event that stands out from normal market conditions as defined in the concept of Value-at-Risk.

Table 7.3 shows that the estimates for σ are very similar across the different estimation methods. By contrast, the estimates for ξ differ widely depending on which method is used. This coefficient shows up with a negative sign most of the time. Interestingly, the elemental

---

[9] As compared to the results of Blum et al. (2003), it should be noted that the estimation procedure and the sample size are different. The study by Blum and colleagues spans the period from January 1994 to December 2002. Furthermore, they report Value-at-Risk figures at the 5% and 0.4% confidence level while the figures we present here refer to the 1% confidence level.

Table 7.3 GPD, parameter estimates for CS/Tremont indices (from January 1994 to December 2006 excluding August to October 1998)

Index	$\hat{\xi}_{MoM}$	$\hat{\xi}_{PWM}$	$\hat{\xi}_{ML}$	$\hat{\xi}_{EPM}$	$\hat{\sigma}_{MoM}$	$\hat{\sigma}_{PWM}$	$\hat{\sigma}_{ML}$	$\hat{\sigma}_{EPM}$	$\hat{\sigma}_{ML,\xi=0}$
Convert.	−0.155	−0.141	−0.205	−0.114	0.012	0.012	0.012	0.012	0.010
Short	−1.473	−1.506	−0.845	−0.854	0.069	0.070	0.069	0.051	0.028
Emerging	−0.325	−0.334	−0.411	−0.289	0.040	0.040	0.040	0.039	0.030
M. Neut.	−0.081	0.000	−0.182	−0.135	0.005	0.004	0.005	0.005	0.004
Event-D.	−0.001	−0.017	−0.016	0.101	0.008	0.008	0.008	0.008	
Fixed I.	−0.108	−0.049	−0.181	−0.076	0.008	0.008	0.008	0.008	0.007
Macro	−0.099	−0.116	−0.135	−0.077	0.022	0.022	0.022	0.022	0.020
L/S	−0.076	−0.107	−0.075	0.146	0.015	0.016	0.015	0.014	
CTA	−0.018	0.046	−0.053	0.030	0.021	0.019	0.021	0.020	
MS	0.132	0.265	0.261	0.237	0.007	0.006	0.006	0.006	

percentile method is still the approach that yields the most sensible figures with regard to the non-negativity constraint.

As expected, the quantiles are lower than those obtained by leaving the stress period of 1998 (see Table 7.4). For Dedicated Short Bias, Equity Market Neutral and Managed Futures, the figures are essentially the same as those obtained with the LTCM event. This is not surprising as these indices took profit from, or were only marginally impacted by, the crisis.

7.1.6 Dealing with Autocorrelation

The limit theorem leading to the GPD assumes independence of the observations. However, one of the stylized facts of hedge fund data

Table 7.4 EVT Value-at-Risk of CS/Tremont indices (from January 1994 to December 2006 excluding August to October 1998)

Index	MoM	PWM	ML	EPM	ML with $\xi = 0$
Convertible Arbitrage	2.7	2.7	2.6	2.8	3.0
Dedicated Short Bias	7.6	7.6	8.3	8.5	12.0
Emerging Markets	9.2	9.2	8.9	9.3	11.0
Equity Market Neutral	1.1	1.1	1.0	1.0	1.1
Event-Driven	2.3	2.2	2.2	2.6	
Fixed Income Arbitrage	1.9	2.0	1.8	2.0	2.0
Global Macro	6.0	5.9	5.9	6.3	6.4
Long/Short Equity	5.1	5.0	5.1	6.4	
Managed Futures	8.0	8.3	7.9	8.4	
Multi-Strategy	2.7	2.9	3.0	2.8	

Table 7.5   CS/Tremont indices first-order autocorrelation coefficients

Index	First-order autocorrelation coefficients
Convertible Arbitrage	0.57
Dedicated Short Bias	0.12
Emerging Markets	0.29
Equity Market Neutral	0.30
Event-Driven	0.33
Fixed Income Arbitrage	0.39
Global Macro	0.06
Long/Short Equity	0.17
Managed Futures	0.05
Multi-Strategy	0.03

is a smoothing phenomenon in the returns reported by the managers. This violation of the assumption of the limit theorem brings into doubt the validity of the threshold excess model for these particular time series.

One way to solve the issue is to remove the typical autocorrelation scheme characterizing hedge funds returns by applying the Geltner transformation[10]

$$ r_t^* = \frac{r_t - \hat{\rho}\, r_{t-1}}{1 - \hat{\rho}} $$

where $\hat{\rho}$ denotes the sample autocorrelation coefficient of order 1 of the observed return series r_t. In that regard, Table 7.5 reports the first-order autocorrelation coefficients for the CS/Tremont indices.

Table 7.6 shows that the estimates for σ are close to each other. Notice, however, that the EPM figure is generally lower than those of the other methods. By contrast, the results differ substantially for ξ. The parameter is negative 3 times out of 10 for the method of moments, 4 for the PWM and ML, and 2 for the EPM.

In terms of Value-at-Risk, the EPM yields the most conservative figure except for the Multi-Strategy Index (see Table 7.7). As expected, the quantiles are higher than those associated to the raw data series. The step up is particularly impressive for Convertible Arbitrage and Emerging Markets.

---

[10] See Geltner (1991, 1993).

Table 7.6 GPD, parameter estimates for CS/Tremont indices (from January 1994 to December 2006). Geltner transformed series

Index	$\hat{\xi}_{MoM}$	$\hat{\xi}_{PWM}$	$\hat{\xi}_{ML}$	$\hat{\xi}_{EPM}$	$\hat{\sigma}_{MoM}$	$\hat{\sigma}_{PWM}$	$\hat{\sigma}_{ML}$	$\hat{\sigma}_{EPM}$	$\hat{\sigma}_{ML|\xi=0}$
Convert.	0.129	0.216	0.179	0.333	0.018	0.016	0.017	0.016	
Short	−1.089	−1.096	−0.719	−0.680	0.060	0.060	0.060	0.048	0.028
Emerging	−0.018	−0.291	−0.017	0.215	0.054	0.069	0.054	0.055	
M. Neut.	0.047	0.018	0.038	0.170	0.006	0.006	0.006	0.006	
Event-D.	0.374	0.434	0.400	0.855	0.009	0.008	0.008	0.007	
Fixed I.	0.183	0.260	0.247	0.522	0.011	0.010	0.011	0.008	
Macro	0.010	0.028	−0.004	0.190	0.024	0.024	0.025	0.022	
L/S	0.124	−0.032	0.086	0.361	0.018	0.021	0.018	0.017	
CTA	−0.074	−0.047	−0.131	−0.060	0.025	0.024	0.025	0.025	0.023
MS	0.182	0.351	0.411	0.410	0.008	0.006	0.006	0.006	

Table 7.8 shows that when the crisis of 1998 is excluded, the results for σ resemble those obtained with the entire history. While the figures for σ do not differ so much across the different methods, the estimates for ξ vary widely depending on the chosen methodology. The number of cases displaying a negative value is larger than for the full sample.

In terms of quantiles, the statistics are greater than those obtained with the raw data series but smaller than those deriving from the full sample, but with the Geltner transformation (see Table 7.9). The figures for the Global Macro strategy, however, are lower than those associated with correlated returns.

Table 7.7 EVT Value-at-Risk of CS/Tremont indices (from January 1994 to December 2006). Geltner transformed series

Index	MoM	PWM	ML	EPM	ML with $\xi = 0$
Convertible Arbitrage	7.4	7.8	7.7	9.2	
Dedicated Short Bias	9.1	9.1	9.7	10.1	13
Emerging Markets	18.7	16.1	18.7	27.3	
Equity Market Neutral	1.9	1.9	1.9	2.3	
Event-Driven	5.7	5.8	5.5	11.7	
Fixed Income Arbitrage	5.0	5.2	5.2	6.8	
Global Macro	8.2	8.3	8.2	10.0	
Long/Short Equity	7.9	7.3	7.8	11.1	
Managed Futures	8.5	8.7	8.3	8.9	8.9
Multi-Strategy	3.3	3.6	3.9	3.8	

Table 7.8 GPD, parameter estimates for CS/Tremont indices (from January 1994 to December 2006 excluding August to October 1998). Geltner transformed series

Index	$\hat{\xi}_{MoM}$	$\hat{\xi}_{PWM}$	$\hat{\xi}_{ML}$	$\hat{\xi}_{EPM}$	$\hat{\sigma}_{MoM}$	$\hat{\sigma}_{PWM}$	$\hat{\sigma}_{ML}$	$\hat{\sigma}_{EPM}$	$\hat{\sigma}_{ML|\xi=0}$
Convert.	0.068	0.155	0.082	0.304	0.016	0.015	0.016	0.013	
Short	−0.949	−0.961	−0.665	−0.596	0.054	0.054	0.054	0.044	0.028
Emerging	−0.632	−0.707	−0.595	−0.500	0.075	0.079	0.075	0.071	0.046
M. Neut.	0.037	−0.006	0.027	0.150	0.006	0.006	0.006	0.005	
Event-D.	0.025	0.085	0.018	0.146	0.009	0.009	0.009	0.009	
Fixed I.	−0.022	0.061	−0.060	0.102	0.010	0.009	0.010	0.009	
Macro	−0.045	−0.022	−0.085	−0.004	0.019	0.018	0.019	0.018	0.018
L/S	−0.174	−0.351	−0.138	−0.003	0.022	0.025	0.021	0.020	0.018
CTA	−0.019	0.051	−0.058	0.067	0.021	0.020	0.021	0.019	
MS	0.154	0.322	0.364	0.329	0.007	0.006	0.006	0.006	

Model Diagnostic

The adequacy of the GPD to fit the data can be assessed through different ways.

The probability plot compares the model probability with the empirical probability. Specifically, it consists of the points $(\hat{G}(y_{(i)}), i/k)$, where $\hat{G}(\cdot)$ denotes the GDP evaluated at the estimated parameters $\hat{\xi}$ and $\hat{\sigma}$. If the model is appropriate, the probability plot should lie close to the unit diagonal. Hence, any substantial departures from linearity are indicative of some failing in the model. It turns out that the fit is

Table 7.9 EVT Value-at-Risk of CS/Tremont indices (from January 1994 to December 2006 excluding August to October 1998). Geltner transformed series

Index	MoM	PWM	ML	EPM	ML with $\xi = 0$
Convertible Arbitrage	6.1	6.4	6.1	7.6	
Dedicated Short Bias	9.1	9.1	9.6	10.0	12.6
Emerging Markets	12.0	11.7	12.3	13.0	16.5
Equity Market Neutral	1.7	1.7	1.7	2.1	
Event-Driven	3.2	3.3	3.2	3.6	
Fixed Income Arbitrage	3.0	3.2	2.9	3.3	
Global Macro	5.6	5.7	5.5	5.7	5.8
Long/Short Equity	6.4	5.9	6.5	7.5	7.0
Managed Futures	8.3	8.6	8.2	8.5	
Multi-Strategy	2.9	3.2	3.4	3.1	

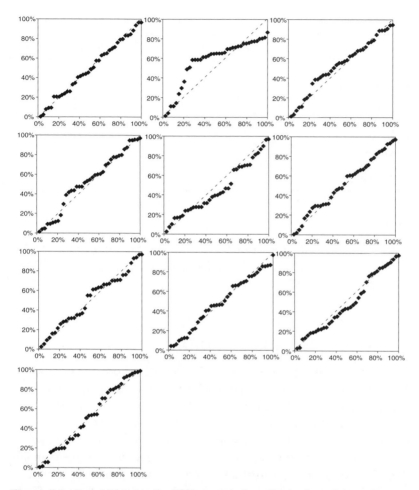

Figure 7.1 Probability plots for CS/Tremont indices (line by line): Convertible Arbitrage, Dedicated Short Bias, Emerging Markets, Equity Market Neutral, Event-Driven, Fixed Income Arbitrage, Global Macro, Long/Short Equity, Managed Futures and Multi-Strategy

fairly good for all the CS/Tremont indices except Dedicated Short Bias. Figure 7.1 tells the story.

More formally, the test of Kolmogorov and Smirnov can be carried out to assess if the distribution really suits the data. The test relies on the statistic

$$D_{KS} = \max_{i=1,...,k} \{|\hat{G}(y_{(i)}) - i/k|, |\hat{G}(y_{(i)}) - (i-1)/k|\}$$

Table 7.10   Kolmogorov–Smirnov statistic. CS/Tremont indices

Index	Full sample	Excluding Aug-98 to Oct-98
Dedicated Short Bias	0.31	0.33
Emerging Markets	0.13	0.16
Equity Market Neutral	0.12	0.13
Event-Driven	0.13	0.15
Fixed Income Arbitrage	0.10	0.09
Global Macro	0.11	0.11
Long/Short Equity	0.12	0.10
Managed Futures	0.10	0.10
Multi-Strategy	0.10	0.11

With 39 data points, the critical value at the 5% confidence level is 0.218. As Table 7.10 shows, only for Dedicated Short Bias is the test statistic above the critical value.

7.2   RISK CONSOLIDATION

Depending on the point of view, the consolidation of push factors through a quadratic form is the weakness or the strength of the Style Value-at-Risk. Statistically, the dependence structure of extremes cannot be captured by a single scalar measure. The quadratic form with a correlation matrix indeed remains a proxy: it is a simple application of the traditional variance–covariance consolidation to a more complex case. For non-elliptical distribution and, as consequence for extremes, marginal distributions and correlation do not determine the joint distribution. A more general form of dependence should be considered in that case. The theory of copulas addresses this issue. A copula can be defined as the mapping that joins a multivariate distribution function to a set of univariate marginal distribution functions. Briefly, the copula[11] function describes the dependence structure of any joint distribution. With copulas, the Value-at-Risk can be determined by applying a Monte Carlo simulation of the risk factors for the relevant copula and Extreme Value Theory in the tails.

---

[11] A more detailed description of copulas is provided in Appendix E.

Even if such a solution is perfectly feasible, practitioners may be reluctant to implement it. If in theory copulas may handle as many dimensions as required by the number of risk factors. There is a clear curse of the dimensionality: the more parameters to be estimated, the fewer the multivariate extremes. Remember that hedge funds samples typically suffer from a small size as only monthly returns are available.[12] In the opposite, risk consolidation through a quadratic form does not require additional data, is easy to perform, and enables a risk budgeting approach based on closed form risk attributions. Practitioners generally have to conduct arbitrage between theoretical accuracy and feasibility. For them, the risk consolidation through a quadratic form is a strength of the model.

Another way to maintain a sustainable level of complexity consists of mixing Extreme Value Theory with historical simulations (thereafter hybrid EVT). A new historical track (synthetic returns) for each hedge fund is computed by combining sensitivity (i.e. β_i) with indices returns. The Extreme Value Theory moves are then computed on this synthetic track. However, the flip side of the coin is that risk attribution at a multi-manager portfolio level can no longer be expressed in a closed form (it thus requires more computations[13]) and tends to underestimate the tail dependence given the restrictive sample size of hedge funds data.

In this section, we first expose a methodology of the hybrid EVT approach. Then, a measure of dependence that focuses exclusively on extremes, and that is linked with copula, is incorporated to the model. This enables us to keep the quadratic consolidation[14] in the model. We also present a modification that takes into account the existence of location parameters due to frequency of the returns.

7.2.1   Hybrid EVT Approach

Consider the style analysis model for hedge fund s:

$$r_{s,t} = \alpha_s + \sum_{i=1}^{10} \beta_{s,i}\, I_{i,t} + \varepsilon_{s,t}$$

---

[12] When the samples cover a time window larger than 15 years, the quality of the information rapidly decreases due to the various sampling biases.

[13] Actually, the level of computation is already increased at the Value-at-Risk level, as the Elementary Percentile should be applied to each synthetic track, while with the quadratic consolidation, the EVT is computed only on the 10 indices.

[14] However, the quadratic consolidation, even based on the tail dependence concept, remains a proxy.

After estimation of the parameters $\left(\hat{\alpha}_s, \left(\hat{\beta}_{s,i}\right)_{i=1,\ldots,10}\right)$, a synthetic track for hedge fund $(\hat{r}_{s,t'})_{t'=0,\ldots,t}$ s can be computed with

$$\hat{r}_{s,t'} = \hat{\alpha}_s + \sum_{i=1}^{10} \hat{\beta}_{s,i} \, I_{i,t'}$$

Obviously, the period used for the constrained regression and the one for the synthetic track do not need to match: we simulate for a larger time window what would have been the track if the hedge fund had maintained the current exposure in the past. Abusively in terms of alternative strategies, the short-term regression captures the current style while the risk is measured on a longer time horizon. So, the Extreme Value Move is computed on the synthetic time series and the synthetic Value-at-Strategy-Risk is

$$\text{VsR}_s^{\text{synthetic}} = \text{VaR}_{\text{EVT}}(\hat{r}_s) \qquad (7.6)$$

7.2.2 Tail Dependence

The simplicity of the hybrid approach should not hide its inner weaknesses: more particularly, without any explicit structure on the extreme dependence, the estimation of the tendency for the joint distribution to generate simultaneous extreme movements is fully dependent on the sample: as empirical percentile computed on a small sample leads to underestimation of the risk, a restrictive number of historical simulations for the construction of the synthetic track induces underestimation of the tail dependence. A natural way of circumventing this problem lies in specifying the tail dependence.

Correlation and Confusion

The most classical measure of linear dependence is known as correlation and its popularity can be explained in several ways. First, correlation is straightforward to calculate. Second, the variance of any linear combination is fully determined by the pairwise covariance between the components, a fact that is commonly exploited in portfolio theory. Third, linear correlation is the natural dependence measure in multivariate normal distribution and, more generally in multivariate spherical and elliptical distributions.

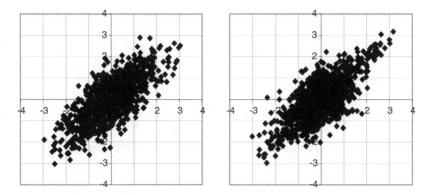

Figure 7.2   Two variables with the same correlation, but different tail dependence

When moving away from elliptical models, the use of linear correlation has several disadvantages. First, while it is well known that correlation is invariant under strictly increasing linear transformations, correlation is not invariant under non-linear strictly increasing transformations. Second, correlation is only defined when the variances of the variables are finite. This causes a problem if heavy-tailed distributions are assumed. Third, the marginal distributions and pairwise correlations of a random vector do not determine its joint distribution. Fourth, and most importantly, low correlation coefficients do not imply weak dependence.

For Bivariate Extreme Value Theory, the key issue is to model not the complete dependence structure but the tenancy for the joint distribution to generate simultaneously extreme values for the random variables. For instance, Figure 7.2 illustrates two bivariate distributions with the same correlation of 0.7.

Clearly, the second pair on the right-hand side exhibit more strength in the association between the two variables at the upper tail than the first one, which exhibits a weaker tail dependence.

Extremal Dependence

So for our framework the relevant measure is an indicator of extreme dependence or, in other words, of the strength of dependence in the tails of a bivariate distribution. Joe (1993, 1997) defines the coefficient of upper tail dependence[15] of two random variables X and Y as the

---

[15] The coefficient of lower tail dependence is defined analogously but refers to the lower tail of the distribution.

probability that X exceeds its u-quantile given that Y exceeds its u-quantile and then considers the limit[16]

$$\chi = \lim_{u \to 1} P\left(F_X(X) > u \mid F_Y(Y) > u\right)$$

with $0 \leq \chi \leq 1$.

If χ correctly measures the strength of the extreme association within the class of asymptotically dependent variables, it fails to provide any measure of discrimination for asymptotically independent variables. Coles et al. (1999) propose the following indicator for the asymptotical independence

$$\begin{aligned}
\overline{\chi} &= \lim_{u \to 1} \frac{2\ln\left(P\left(F_X(X) > u\right)\right)}{\ln\left(P\left(F_X(X) > u, F_Y(Y) > u\right)\right)} - 1 \\
&= \lim_{u \to 1} \frac{2\ln(1 - u)}{\ln\left(P\left(F_X(X) > u, F_Y(Y) > u\right)\right)} - 1
\end{aligned}$$

with $-1 < \overline{\chi} \leq 1$, $\overline{\chi} = 1$ for asymptotically dependent variables, $\overline{\chi} = 0$ for independent variables and a value of $\overline{\chi} > 0$ (respectively $\overline{\chi} < 0$) loosely corresponding to positively associated variables (respectively negatively associated).

Estimation

To estimate $\overline{\chi}$, Poon et al. (2002) propose to apply the Hill estimator. First, the bivariate return (X, Y) are transformed into a Fréchet unit (M_X, M_Y) in order to remove the influence of the marginal aspects of initial random variables:

$$M_X = -\frac{1}{\ln\left(F_X(X)\right)} \qquad M_Y = -\frac{1}{\ln\left(F_Y(Y)\right)}$$

---

[16] Tail dependence may be understood as an asymptotic property of the copula. Indeed, using elementary conditional probability, we can deduce

$$\chi = \lim_{u \to 1} P\left(F_X(X) > u \mid F_Y(Y) > u\right) = \lim_{u \to 1} \frac{= 1 - 2u + C(u, u)}{u}$$

where $C(u, u)$ is a copula. Provided that $\theta > 1$, the Gumbel copula (see Appendix E) has upper tail dependence. The coefficient of lower tail dependence for the Clayton copula may be shown to be $\lambda_l = 2^{-1/\theta}$ for $\theta > 0$. The Gauss copula is asymptotically independent in both tails, which means that regardless of how high a correlation we choose, if we go far enough into the tail, extreme events appear to occur independently in each margin. The t copula has both upper and lower tail dependence of the same magnitude.

In practice F_X and F_Y are the empirical distribution functions. Then consider $Z^{[X,Y]} = \min(M_X, M_Y)$; this variable enables us to represent the conjoint probability in an univariate distribution whose tail index can, under weak conditions, be estimated by

$$\hat{\bar{\chi}}(X, Y) = \frac{2}{n_u} \left(\sum_{\ell=1}^{n_u} \ln \left(\frac{z_\ell^{[X,Y]}}{u} \right) \right) - 1$$

with the following variance

$$\mathrm{var}(\hat{\bar{\chi}}(X, Y)) = \frac{\left(\hat{\bar{\chi}}(X, Y) + 1\right)^2}{n_u}$$

Then if $\hat{\bar{\chi}}(X, Y) + 1.96\sqrt{\mathrm{var}(\hat{\bar{\chi}}(X, Y))} > 1$, we infer X and Y to be asymptotically dependent and we set $\hat{\bar{\chi}}(X, Y) = 1$. If $\hat{\bar{\chi}}(X, Y)$ is positive and significantly different from 1, the two random variables are not asymptotically positively dependent. Then the negative dependence should also be tested. This step of the algorithm is a typical consequence of assuming an asymmetric distribution of returns: one tail could not be used to proxy the other tail for asymmetric distributions. One might be tempted to think that a negative relationship is sufficiently rare and we do not need to worry about it. This would be a mistake as a negative relationship is highly probable between the CS/Tremont Short Bias Index and all the other alternative style indices with a long equity bias such as the CS/Tremont Equity Long/Short Index. Moreover, this type of negative dependence may be frequent in a more general framework than the one presented in the last part of this book. So, if, for instance, $\hat{\bar{\chi}}(X, Y) < 0$ and $\hat{\bar{\chi}}(-X, Y)$ is not significantly different from 1, there is an asymptotic negative dependence between $-X$ and Y. For the cases when there is no significant evidence to reject $\overline{\chi}(X, Y) = \overline{\chi}(-X, Y) = 1$, the estimation of $\chi(I_i, I_j)$ and $\chi(-X, Y)$ is performed under the assumption of asymptotical dependence using the following formula:

$$\hat{\chi}(X, Y) = \frac{u\, n_u}{n}$$

This estimator of $\hat{\chi}$ reflects the empirical frequency of extreme co-movements and discriminates between the two asymptotical dependences.

For the cases of negative asymptotic dependence, the Value-at-Strategy-Risk (equation 6.2) should also be changed in terms of

Value-at-Risk of the indices. As a matter of fact, despite the fact that it is often omitted, the asymmetric aspect of the distributions should also be taken into account here. The procedure is as follows if the asymptotic negative dependence is uniquely due to the bivariate $(-X, Y)$ then the Extreme Value Value-at-Risk of $-X$ should be used and respectively the Value-at-Risk of $-Y$ if the asymptotic negative dependence comes from $(X, -Y)$; if both pairs exhibit significative asymptotic dependence, the Value-at-Risk of the opposite index used is that of the index that exhibits the larger number of negative $\hat{\bar{\chi}}_{XY}$.

Finally, when there is no evidence to accept positive or negative asymptotic dependence, the degree of independence is given by $\hat{\bar{\chi}}(X, Y)$.

So, if we denote $\tilde{F}_i^{[j]}$ the move of index i and $\tilde{\bar{\chi}}_{i,j}$ the extremal dependence indicator obtained with the above algorithm, the Value-at-Strategy-Risk is

$$
\text{VsR}_s = \sqrt{\sum_{i=1}^{10} \sum_{j=1}^{10} \tilde{\bar{\chi}}_{i,j} \, \hat{\beta}_{s,i} \, \tilde{F}_i^{[j]} \, \hat{\beta}_{s,j} \, \tilde{F}_j^{[i]}}
\tag{7.7}
$$

7.2.3 Location Parameters

Indices Means

The quadratic consolidation finds its roots both in the normal Value-at-Risk for daily data $(\text{VaR}_{1\%}(X) = 2.33 \, \hat{\sigma}_X)$ and in the following property of the variance:

$$
\text{var}\left(\sum_i^n \omega_i \, X_i\right) = \sum_i^n \sum_j^n \omega_i \, \omega_j \, \hat{\sigma}_{X_i} \, \hat{\sigma}_{X_j} \hat{\rho}_{i,j}
$$

On the other hand, hedge funds provide monthly data and one crucial effect of increasing the time horizon lies in the decreasing relevancy of the zero mean assumption.[17] In other words, for monthly data, the normal Value-at-Risk should incorporate the location parameter $\text{VaR}_{1\%}(X) = \hat{\mu} + 2.33\hat{\sigma}_X$. This means that even with the normal assumption, risk consolidation cannot be performed through a quadratic form without some sort of transformation. Indeed, consider that the loss/profit arithmetic returns of two indices I_i and I_j are distributed according two normal laws. Then the percentiles and EVT moves for

---

[17] See the next chapter for a more detailed discussion on the impact of an extension of the time horizon.

each variable for a given α should not differ in expected terms from the normal Value-at-Risk, i.e.

$$F_i = \hat{\mu}_i + 2.33\,\hat{\sigma}_i \qquad F_j = \hat{\mu}_j + 2.33\,\hat{\sigma}_j$$

and the equation of the Value-at-Strategy-Risk (equation 6.2) becomes

$$\mathrm{VsR}_s^{[\text{Normal False}]} = \sqrt{\sum_{i=1}^{10}\sum_{j=1}^{10}\hat{\rho}_{i,j}\hat{\beta}_{s,i}\,(\hat{\mu}_i+2.33\,\hat{\sigma}_i)\,\hat{\beta}_{s,j}\,(\hat{\mu}_j+2.33\hat{\sigma}_j)}$$

while the correct risk consolidation should be

$$\mathrm{VsR}_s^{[\text{Normal True}]} = \sum_{i}^{10}\hat{\beta}_{s,i}\,\hat{\mu}_i + \sqrt{\sum_{i=1}^{10}\sum_{j=1}^{10}\hat{\rho}_{i,j}\,\hat{\beta}_{s,i}\,2.33\,\hat{\sigma}_i\,\hat{\beta}_{s,j}\,2.33\,\hat{\sigma}_j}$$

Obviously $\mathrm{VsR}_s^{[\text{Normal False}]} \neq \mathrm{VsR}_s^{[\text{Normal True}]}$ and differences may be substantial depending on the value of the averages and of the correlations. In the case of negative averages (of the loss/profit series, i.e. of positive average return) and positive correlations, $\mathrm{VsR}_s^{[\text{Normal False}]} > \mathrm{VsR}_s^{[\text{Normal True}]}$ and when the hedge fund s exhibits only one non-null beta, the Value-at-Strategy-Risks are equal.

By analogy, when the normality assumption is relaxed, the quadratic consolidation should be performed on the centred moves of the indices and then the average effects should be added. For the original model, let us define the centred percentile $F_i^{[c]} = F_i - \hat{\mu}_i$, then

$$\mathrm{VsR}_s^{[\text{P False}]} = \sqrt{\sum_{i=1}^{10}\sum_{j=1}^{10}\hat{\rho}_{i,j}\,\hat{\beta}_{s,i}\,F_i\,\hat{\beta}_{s,j}\,F_j}$$

while the correct risk consolidation should be

$$\mathrm{VsR}_s^{[\text{P True}]} = \sum_{i}^{10}\hat{\beta}_{s,i}\,\hat{\mu}_i + \sqrt{\sum_{i=1}^{10}\sum_{j=1}^{10}\hat{\rho}_{i,j}\,\hat{\beta}_{s,i}\,F_i^{[c]}\,\hat{\beta}_{s,j}\,F_j^{[c]}}$$

Consider now the relative error defined as the following ratio:

$$\text{Relative Error} = \frac{\mathrm{VsR}_s^{[\text{P False}]} - \mathrm{VsR}_s^{[\text{P True}]}}{\mathrm{VsR}_s^{[\text{P True}]}}$$

then Table 7.11 provides the distribution of this relative error for the Value-at-Strategy-Risk computed for the backtest from January 1994

Table 7.11   Distribution of the relative error of the Value-at-Strategy-Risk

	<0%	[0%, 20%[	[20%, 50%[	[50%, 75%[	[75%, 100%[	≥100%
Relative Error	0.97%	38.26%	45.49%	5.87%	2.82%	6.6%

to December 2006 (see section 6.3). The underestimation had little effect (less than 1%) while the overestimation was important (say, above 20%) for more than 60.8% of the cases. In other words, the conservative risk consolidation helped to improve the hedge funds backtesting results by dampening the weakness of the percentile approach as demonstrated by the high number of exceptions at the 10 indices level (see Table 6.12).

Finally, the Value-at-Strategy-Risk computed with the Extreme Value Theory and tail dependence (as in equation 7.7) should also correctly reflect the effect of the location parameters. Thus the Value-at-Strategy-Risk of the new model is

$$
\text{VsR}_s = \sum_i^{10} \hat{\beta}_{s,i}\, \hat{\mu}_i + \sqrt{\sum_{i=1}^{10}\sum_{j=1}^{10} \tilde{\tilde{\chi}}_{i,j}\, \hat{\beta}_{s,i}\, (\tilde{F}_i - \hat{\mu}_i)\, \hat{\beta}_{s,j}\, (\tilde{F}_i - \hat{\mu}_i)}
$$

with $\tilde{F}_i$ and $\tilde{\tilde{\chi}}_{i,j}$ obtained with the algorithm described in section 7.2.2 and will be formally defined in section 7.3.1 with equations (7.9) and (7.10).

Alpha

Moreover, a second location parameter due to the frequency of the returns exists: the value of the constant α of the style regression. Table 7.12 exhibits the distribution of the 171 188 α_s of the backtesting of section 6.3.

If the Style Model for hedge funds was the strict equivalent of the Sharpe Style Model for a traditional investment vehicle, and if all styles

Table 7.12   Distribution of the constant of the style regression on loss/profit

	<−2%	[−2%, −1%[	[−1%, 0%[	[0%, 1%[	[1%, 2%[	≥2%
% of α	0.5%	3.5%	28.4%	35.6%	16.1%	15.8%

were represented by an index, the α of the regression would reflect the manager's skill to implement the various strategies. This ability, from a risk management point of view, may be assimilated to simple luck and should be neglected in the risk computation. However, alternative style indices are not representative, comprehensive or explicit factors. Thus, the alpha can be interpreted as a scaling factor of the latent variables or as the average of factor risks that are not included in the model. With 67% of positive α on the loss/profit series, the risk is therefore underestimated for an important set of hedge funds. So the Value-at-Idiosyncratic-Risk should incorporate the constant of the regression and equation (6.3) should be modified in the following way:

$$\text{ViR}_s = \hat{\alpha}_s + 2.33\,\hat{\sigma}_{s,\hat{\varepsilon}}$$

7.2.4 Extreme Value-at-Idiosyncratic-Risk

A final modification of the risk consolidation consists of relaxing the normality assumption on residuals and estimating the Extreme Value quantile. So the Value-at-Idiosyncratic-Risk becomes

$$\text{ViR}_s = \hat{\alpha}_s + \text{VaR}_{\text{EVT}}\,(r_s - \hat{r}_s)$$

7.3 THE NEW STYLE MODEL

7.3.1 The Model

The Value-at-Strategy-Risk of a hedge fund s is now defined by the following system:

$$\text{VsR}_s = \sum_{i}^{10} \hat{\beta}_{s,i}\,\hat{\mu}_i + \sqrt{\sum_{i=1}^{10}\sum_{j=1}^{10} \tilde{\tilde{\chi}}_{i,j}\,\hat{\beta}_{s,i}\,(\tilde{F}_i^{[j]} - \hat{\mu}_i)\,\hat{\beta}_{s,j}\,(\tilde{F}_j^{[i]} - \hat{\mu}_j)}$$

$$(7.8)$$

where

$$\tilde{F}_i^{[j]} = \text{VaR}_{\text{EVT}}(I_i) \quad \text{if } \tilde{\tilde{\chi}}_{i,j} \geq 0$$
$$\quad\quad = \text{VaR}_{\text{EVT}}(-I_i) \text{ if } \tilde{\tilde{\chi}}_{i,j} < 0$$

$$(7.9)$$

with[18]

$$\hat{\hat{\chi}}_{i,j} = 1 \qquad \text{if} \quad \hat{\hat{\chi}}(I_i, I_j) + 1.96\sqrt{\text{var}(\hat{\hat{\chi}}(I_i, I_j))} > 1$$
$$\text{and} \quad \hat{\hat{\chi}}(-I_i, I_j) + 1.96\sqrt{\text{var}(\hat{\hat{\chi}}(-I_i, I_j))} < 1$$

$$= 1 \qquad \text{if} \quad \hat{\hat{\chi}}(I_i, I_j) + 1.96\sqrt{\text{var}(\hat{\hat{\chi}}(I_i, I_j))} > 1$$
$$\text{and} \quad \hat{\hat{\chi}}(-I_i, I_j) + 1.96\sqrt{\text{var}(\hat{\hat{\chi}}(-I_i, I_j))} > 1$$
$$\text{and} \quad \hat{\chi}(I_i, I_j) > \hat{\chi}(-I_i, I_j)$$

$$= -1 \qquad \text{if} \quad \hat{\hat{\chi}}(I_i, I_j) + 1.96\sqrt{\text{var}(\hat{\hat{\chi}}(I_i, I_j))} < 1$$
$$\text{and} \quad \hat{\hat{\chi}}(-I_i, I_j) + 1.96\sqrt{\text{var}(\hat{\hat{\chi}}(-I_i, I_j))} > 1$$

$$= -1 \qquad \text{if} \quad \hat{\hat{\chi}}(I_i, I_j) + 1.96\sqrt{\text{var}(\hat{\hat{\chi}}(I_i, I_j))} > 1$$
$$\text{and} \quad \hat{\hat{\chi}}(-I_i, I_j) + 1.96\sqrt{\text{var}(\hat{\hat{\chi}}(-I_i, I_j))} > 1$$
$$\text{and} \quad \hat{\chi}(I_i, I_j) < \hat{\chi}(-I_i, I_j)$$

$$= \hat{\hat{\chi}}(I_i, I_j) \quad \text{if} \quad \max\left(\hat{\hat{\chi}}(I_i, I_j) + 1.96\sqrt{\text{var}(\hat{\hat{\chi}}(I_i, I_j))}, \right.$$
$$\left. \hat{\hat{\chi}}(-I_i, I_j) + 1.96\sqrt{\text{var}(\hat{\hat{\chi}}(-I_i, I_j))} \right) < 1$$
$$\text{and} \quad \hat{\hat{\chi}}(I_i, I_j) > 0 \text{ and } \hat{\hat{\chi}}(I_i, I_j) > \hat{\hat{\chi}}(-I_i, I_j)$$

$$= -\hat{\hat{\chi}}(-I_i, I_j) \text{ if} \quad \max\left(\hat{\hat{\chi}}(I_i, I_j) + 1.96\sqrt{\text{var}(\hat{\hat{\chi}}(I_i, I_j))}, \right.$$
$$\left. \hat{\hat{\chi}}(-I_i, I_j) + 1.96\sqrt{\text{var}(\hat{\hat{\chi}}(-I_i, I_j))} \right) < 1$$
$$\text{and} \quad \hat{\hat{\chi}}(-I_i, I_j) > 0 \text{ and } \hat{\hat{\chi}}(-I_i, I_j) > \hat{\hat{\chi}}(I_i, I_j)$$

$$= 0 \qquad \text{if} \quad \max\left(\hat{\hat{\chi}}(I_i, I_j) + 1.96\sqrt{\text{var}(\hat{\hat{\chi}}(I_i, I_j))}, \right.$$
$$\left. \hat{\hat{\chi}}(-I_i, I_j) + 1.96\sqrt{\text{var}(\hat{\hat{\chi}}(-I_i, I_j))} \right) < 1$$
$$\text{and} \quad \hat{\hat{\chi}}(I_i, I_j) < 0 \text{ and } \hat{\hat{\chi}}(-I_i, I_j) < 0 \tag{7.10}$$

---

[18] Contrary to the correlation matrix, the tail dependence matrix is not as symmetric as $\hat{\hat{\chi}}_{i,j} \neq \hat{\hat{\chi}}_{j,i}$.

The Value-at-Idiosyncratic-Risk is defined as

$$\text{ViR}_s = \hat{\alpha}_s + \text{VaR}_{\text{EVT}}\,(r_s - \hat{r}_s) \qquad (7.11)$$

Finally the Value-at-Risk for hedge fund s is

$$\text{VaR}_s = \hat{\alpha}_s + \sum_i^{10} \hat{\beta}_{s,i}\,\hat{\mu}_i + \sqrt{(\text{ViR}_s - \hat{\alpha}_s)^2 + \left(\text{VsR}_s - \sum_i^{10} \hat{\beta}_{s,i}\,\hat{\mu}_i\right)^2} \qquad (7.12)$$

In the same spirit, using equation (7.6), we may define the Synthetic Value-at-Risk as

$$\text{VaR}_s^{\text{Synthetic}} = \hat{\alpha}_s + \sum_i^{10} \hat{\beta}_{s,i}\,\hat{\mu}_i + \sqrt{(\text{ViR}_s - \hat{\alpha}_s)^2 + \left(\text{VsR}_s^{\text{Synthetic}} - \sum_i^{10} \hat{\beta}_{s,i}\,\hat{\mu}_i\right)^2} \qquad (7.13)$$

7.3.2 Backtesting

In order to perform a backesting, we compute the new Style Value-at-Risk on the same data sample (with the exclusion of August 1998 to October 1998) as in section 6.3 with the constrained regressions being conducted over a 36-month rolling window while Extreme Moves of the Indices and Tail Dependence Estimators are computed on a 96-month rolling window dependence. This distinction in the time window enables us to take into account current risk exposure and to compute the level of risk on a larger horizon.

For each CS index, none of the 48 monthly returns (four out of the estimation sample years) exceeded the extreme move estimated the month before. Because of the asymmetry of the tail dependence, the extreme moves of the profit were also tested. Here also, none of the 10 CS sub-indices experienced any Value-at-Risk exception during the four years. This absence of exception is totally in line with the level of exceedances as expected with a Kupiec test, the null hypothesis being rejected for zero exception with a sample of at least 440 data. Clearly, elemental percentile (excluding August 1998 to October 1998) on eight years totally erases the major source of risk underestimation of the original approach.

Table 7.13 details the percentage of exceptions from 2003 to 2006 and compares this with the results of the original model for the hedge

Table 7.13   Annual exception rates

	2003	2004	2005	2006	Total
New Style VaR	0.21%	0.18%	0.31%	0.36%	0.27%
Synthetic Style VaR	0.26%	0.32%	0.76%	0.59%	0.51%
Original Style VaR	0.51%	0.87%	1.37%	1.77%	1.16%

funds sample. For the four years, the average exception rate of the New Style Value-at-Risk decreases from 1.16% to 0.25%.

This significant improvement is particularly obvious in 2005 and in 2006, when hedge funds classified as Convertible Arbitrage, Event-Driven, Multi-Strategy, Emerging Markets and some Long/Shot managers experienced some difficult months (see Table 6.8). More precisely, March 2005 and April 2005 were particularly difficult for Convertible Arbitrage hedge funds after the downgrade of GM and Ford debt to junk status. This news initiated a sharp sell-off in US credit markets, a challenging stock borrowing environment and a deterioration in convertible market sentiment followed by de-leveraging effects. For the Original Style Value-at-Risk, 33 out of 90 Convertible Arbitrage hedge funds experienced a VaR exception in April, while 9 of them had already experienced a loss larger than the Value-at-Risk in March 2005. Moreover, 6 convertible hedge funds experienced an exception in May. During these particularly difficult months, it was possible to compute the Value-at-Risk for 125 Multi-Strategy hedge funds and 993 Long/Short; in March, for the Multi-Strategy funds, there were 4 exceptions, 20 in April and 6 in May while there were 11, 40 and 9 exceptions for the Long/Short Equity managers. With the New Style Model, only one Convertible Arbitrage investment vehicle, two Multi-Strategy funds and four Long/Short recorded a larger loss of the Value-at-Risk during these three months.

Another difficult environment was the October 2005 equity correction with the merger spread tightening after some bad expectations for the Guidant/Johnson & Johnson deal (due to a broad product recall for Guidant's defibrillator). Out of 247 Event-Driven hedge funds, 45 experienced Original Style Value-at-Risk exception and 80 Long/Short managers out of 1000 registered a return below this risk indicator. These figures shrink to 3 and 4, respectively, with the New Style Value-at-Risk. A more important equity correction occurred in May 2006 with the MSCI World Index registering a -4.26% return and emerging markets

Table 7.14 Exception rate during two difficult months of 2007 for each style

Index	August 2007			November 2007		
	Original Style VaR	New Style VaR	Synthetic Style VaR	Original Style VaR	New Style VaR	Synthetic Style VaR
Total	13.2%	3.84%	4.55%	15.3%	4.70%	4.07%
Convertible Arb.	21.7%	0.0%	0.0%	38.2%	0.0%	0.0%
Short Bias	0%	0.0%	0.0%	0.0%	0.0%	0.0%
Emerging Markets	5.7%	4.3%	4.3%	6.8%	0.0%	1.7%
Eq. Market Neutral	11.5%	8.2%	8.3%	4.0%	0.0%	0.0%
Event-Driven	15.9%	3.7%	7.3%	25%	5.1%	5.1%
Fixed Income	31.0%	12.6%	11.5%	17.1%	3.9%	3.9%
Global Macro	21.3%	5.0%	5.0%	13.8%	4.6%	4.7%
Long/Short	8.0%	0.9%	1.9%	17.0%	7.3%	5.7%
Managed Futures	13.0%	8.7%	5.2%	0.0%	0.0%	0.0%
Mulit-Strategy	20.0%	6.0%	8.0%	11.5%	3.4%	3.4%

were particularly hit. With the original model, there were 27 exceptions for emerging markets managers (out of 116) and 96 for Long/Short funds (out of 925). With the new model, these figures decrease to 3 and 22.

Obviously, the new model is more correctly positioned to provide a forecast for endogenous stressed periods. This is confirmed by Table 7.14 for two months of our testing sample: August 2007 for the statistical arbitrage and de-leveraging crisis, November 2007 for the equity and credit correction.

As a conclusion, the New Style Model provided the opportunity to implement three changes in the Style Model. The first consists of using the elemental percentile method on a 8-year time frame to estimate the extreme move of both the index and the idiosyncratic risk. This enables us to correct the source of risk underestimation in the original model at the factor level and to incorporate a more realistic assumption on the real nature of the residuals of the regression. The second change distinguishes location effects from dispersion effects. This ends up in a more realistic risk consolidation but also provides a correct framework for the annualization of the Value-at-Risk, as described in the next chapter. Finally, if the peak over threshold is the natural way to model return exceedances, the tail dependence is the application of the same philosophy on the extreme co-movement. Moreover, the incorporation of such an extreme dependence indicator enables us to conduct risk budgeting on closed form risk attribution, as will be shown in Chapter 11.

However, there remains one issue that was not addressed by the new version of the Style Value-at-Risk: how to improve the low average R-square of the constrained regression. Obviously, any improvement should go beyond the basis of the Style Model. This re-modelling is the subject of the third part of this book.

7.4 APPENDIX D: ALGORITHMS FOR THE ELEMENTAL PERCENTILE METHOD

Following the authors, let's define the procedure in terms of $\delta = -\sigma/\xi$.

Algorithm 1

1. Select any two distinct order statistics, $y_{(i)} < y_{(j)}$, and compute

$$C_i = \log \left(1 - \frac{i}{k+1} \right)$$

as well as C_j for $y_{(j)}$.

2. Let

$$d = C_j \, y_{(i)} - C_i \, y_{(j)}.$$

If $d = 0$, then let $|\hat{\delta}| = \infty$, $\hat{\xi}(i, j) = 0$ and go to Step 5; otherwise go to Step 3.

3. Compute $\delta_0 = y_{(i)} \, y_{(j)} (C_j - C_i)/d$. If $\delta_0 > 0$, then $\delta_0 > y_{(j)}$. Thus use the bisection method[19] on the interval $[y_{(j)}, \delta_0]$ to obtain a solution $\hat{\delta}(i, j)$ by $C_i \log(1 - y_{(j)}/\delta) = C_j \log(1 - y_{(i)}/\delta)$ and go to Step 5; otherwise go to Step 4.

4. Use the bisection method on the interval $[\delta_0, 0]$ to solve (7.3) and obtain $\hat{\delta}(i, j)$.

5. Use $\hat{\delta}(i, j)$ to compute $\hat{\xi}(i, j)$ and $\hat{\sigma}(i, j)$ using

$$\hat{\xi}(i, j) = -\log \left[1 - y_{(i)}/\hat{\delta}(i, j) \right]/C_i$$

and

$$\hat{\sigma}(i, j) = -\hat{\xi} \, \hat{\delta}(i, j)$$

---

[19] Recall that the bisection method is a root-finding algorithm that works by repeatedly dividing an interval in half and then selecting the subinterval in which the root exists.

The estimates found in Algorithm 1 are based on only two order statistics. More efficient estimators are obtained using Algorithm 2.

Algorithm 2

1. Use Algorithm 1 to compute $\hat{\xi}(i, j)$ and $\hat{\sigma}(i, j)$ for all distinct pairs $y_{(i)} < y_{(j)}$.
2. Use the median of each of the foregoing sets of estimators to obtain a corresponding overall estimator of ξ and σ, that is

$$\hat{\xi}_{EPM} = \text{median}(\hat{\xi}(1, 2), \hat{\xi}(1, 3), \ldots, \hat{\xi}(k - 1, k))$$

$$\hat{\sigma}_{EPM} = \text{median}(\hat{\sigma}(1, 2), \hat{\sigma}(1, 3), \ldots, \hat{\sigma}(k - 1, k))$$

7.5 APPENDIX E: COPULAS

The concept of copulas is intimately related to Sklar's theorem. Sklar's theorem shows that a joint distribution function can be broken down into its marginal distributions. Formally, Sklar's theorem states that any joint distribution function F with margins $F_1, \ldots, F_d$ admits the decomposition

$$F(x_1, \ldots, x_d) = C(F_1(x_1), \ldots, F_d(x_d))$$

where C is the so-called copula. In other words, the theorem shows that joint distributions are formed by coupling together marginal distributions with a copula.

Since the copula determines how the different random variables interact with each another, the copula appears as a natural measure of dependence. In fact, Sklar's theorem reveals that copulas express dependence on a quantile scale. Specifically, let $u_i = F_i(x_i)$, $0 \le u_i \le 1$, $i = 1, \ldots, d$. We have

$$C(u_1, \ldots, u_d) = F(x_1, \ldots, x_d) \tag{7.14}$$

$C(u_1, \ldots, u_d)$ is the joint probability that X_1 lies below its u_1-quantile, X_2 lies below its u_2-quantile, and so forth.

- By determining how the marginal distributions are interrelated to define the joint distribution, copulas appear as a natural measure of dependence.

- The importance of the concept of copulas in the study of multivariate distribution is that it allows to break down any joint distribution function into marginal distributions.
- Sklar's theorem shows that in the case of continuous margins, it is natural to define the notion of the copula of a distribution; that is, if the random vector X has joint distribution function F with continuous marginal distributions $F_1, \ldots, F_d$, then the copula of F (or X) is the distribution function C of $(F_1(X_1), \ldots, F_d(X_d))$.
- A copula describes how the marginal distributions are tied together in the joint distribution. In this way, the joint distribution is decomposed into the marginal density functions and a copula.

In view of equation (7.14), a copula is defined as follows: a d-dimensional copula is a distribution function on $[0; 1]^d$ with standard uniform marginal distributions. We list below some important properties of copulas.

- *Uniqueness*: If the marginal distribution functions are continuous, then C is unique; otherwise C is uniquely determined on the range of F_i.
- *Invariance*: By contrast to linear correlation coefficients, it can be shown that if $(X_1, \ldots, X_d)$ is a random vector with continuous margins and copula C and $T_1, \ldots, T_d$ are d strictly increasing functions, then $(T_1(X_1), \ldots, T_d(X_d))$ has also copula C. In other words, copulas are invariant to . . .
- *Boundaries*: For every copula $C(u_1, \ldots, u_d)$, we have the so-called Fréchet bounds

$$\max \left\{ \sum_{i=1}^{d} u_i + 1 - d, 0 \right\} \leq C(u) \leq \min\{u_1, \ldots, u_d\}.$$

- *Independence*: If $X_1, \ldots, X_d$ are independent, then $C(u_1, u_2, \ldots, u_d) = u_1 \cdot u_2 \cdot \ldots \cdot u_d$.

Several interesting special cases are worth noting. The independence copula is the copula for independent distributions. The co-monotonicity copula is for perfectly positively dependent variables (note that this is the Fréchet upper bound copula). The counter-monotonicity copula is the two-dimensional Fréchet lower bound copula that stands for perfectly negatively dependent variables. Note that copulas do not always have simple closed forms. In particular, the Gaussian and the t copulas do not have one but the bivariate Gumbel copula has the explicit expression

$$C_\theta^{\text{Gumbel}} = \exp\{-((- \ln u_1)^\theta + (- \ln u_2)^\theta)^{1/\theta}\} \quad 1 \le \theta < \infty$$

Another example of a closed form is given by the bivariate Clayton copula

$$C_\theta^{\text{Clayton}} = (u_1^{-\theta} + u_2^{-\theta} - 1)^{-1/\theta} \quad 0 < \theta < \infty$$

Interestingly, the Gumbel copula interpolates between independence (when $\theta = 1$) and perfect positive dependence (when $\theta \to \infty$). Similarly to the Gumbel copula, the Clayton copula approaches the independence copula when $\theta \to 0$ while it approaches perfect positive dependence as $\theta \to \infty$.

The converse of Sklar's theorem states that if C is a copula and $F_1, \ldots, F_d$ are distribution functions, then H, defined as

$$H(x_1, \ldots, x_d) = C(F_1(x_1), \ldots, F_d(x_d)) \tag{7.15}$$

is a joint distribution function with marginal density functions $F_1, \ldots, F_d$.

As such, the converse of Sklar's theorem allows the construction of multivariate distributions with arbitrary margins and copulas. A distribution that has been created in this manner is called a *meta* distribution. For example, the *meta*-Gumbel distribution has the Gumbel copula and arbitrary margins.

Interestingly, creating meta distributions allows the modeller to design multivariate distributions with specific characteristics. In particular, the meta-Gumbel distribution with Gaussian margins features upper tail dependence by which there is much more of a tendency for one variable to take an extremely high value when the other is also extremely high and vice versa. The Clayton copula turns out to have lower tail dependence and the t copula to have both lower and upper tail dependence. In contrast, the Gauss copula does not have tail dependence.

A skewed normal mixture copula is the copula of any normal mixture distribution that is not elliptically symmetric. An example is provided by the skewed t copula. The main advantage of the skewed t copula over the ordinary t copula is that its asymmetry allows us to have different levels of tail dependence in 'opposite corners' of the distribution. In the context of market risk, it is often claimed that joint negative returns on stocks show more tail dependence than joint positive returns.

Threshold copulas are natural limiting models for the dependence structure of multivariate exceedances. For the bivariate case, the Clayton copula is a limiting lower threshold copula while the limiting upper threshold copula is the Clayton survival copula.

It is often very difficult to find a good multivariate model that describes both marginal behaviour and dependence structure effectively. That is why it is a good idea to separate the marginal-modelling and dependence-modelling. The main method is maximum likelihood. However, a simpler method-of-moments procedure using sample rank correlation estimates can be exploited. This method has the advantage that marginal distributions do not need to be estimated, and consequently inference about the copula is in a sense margin-free. In this case, empirical estimates of either Spearman's or Kendall's rank correlation is used to infer an estimate of the copula parameter. Obviously, we assume that there are *a priori* grounds for considering the chosen copula to be an appropriate model, such as symmetry or the lack of it and the presence or absence of tail dependence.

8

Annualization Problem

In practice, risk managers are often asked to extend the time horizon of Value-at-Risk computed on hedge funds or traditional financial assets. In its amendment of January 1996,[1] the Basel Committee suggests that Value-at-Risk may be estimated for the minimum 10-day holding period by applying the square-root of time rule to Value-at-Risk 99% ($VaR_{99\%}$) calculated on daily data.

$$VaR_{99\%}^{[10\,\text{days}]} = \sqrt{10}\; VaR_{99\%}^{[\text{daily}]} \tag{8.1}$$

In theory, this methodology should only be applied to centred normal conditional[2] distributions that are independently and identically distributed per unit of time. For daily data, the zero mean assumption is not too unrealistic, but it is not easily extended to longer time horizons. Moreover, as we will see later, if distribution is not normal but is characterized by heavier tails, the approach tends to overestimate the risk for longer time horizons. This is why it is not necessary for the supervisory authorities to explicitly insist on the conditional aspect of this approach.

Use of the square-root of time rule has become widespread among a broad range of financial players. Because it is easy to use and accepted by the supervisory authorities, it has also been unconditionally imposed for longer time horizons. For example, in the case of insurers it is common to calculate risk over one year by applying the square-root of

---

[1] Page 44, section B.4, paragraph c.

[2] This confusion between conditional and unconditional distribution is fairly common. People tend to forget rather too quickly that many formulae for calculating risk indicators are only valid for previously filtered data. This introductory stage results in what are known as conditional distributions. The unconditional application of formulae developed for filtered variables can lead to wrong assessments being made. The opinion, for instance, that in theory all returns are supposed to be normally distributed is an example of this type of error. First of all, it is worth remembering that in financial theory there are other distributions in addition to the one that presents most simply the necessary concepts for its development. More importantly, a normal variable to which a memory process is added produces a completely different distribution. For example, if successive returns are obtained under different volatility regimes, the distribution that the investor faces (unconditional distribution) may be characterized by very heavy tails. However, once adjusted (conditionally) for changes in volatility, losses and profits can be normally distributed.

However, in practice there are sometimes good reasons to look at data in an unconditional way. For example, a complex and rigorous conditional methodology can only slightly improve the results of a simple model while requiring a level of calculation and time resources incompatible with the continuous production of indicators. Risk managers also deliberately omit the filtering stage when the relationship between transparency and the value added by complexity favours simplicity.

time to harmonize the time horizons. However, this practice can produce major errors, even under the favourable hypotheses of independent and identically distributed returns per unit of time. We might at first glance think that applying a single biased methodology to the measurement of risk in respect of all financial assets is not that serious a problem, and represents a process of error standardization that treats all assets impartially. Unfortunately, the standardization of error does not exist: the more imperfect the approximation, the greater the inequality of treatment in the assessment of risk. As pointed out by Popper (1960),

In our infinite ignorance we are all equal.

As we will see, the square-root of time rule applied to a Value-at-Risk calculated assuming independently and identically distributed (i.i.d.) returns penalizes hedge funds between 7.9 and 21.9 times more than equities, and between 4.9 and 9 times more than bonds. When the i.i.d. assumption is excluded, the square-root of time rule penalizes hedge funds between 5.2 and 13.8 times more than equities and around 5 times more than bonds.

This inequality of treatment is explained by the time structure of hedge fund risk: after several months, the risk no longer increases and the annual Value-at-Risk can be lower than the monthly risk. This time structure can actually be observed by simple empirical analysis. For example, the greatest cumulative loss for hedge funds (maximum drawdown) is 1.6 times the worst monthly loss and lasts 3 months. For equities, the maximum drawdown is 4 times higher than the worst monthly loss and lasts 31 months. The length of the longest cumulative loss for hedge funds is 17 months, whereas it is 86 months in the case of equities.

We have to remember that hedge funds are managed whereas market indices are not. In particular, the investment process established for hedge funds generally incorporates management procedures that reduce the cumulative risks. When the technology bubble burst, for example, long/short-type funds were at first badly hit by the market reversal, but then their absolute approach enabled them to drastically reduce their global portfolio exposure and their allocations to the most sensitive sectors. In contrast, the corresponding reduction in market indices (or the loss posted by index managers) was largely the result of capital destruction.

In this chapter we will propose a method to annualize the new Style Value-at-Risk. As this methodology may be applied to the most common approaches to Value-at-Risk, we propose to examine the impact of the approximation errors for different risk indicators and among hedge funds, equities and international bonds for the 1994 to 2006 period.[3] So in the first section of this chapter, we look at the annualization of the main statistical indicators. Then, the approximation errors for the most common Value-at-Risk models are examined and we consider the annualization of Value-at-Risk for 1951 hedge funds.

8.1 ANNUALIZATION OF THE MAIN STATISTICAL INDICATORS ASSUMING I.I.D.

In finance, the most common annualization methods are based on the assumption of independently and identically distributed (i.i.d.) returns[4] X per unit of time.

8.1.1 Annualization of the Mean

In general, the mean of the sum of variables X_i identically distributed is equal to the sum of the means of the variables:[5]

$$E(X_i) = \mu \, \forall i \implies E\left(\sum_{i=1}^{n} X_i\right) = n\mu$$

X_i is defined as the continuous monthly returns independently and identically distributed and $X_{[annual]}$ as the annual return obtained by the sum of the monthly returns for the 12 months of the year:

$$X_{[annual]} = \sum_{1=1}^{12} X_i$$

The identical distribution assumption allows the annual mean to be deduced from the monthly mean (identical for all X_i variables) by means of a multiplication factor:

$$E(X_i) = \mu \;\; \forall i \;\; \text{then} \;\; E(X_{[annual]}) = E\left(\sum_{i=1}^{12} X_i\right) = \sum_{i=1}^{12} E(X_i)$$

---

[3] As in the previous chapters, the period from August 1998 to October 1998 is excluded so as not to reflect fluctuations attributable to exogenous shocks.

[4] In comparing returns calculated for given time frequencies, the effect of compounding returns must be taken into account. The analysis set out below is therefore carried out on the basis of continuous returns and the results expressed as a log differential of prices.

[5] To simplify the presentation of this first section, the statistical moments are those of the population.

We therefore have the following annualization:

$$\mu_{[\text{annual}]} = 12\mu_{[\text{monthly}]} \tag{8.2}$$

The mean increases with temporal aggregation.

8.1.2   Annualization of Volatility

The identical distribution assumption implies that the X_i variables have the same variance, i.e.

$$\text{Var}(X_i) = \sigma^2 \; \forall i$$

In addition, the variance of a sum of independent variables is equal to the sum of the variances, i.e.

$$\text{Var}\left(\sum_{i=1}^{n} X_i\right) = \sum_{i=1}^{n} \text{Var}(X_i)$$

Bringing together these two properties therefore gives

$$\text{Var}(X) = \text{Var}\left(\sum_{i=1}^{n} X_i\right) = \sum_{i=1}^{n} \text{Var}(X_i) = \sum_{i=1}^{n} \sigma^2 = n\sigma^2$$

In finance, the standard deviation of the data (in other words the square root of the variance) is called volatility and, in the case of hedge funds, what we are interested in is annualizing the volatility of the monthly data. So

$$\sigma_{[\text{annual}]} = \sqrt{\text{Var}\left(\sum_{i=1}^{12} X_i\right)} = \sqrt{\sum_{i=1}^{12} \text{Var}(X_i)} = \sqrt{12\sigma^2_{[\text{monthly}]}}$$

The annualization of volatility assuming i.i.d returns is therefore

$$\sigma_{[\text{annual}]} = \sqrt{12}\,\sigma_{[\text{monthly}]} \tag{8.3}$$

Volatility increases with temporal aggregation, though not as quickly as does the mean.

8.1.3   Annualization of Skewness

As well as its measure of central tendency and its dispersion, a statistical distribution can be described by its shape, the first characteristic of which is skewness (S). When skewness is zero, there is perfect symmetry and when skewness is positive (negative), the distribution is skewed to the right (left). Skewness is calculated on the basis of the cube of mean deviations (third central moment) divided by the cubed standard deviation.

$$S(X_i) = \frac{E\,(X_i - E(X_i))^3}{\sigma^3}$$

If $X = \sum X_i$ is the sum of independent and identically distributed variables, then skewness can be deduced as follows:

$$S(X) = \frac{E\left(\sum_{i=1}^{n} X_i - E\left(\sum_{i=1}^{n} X_i\right)\right)^3}{\sqrt{\mathrm{Var}(X)^3}} = \frac{nE\,(X_i - E(X_i))^3}{\sqrt{n^3\mathrm{Var}(X)^3}}$$

$$= \frac{1}{\sqrt{n}}S(X_i)$$

The skewness is annualized on the basis of independent and identically distributed monthly data as follows:

$$S_{[\text{annual}]} = \frac{1}{\sqrt{12}}S_{[\text{monthly}]} \tag{8.4}$$

Skewness diminishes with temporal aggregation.

8.1.4   Annualization of the Kurtosis Coefficient

The second statistical indicator of the distribution shape is kurtosis (given as $\check{K}$) which measures the fatness of the distribution tails. In finance, the measure of kurtosis generally used is

$$\check{K}(X_i) = \frac{E\,(X_i - E(X_i))^4}{\sigma^4}$$

In a normal distribution the kurtosis is equal to 3. All distributions with fatter distribution tails (and therefore a sharper peak around the mean) than normal ($\check{K} > 3$) are known as leptokurtic distributions, while distributions with thinner tails than normal (and therefore a smaller peak around the mean) are known as platykurtic distributions. Excess kurtosis (K) is defined as the difference between the kurtosis of the distribution examined and that of the normal distribution (always equal to 3):

$$K(X_i) = \check{K}(X_i) - 3$$

The concept of excess kurtosis not only enables us to express the fatness of the distribution tails relative to the mean, but also allows a simple annualization[6] for i.i.d. variables

$$K_{[\text{annual}]} = \frac{1}{12} K_{[\text{monthly}]} \tag{8.5}$$

With temporal aggregation, the fatness of the distribution tails tends towards that of normal distribution tails; in other words, the distribution tails become fatter if the initial distribution is platykurtic and thinner if the initial distribution is leptokurtic.

In statistics, a more recent definition of kurtosis $\tilde{K}$ consists of measuring the arrangement of probability masses around the centre, excluding the dispersion effect, by the ratio between the fourth cumulant and the square of the second cumulant. This new approach, which replaces central moments by cumulants, has two advantages. First, the kurtosis $\tilde{K}$ of normal distribution is equal to 0. Moreover, as the additivity property of the indicators of the sum of independent variables is valid for cumulants of all orders of magnitude (it only applies to moments below the fourth order of magnitude), kurtosis $\tilde{K}$ is annualized as follows:

$$\tilde{K}_{[\text{annual}]} = \frac{1}{12} \tilde{K}_{[\text{monthly}]} \tag{8.6}$$

8.1.5 Annualization of Coefficients above the Fourth Order of Magnitude

As a general rule, the coefficient C_m of order of magnitude m can be defined as the ratio between the cumulant L_m of order of magnitude m and the second cumulant to the power of $m/2$:

$$C_m(X_i) = \frac{L_m}{\sqrt{L_2^m}}$$

The coefficient is therefore annualized as follows:

$$C_m^{[\text{annual}]} = 12^{1-\frac{m}{2}} C_m^{[\text{monthly}]} \tag{8.7}$$

8.1.6 Application to Finance

Cataloguing all the various annualizations under the i.i.d. assumption highlights the heterogeneity of the methods used: even though the multiplication factor is a function of the coefficient's order of magnitude, there is no single annualization factor, as shown by equations (8.2)–(8.7). This absence of standardization does not at first sight have a major impact in terms of its application to finance, as statistical indicators considered

---

[6] This is demonstrated in Appendix F.

individually are generally the focus of interest. In this respect, calculating the mean for a sample of returns supposes the existence of a single mean. Annualization by means of a multiplication factor of 12 is the natural corollary of this assumption. Similarly, the annualization of monthly volatility by the square root of 12 ($\sqrt{12}$) – very common in finance – is completely consistent with the assumption of independent and identically distributed returns. But theoretical consistency in no way guarantees the empirical validity of assumptions and, as we will see in the fourth section, the financial data observed contradicts the assumption of i.i.d. returns.

It would also be an error to believe that the heterogeneity of annualization factors has no consequences as far as finance is concerned, because in this sphere as in many others, $G(X_i)$ indicators linking different statistical coefficients together are also of interest. Equations (8.2)–(8.7) imply that the annualization of a statistical indicator $G(X_i)$ by a common multiplication factor is only possible, other than on a one-off basis, if

$$\forall m > 2 \text{ if } C_m \text{ exists } \frac{\partial G}{\partial C_m}$$

$$= \begin{cases} 0 & \text{or} \\ 12^{-\frac{m-j}{2}} \frac{\partial G}{\partial C_j} & \forall j, 2 < j < m \text{ if } \frac{\partial G}{\partial C_j} \neq 0 \\ 12^{\frac{m}{2}} \frac{\partial G}{\partial \mathrm{Var}(X)} & \text{if } V(X) \text{exists and } \frac{\partial G}{\partial \mathrm{Var}(X)} \neq 0 \\ 12^{\frac{m}{2}} \frac{\partial G}{\partial E(X)} & \text{with } \frac{\partial G}{\partial E(X)} \neq 0 \end{cases}$$

with $C_3 = S$ and $C_4 = K$ and if variance exists:

$$\frac{\partial G}{\partial \mathrm{Var}(X)} = \begin{cases} 0 & \text{or} \\ \frac{\partial G}{\partial E(X)} & \text{if not} \end{cases}$$

There is no need to conduct an extensive analysis in order to conclude that only a limited number of financial indicators will meet this constraint. As we shall see in the next section, Value-at-Risk certainly does not.

8.2 ANNUALIZATION OF VALUE-AT-RISK ASSUMING I.I.D.

In this section, the impact on Value-at-Risk of the square-root of time rule assuming i.i.d. returns is empirically assessed in comparison with an indicator respecting equations (82)–(8.7) for hedge funds, European equities and European bonds. We have adopted standard notation for

Table 8.1   Statistics calculated on the log differences of monthly returns

| | January 1994 to December 2006 | | |
Monthly data	CS HF Index	MSCI World Index	City World GVT AM
Average	−0.98%	−0.61%	−0.42%
Standard deviation	2.03%	3.75%	1.81%
Skewness	−0.46	0.63	−0.28
Excess kurtosis	1.86	0.41	0.40

profits and losses in risk management: variable X represents losses when positive and profits when negative. Since Value-at-Risk is a maximum loss, it is therefore generally positive using this notation.

Table 8.1 gives the value of the statistical coefficients calculated on monthly profits and losses from January 1994 to December 2006 for hedge funds and international securities indices.

8.2.1   Annualization of Normal Value-at-Risk

Normal Value-at-Risk at a 99% confidence level is defined as follows:

$$VaR_{99\%} = \mu + 2.33\sigma$$

If Value-at-Risk is calculated on the basis of daily data, zero mean returns are assumed and normal Value-at-Risk amounts to an indicator proportional to volatility

$$VaR_{99\%} = +2.33\sigma$$

Under this assumption, Value-at-Risk is annualized by applying a multiplication factor. It is however important to remember that this methodology remains an approximation (assumption of zero mean returns) that only works for a very short time horizon. Sometimes Value-at-Risk 99% is defined as the deviation from the mean return that might be expected to be exceeded in 1 case out of 100. In this case too, VaR is proportional to volatility and the problem of annualization does not arise. But once the deviation has been annualized, it should be set against the annual mean return to obtain the loss that can be expected to be exceeded once in every 100 cases.

For monthly returns, it is not realistic to assume zero mean returns and normal Value-at-Risk is therefore calculated according to the following formula

$$VaR_{99\%}^{[monthly]} = \mu_{[monthly]} + 2.33\sigma_{[monthly]}$$

The annualization of normal Value-at-Risk must take into account the difference between mean annualization factors and factors for annualizing volatility. Rather than simply multiplying the monthly Value-at-Risk by $\sqrt{12}$, the following calculation should be carried out

$$VaR_{99\%}^{[\text{annual}]} = 12\mu_{[\text{monthly}]} + 2.33\sqrt{12}\,\sigma_{[\text{monthly}]} \tag{8.8}$$

The higher the ratio between mean and volatility, the greater the approximation error using the square-root of time rule (i.e. the difference between $\sqrt{12}$VaR and the Value-at-Risk calculated according to equation (8.8)). In effect, as shown by equation (8.8), when annualization is carried out correctly under the i.i.d. assumption, there are two offsetting effects: the mean increases at a rate equal to 12 and the mean deviation at a rate of 8.07. So, if the ratio between the average in absolute terms and the standard deviation is 67.26%, annualization reduces the Value-at-Risk. Clearly, none of the indices considered here has such a ratio, but as Table 8.2 shows, the ratios between mean and volatility are very different for traditional indices and hedge funds. We can legitimately expect that the approximation error arising from annualization by the square-root of time rule more strongly penalizes the valuations with the highest ratios, i.e. hedge funds, relative to traditional funds.

The charts in Figure 8.1 plot the Value-at-Risk calculated using the square-root of time rule and those obtained using the formula in equation (8.8) in relation to the number of months (1 to 24), with 12 months corresponding to the annualization. It is clear that:

• The approximation of Value-at-Risk using the square-root of time rule differs rapidly and significantly from the correct Value-at-Risk.
• The correct Value-at-Risk of hedge funds has a peak: the risk begins to fall as from the sixth month. This phenomenon is clearly impossible to capture using the square-root of time rule.

Table 8.2 Ratios between average and standard deviation calculated on the basis of continuous monthly returns

	January 1994 to December 2006		
Monthly data	CS HF Index	MSCI World Index	City World GVT AM
Ratio between average and standard deviation	48.29%	16.33%	22.99%

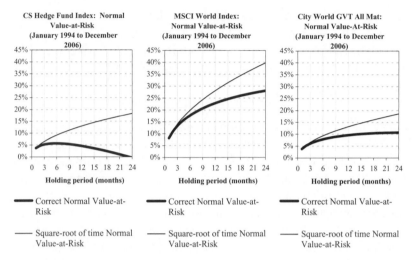

Figure 8.1 Normal Value-at-Risk and its approximation in relation to the time horizon

- The Value-at-Risk of the CS Hedge Fund Index becomes negative as from the 23rd month. In other words, assuming normal distribution and independence, there is less than one chance in 100 of suffering a loss over 24 months. The square-root of time rule is unable to represent this either.

The charts in Figure 8.2 represent the relative approximation error, in other words the differential between the approximation of the Value-at-Risk and the correct Value-at-Risk divided by the latter. It appears that the relative approximation error increases over time: after three months, the Value-at-Risk approximated using the square-root of time rule does not provide acceptable approximations for hedge funds. What is more, the approximation error differs significantly depending on the index in question. Thus, the annualized Value-at-Risk of equities is overestimated by 22.86%, whereas in the case of bonds it is overestimated by 37.02%. For hedge funds, Value-at-Risk is simply multiplied by a factor of 2.81. In other words, the annualization of normal Value-at-Risk using the square-root of time rule penalizes hedge funds 7.94 times more than equities and 4.9 times more than bonds.

8.2.2 Annualization of Value-at-Risk for Leptokurtic Distributions

One of the weaknesses for risk management of the normal approach is that it is unable to model fat tail distributions. If normal Value-at-Risk is

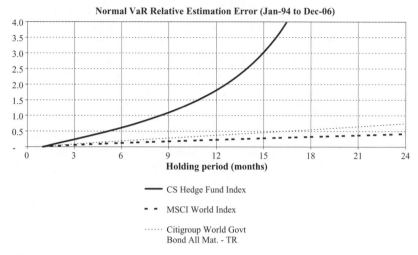

Normal VaR Relative Estimation Error (Jan-94 to Dec-06)

Holding period (months)

——— CS Hedge Fund Index

- - MSCI World Index

······ Citigroup World Govt
Bond All Mat. - TR

Figure 8.2   Relative approximation error, i.e. the difference between the approximated normal VaR and the correct normal VaR, divided by the correct VaR, in relation to the time horizon

calculated on the basis of monthly data from a leptokurtic distribution, the risk is underestimated for one month. On the other hand, as shown by Dacorogna et al. (2001), the extrapolation of Value-at-Risk for longer time horizons overestimates the risk: assuming i.i.d. returns, there is less diversification at the centre than at the extremes. This retrospectively explains the position of the supervisory authorities: extrapolation over a longer time horizon using the square-root of time rule penalizes those that have chosen an over-favourable measure of risk in the short term.

Because they share many properties with the normal distribution, Student distributions with ν degrees of freedom are generally used to model distributions with fatter tails than those of the normal distribution. As the mean of a Student variable is zero and its variance stands at $\nu/(\nu - 2)$ for $\nu \geq 2$, the Student ν Value-at-Risk is defined as follows:

$$Var^{[\text{monthly}]}_{99\%} = \mu_{[\text{monthly}]} + t_{99\%,\nu}\sqrt{\frac{\nu - 2}{\nu}}\sigma_{[\text{monthly}]}$$

The excess kurtosis of a Student's distribution with ν degrees of freedom is $K = [3(\nu - 2)/\nu - 4] - 3$. Student distributions in fact enable variables to be modelled with excess kurtosis ranging from 0 (where $\nu \to \infty$ Student distribution is equal to the normal distribution) to 6 ($\nu = 5$), since Student distributions with fewer degrees of freedom do not have kurtosis. The number of degrees of freedom ν of the Student distribution of a variable is therefore determined by its kurtosis:

$$\nu(X_i) = 5 \qquad\qquad \text{if } K(X_i) \geq 6$$
$$= \text{Integer}\left(4 + \frac{6}{K(X_i)}\right) \text{ if } 6 \geq K(X_i) \geq 0$$

For all cases where $K(X_i) \leq 3$, normal distribution is used.

Although the Student distribution is only stable[7] for $\nu = 1$ and $\nu \rightarrow \infty$, the combination of Student variables i.i.d. is in practice sometimes considered[8] to be a Student variable. Under this assumption, the number of degrees of freedom must change as excess kurtosis increases or decreases. The operator ϑ needs to be defined:

$$\vartheta\left(\sum_{i=1}^{n} X_i\right) = 5 \qquad\qquad \text{if } \frac{K(X_i)}{n} \geq 6$$
$$= \text{Integer}\left(4 + \frac{6n}{K(X_i)}\right) \text{ if } 6 \geq \frac{K(X_i)}{n} > 0$$
$$= 1,000 \qquad\qquad \text{if } \frac{K(X_i)}{n} \leq 0$$

The Student Value-at-Risk is then annualized as follows:

$$VaR_{99\%}^{[\text{annual}]} = 12\mu_{[\text{monthly}]}$$
$$+ t_{99\%, \vartheta(\sum_{i=1}^{12} X_i)}\sqrt{\frac{\vartheta(\sum_{i=1}^{12} X_i) - 2}{\vartheta(\sum_{i=1}^{n} X_i)}} \sqrt{12}\, \sigma_{[\text{monthly}]} \qquad (8.9)$$

Student Value-at-Risk calculated for one month is significantly different from normal Value-at-Risk only for those variables with high excess kurtosis. We can therefore expect monthly Student Value-at-Risk to be significantly higher for hedge funds than for other indices.

However, the property established by Dacorogna, et al. (2001) indicates that the differences between the two risk indicators become smaller over time. In the operator ϑ the diversification of tails is expressed by the speed at which the excess kurtosis decreases according to the time horizon (i.e. at a factor of $1/n$). In fact, normal Value-at-Risk and Student Value-at-Risk tend quickly to converge as shown by the charts in Figure 8.3. As a consequence, the approximation error for Student Value-at-Risk calculated according to equation (8.9) and the square-root of time rule is very similar to the approximation error of normal Value-at-Risk.

---

[7] The first case is a Cauchy distribution, while the second is a normal distribution.

[8] For the exact determination of the combination of independent Student variables, see Walker and Saw (1978).

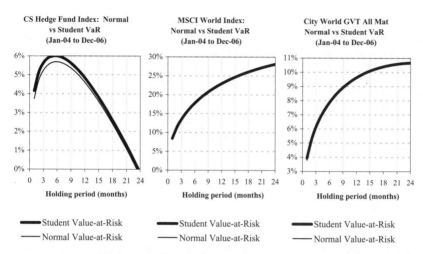

Figure 8.3   Normal Value-at-Risk and Student Value-at-Risk in relation to the time horizon

8.2.3   Annualization of Cornish–Fisher Value-at-Risk

The Cornish–Fisher expansion is a formula for approximating the percentiles of distributions that are almost normal by adjusting the normal distribution percentile according to their skewness and kurtosis. Although this type of expansion is only valid for small deviations from the normal distribution, the approach is widely used to estimate the Value-at-Risk of hedge funds and is formulated as follows[9] for profits and losses:

$$VaR_{99\%}^{[\text{monthly}]} = \mu_{[\text{monthly}]} + \big[2.33 + 0.74 S_{[\text{monthly}]}$$

$$\times \big(1 - 0.512 S_{[\text{monthly}]}\big) + 0.23 K_{[\text{monthly}]}\big] \, \sigma_{[\text{monthly}]}$$

So a distribution with fat tails and with losses (here given as positive figures) more highly skewed than profits increases Value-at-Risk. However, if the skewness is very high ($S > 0.512^{-1} = 1.694$) and the distribution therefore deviates strongly from the normal distribution, the expansion gives contradictory results, with highly skewed losses in this case reducing Value-at-Risk.

---

[9] The Cornish–Fisher expansion can be expressed more conventionally as

$$\left[2.33 + \frac{2.33^2 - 1}{6} S_{[\text{monthly}]} + 2.33 \frac{2.33^2 - 3}{24} K_{[\text{monthly}]} - 2.33 \frac{2 \cdot 2.33^2 - 5}{36} S_{[\text{monthly}]}^2\right] \sigma_{[\text{monthly}]}$$

The transition from one formula to the other is algebraically simple and incorporates the fact that the skewness of profits and losses is the opposite of the skewness of losses and profits, i.e. $S(-X) = -S(X)$.

Cornish–Fisher Value-at-Risk incorporates the first four statistical moments. The application of the square-root of time rule clearly does not take into account the different rates of annualization of these indicators as given by equations (8.2)–(8.5). The correct procedure for annualizing Cornish–Fisher Value-at-Risk assuming i.i.d. returns is therefore as follows:

$$
VaR_{99\%}^{[\text{annual}]} = 12\mu_{[\text{monthly}]} + \left[2.33 + \frac{0.74}{\sqrt{12}} S_{[\text{monthly}]} \right.
$$
$$
\left. \times \left(1 - \frac{0.512}{\sqrt{12}} S_{[\text{monthly}]} \right) + \frac{0.23}{12} K_{[\text{monthly}]} \right] \sqrt{12}\sigma_{[\text{monthly}]}
$$

(8.10)

Figure 8.4 plots Cornish–Fisher Value-at-Risk in relation to the time horizon. This is similar to normal Value-at-Risk, except that certain characteristics are magnified. As well as the mean effects that existed in normal Value-at-Risk, Cornish–Fisher Value-at-Risk also includes the skewness and kurtosis effects of the distribution tails. Thus, there are in general greater absolute differences vis-à-vis the square-root of time rule and the relative and absolute differences are multiplied for all the indices. In the case of hedge funds, the local peaks are reached more rapidly, after five months. The square-root of time rule fails to reflect the

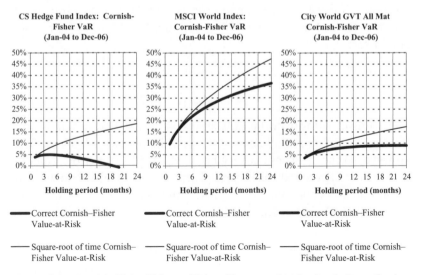

Figure 8.4 Cornish–Fisher Value-at-Risk and its approximation in relation to the time horizon

existence of Value-at-Risk peaks in relation to the time horizon, and the earlier the Value-at-Risk decreases, the less efficient the approximation. In addition, the Values-at-Risk of hedge funds for time horizons in excess of nine months (and therefore 12 months) are lower than the monthly risk. The annualization of Cornish–Fisher Value-at-Risk using the square-root of time rule is therefore totally inadequate for hedge funds, penalizing them 20.9 times more than equities and 7.52 times more than bonds.

Calculated for the January 1999 to December 2006 period, the relative errors for hedge funds (9.94% with the square-root of time rule and 0.84% with the Cornish–Fisher formula (8.10), i.e. relative error of over 1200%), as well as the level of risk calculated according to this methodology (0.84% over 12 months) also reveal the inadequacy of the Cornish–Fisher expansion for hedge funds. But, as we will show later, some characteristics of the time structure of Value-at-Risk highlighted by this methodology remain even when the assumptions underlying these models are no longer applied.

8.2.4 Annualization of Value-at-Risk Based on Historical Percentiles

One of the methodologies most commonly used to calculate Value-at-Risk is to make no assumptions[10] about the underlying distribution of the population with the exception of one, which states that returns are independently and identically distributed. The historical method involves using solely the information relating to the percentile contained in the sample. This method therefore depends on the quality of the sample available and more particularly its size. When there is a very large flow of information, approximations based on the sample's historical percentiles prove to be very conservative. This property of historical Value-at-Risk explains why it is popular with practitioners, as demonstrated by Finger (2006). The temptation to use it for hedge funds was great, but with monthly returns, the size of the samples available for hedge funds is not appropriate to the historical Value-at-Risk approach and approximations are not very robust.

If no assumptions are made about the population, the time horizon window can only be extended by re-sampling. If there is a limited

---

[10] As long as the data has previously been filtered efficiently.

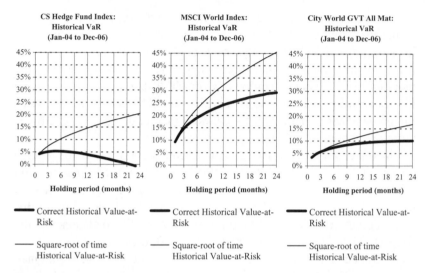

Figure 8.5 Value-at-Risk based on historical percentiles and its approximation in relation to the time horizon

amount of data available[11] and the assumption of independently and identically distributed monthly returns applies, bootstrap simulations are particularly appropriate for calculating a Value-at-Risk for longer time horizons. So for annualization, the algorithm consists of choosing 12 returns randomly from the 156 monthly returns, assuming the i.i.d. of monthly returns for each sampling with replacement. Then the cumulative return for these 12 months is calculated. The procedure is repeated until a sample of 1000 pieces of annual data is obtained. The approximation of historical Value-at-Risk is carried out on this sample. The operation is repeated 500 times, thereby obtaining a sample of 500 historical Value-at-Risk. The mean of these gives the annual Value-at-Risk.

The charts in Figure 8.5 plot the risk in relation to the time horizon. For hedge funds, risk peaks and starts to head downwards after five months and the annual Value-at-Risk is lower than the monthly level. The square-root of time rule is totally inappropriate to reflect this: the approximated annual Value-at-Risk is around 3.7 times higher than the real risk. The relative approximation error for hedge funds is 8.2 times higher than for European equities and 9 times higher than for bonds.

---

[11] Or the use of excessively old data is not relevant.

But in reality these figures underestimate the approximation error. In effect, the calculation for one month is carried out on the original sample without simulation. The size of this sample is much smaller than for longer time horizons. It contains 96 data for the 1-month comparison whereas for the other horizons, there are 1000 data. Given that the historical method is not very reliable for small samples, the Value-at-Risk for one month is significantly underestimated and there are certain irregularities at the start of the risk curves. The time structure of risk, by means of the feedback effect, provides a solution to the problem of approximating Value-at-Risk by historical simulation in the case of small samples. The risk curve between 2 and 24 months is determined by bootstrap simulations as described above. Then this risk curve is modelled and the Value-at-Risk at one month is extrapolated.

As regards analysing the efficiency of approximation using the square-root of time rule, applying this approach increases approximation errors since the square-root of time multiplies a higher monthly Value-at-Risk.

8.3 ANNUALIZATION WITHOUT ASSUMING I.I.D.

8.3.1 Annualization of Extreme Value Theory Value-at-Risk

In reality, returns are rarely identically and independently distributed. First of all, financial data can be highly autocorrelated. In the case of alternative funds, Getmansky, et al. (2003) have demonstrated that, in addition to traditional sources of autocorrelation, other sources include smoothing effects and major exposure to illiquid assets. De-autocorrelation is therefore an essential stage in any measurement of hedge fund risk. As we saw in the previous chapter, this filtering step was implemented in the New Style Value-at-Risk for hedge funds as a prerequisite for the application of Extreme Value Theory. Once de-autocorrelated, data are i.i.d. and bootstrap simulations on filtered data are an obvious method for annualizing EVT Value-at-Risk. The charts in Figure 8.6 show EVT Value-at-Risk in relation to the time horizon. The risk for hedge funds stops increasing as from the five-month time horizon. As from 11 months it becomes lower than the one-month risk. Thus, the EVT Value-at-Risk for hedge funds stands at 4.17% for one month but at 4.05% on an annualized basis. As with the Cornish–Fisher expansion or historical VaR, the square-root of time rule proves completely inadequate to represent this behaviour in the Value-at-Risk of hedge funds. In terms of relative approximation error, annualizing EVT

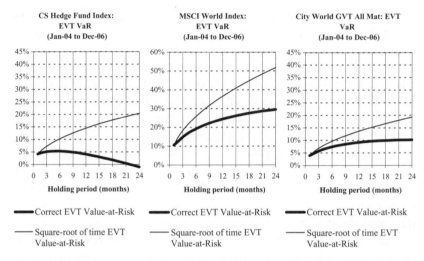

Figure 8.6 Extreme Value Theory Value-at-Risk and its approximation in relation to the time horizon

Value-at-Risk by the square-root of time rule penalizes hedge funds 5.2 times more than equities or bonds.

8.3.2   Annualization of *GARCH* Value-at-Risk

Heteroscedasticity is another source of non-i.i.d. returns. The current variance of the markets can therefore be seen as a weighted average of past variances and levels of past returns. In this case, volatility is explained by a *GARCH*(p, q)-type process.

In the case of *GARCH*(1, 1), the Drost and Nijman (1993) theorem[12] analytically links the parameters of a process for one unit of time with those of a process for h units of time. The formula proves to be much more complex than a simple square-root of time. In addition, the process generates a property that runs counter to the method proposed by the supervisory authorities. While the process allows variations in variance to be explained over a short period of time, the Drost and Nijman formula (1993) shows that by extending the time horizon, the variance tends to stabilize. It is therefore an error to apply the square-root of time to a variance that is very reactive to recent market conditions (conditional

---

[12] A version of the Drost and Nijman (1993) theorem for the issue of annualization is provided in Appendix B.

variance of the process) to approximate a stable long-term variance.[13] Even if on average (i.e. when the volatility spikes have been smoothed) the approximation is good, the longer the time horizon, the more the variations increase, whereas in practice they should diminish. In fact, the square-root rule applied to conditional standard deviation may for a certain time overestimate, and then underestimate, volatility, depending on market conditions. The inequality of treatment in the approximation error therefore depends on the level of conditional volatility, a parameter that is different for each asset class.

For more complex processes, there is no analytical formula. It has also been demonstrated that processes which are asymmetrical in relation to level variations reflect movements in conditional variances more efficiently. The annualization of *GARCH* Value-at-Risk can be carried out by means of a bootstrap simulation where the data is adjusted for the underlying process.[14] So, for the three indices considered here, we initially select the model for which the $GARCH(p, q)$ parameters are all significant, as well as estimating the conditional variances and regression constant. In the second stage, the returns are standardized in relation to the respective centred conditional standard deviations. The sample obtained meets the prerequisite for a bootstrap simulation, since it is composed of independently and identically distributed elements. The algorithm begins with the approximation of volatility for the following period. A standardized return randomly sampled (with replacement) is multiplied by this conditional standard deviation. The new performance allows the new variance to be determined and the operation is repeated for the other 11 months. The 12-month cumulative return is then calculated and by reiterating the operation 10 000 times, a historical Value-at-Risk is calculated on the basis of this bootstrap sample.

The charts in Figure 8.7 plot the risk for the three indices. Assuming a symmetrical *GARCH* process, the annual Value-at-Risk of hedge funds is lower than the monthly Value-at-Risk. Approximation using the square-root of time rule therefore overestimates the real level of risk by 484 basis points, i.e. the relative error is 385%, compared with 27.91% for equities and 79.23% for bonds. In other words, at the end

---

[13] Long-term volatility for substantial time horizons tends towards the constant of the process, with ARCH and *GARCH* parameters tending towards zero. For long time horizons, the square-root of time rule should therefore be applied to long-term volatility rather than to the volatility arising from current market conditions.

[14] This type of bootstrapped historical simulation is proposed by Barone-Adesi, et al. (1998). With reference to a Monte-Carlo simulation of the $GARCH(p, q)$ process with Gaussian or Student's white noise, no assumption is made on the noise-generating function. This is approximated by empirical distribution.

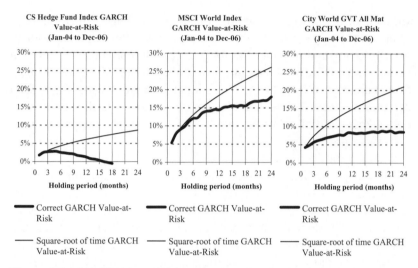

Figure 8.7 *GARCH* Value-at-Risk and its approximation in relation to the time horizon

of December 2006, the annualization of *GARCH* Value-at-Risk using the square-root of time rule penalizes hedge funds 13.8 times more than equities and 4.86 times more than bonds.

8.4   APPLICATIONS TO THE STYLE VALUE-AT-RISK

The annualization of the original Style Value-at-Risk is obtained through bootstrap simulations for the risk factors (annual percentiles of the CS/Tremont indices denoted by $F_{i,[annual]}$) and the application of the square-root of time rule for the idiosyncratic risk. The annual Value-at-Risk of the hedge fund s is therefore defined by

$$\text{VaR}_{s,[annual]} = \sqrt{12 \, (2.33\hat{\sigma}_{\hat{\varepsilon}})^2 + \sum_{i=1}^{10} \sum_{j=1}^{10} \hat{\rho}_{i,j} \, \hat{\beta}_{s,i} \, F_{i,[annual]} \, \hat{\beta}_{s,j} \, F_{j,[annual]}}$$

$$(8.11)$$

The first chart of Figure 8.4 shows the relative approximation errors using the square-root of time rule for the Value-at-Risk annualizations for 1951 hedge funds as at December 2006. On average, the relative approximation error comes to 155% (the Value-at-Risk is multiplied by 2.55 on average). Approximation using the square-root of time generates annual Values-at-Risk that are less than double the correct level of risk only in the case of 307 funds.

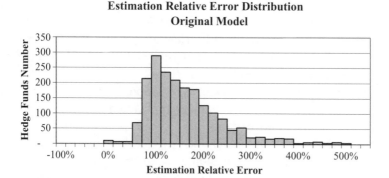

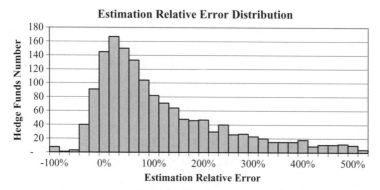

Figure 8.8 Relative error distribution for 1951 hedge funds as at December 2006

As a matter of fact, such error levels come partly from the square-root of time rule and partly from the magnification of an approximation in the aggregation of mean effects and scale factor effects. However, the New Style Value-at-Risk enables us to distinguish these effects as this new risk indicator takes into account the scale factor of the implicit factors as well as the mean impacts. So let $\tilde{F}^{[j]}_{i,[\text{annual}]}$ be the Extreme Value Annual Move of CS/Tremont Index i obtained through bootstrap simulations and equation (7.9). $\text{VaR}^{[\text{annual}]}_{[\text{EVT}]}(\hat{\varepsilon}_s)$ denotes the Extreme Value move of the residuals of the regression annualized through bootstrap simulations. The correct annualized New Style Value-at-Risk is thus defined by

$$\text{VaR}_s = 12\left(\alpha_s + \sum_i^{10}\beta_{s,i}\mu_i\right)$$
$$+\sqrt{\left(\text{VaR}^{[\text{annual}]}_{[\text{EVT}]}(\hat{\varepsilon})\right)^2 + \left(\sum_{i=1}^{10}\sum_{j=1}^{10}\tilde{\tilde{\chi}}_{i,j}\,\beta_{s,i}\left(\tilde{F}^{[j]}_{i,[\text{annual}]} - 12\mu_i\right)\beta_{s,j}\left(\tilde{F}^{[i]}_{j,[\text{annual}]} - 12\mu_j\right)\right)^2}$$

However, formula (8.4) shows the limit of the proposed approach: the Value-at-Strategy-Risk and the Value-at-Risk may be not defined as the underlying number of the square root is negative. Then a prudent approach recommends taking into account only the idiocratical risk. In such a framework, the second chart in Figure 8.4 illustrates the distribution of the estimation error. Here also, even with a conservative approach, the underestimation is important and 16% of the hedge funds have a negative annualized Value-at-Risk.

The combination of the bootstrap simulation, the Extreme Value Theory and the Style Model finds another application in the determination of the maximum cumulative loss that can be expected. Indeed, compute for each CS/Tremont sub-index the Extreme Value on two-month return, three-month return, four-month return and so on using bootstrap simulations. Do the same for the idiosyncratic risk and determine for each time horizon the Value-at-Risk. As the extreme moves for alternative investment strategies are concave with respect to the time horizon, there may exist a maximum Value-at-Risk. This figure can be seen as an estimate of the maximum cumulative loss the fund can expect to exceed. The length of the drawdown is given by the time horizon of the Value-at-Risk.

8.5   APPENDIX F: ANNUALIZATION OF EXCESS KURTOSIS

If we take an independent and identically distributed variable X_i and denote the mth central moment of this variable (if it exists) as $\mu_m(X_i) = E(X_i - E(X_i))^m$ and the mth cumulant as $L_m(X_i)$), and if we define the excess kurtosis K as the ratio between the fourth central moment and the squared second central moment (in other words the squared variance) minus 3, then the annualization of the kurtosis consists of the annualization of the fourth moment.

One of the advantages of cumulants is the additivity property, i.e. the cumulant of a sum of independent variables is equal to the sum of the cumulants. For the i.i.d. X_i variables, we therefore have

$$L_m\left(\sum_{i=1}^{n} X_i\right) = nL_m(X_i)$$

Note that for all distributions, the central moments and the cumulants are no longer equal, as from the order of magnitude $m = 3$. For the fourth order of magnitude, we have

$$\mu_4(X_i) = L_4(X_i) + 3\mu_2^2(X_i)$$

So

$$\mu_4 \left(\sum_{i=1}^{n} X_i \right) = L_4 \left(\sum_{i=1}^{n} X_i \right) + 3\mu_2^2 \left(\sum_{i=1}^{n} X_i \right)$$

$$= nL_4(X_i) + 3n^2\mu_2^2(X_i)$$

$$= nL_4(X_i) + 3n\mu_2^2(X_i) - 3n\mu_2^2(X_i) + 3n^2\mu_2^2(X_i)$$

$$= n(L_4(X_i) + 3\mu_2^2(X_i)) - 3n\mu_2^2(X_i) + 3n^2\mu_2^2(X_i)$$

$$= n\mu_4(X_i) - 3n\mu_2^2(X_i) + 3n^2\mu_2^2(X_i)$$

$$= n\mu_4(X_i) + 3n\mu_2^2(X_i)(n-1)$$

which implies for excess kurtosis K

$$K \left(\sum_{i=1}^{n} X_i \right) = \frac{\mu_4(\sum_{i=1}^{n} X_i)}{\mu_2^2(\sum_{i=1}^{n} X_i)} - 3 = \frac{\mu_4(\sum_{i=1}^{n} X_i)}{n^2\mu_2^2(X_i)} - 3$$

$$= \frac{n\mu_4(X_i) + 3n\mu_2^2(X_i)(n-1)}{n^2\mu_2^2(X_i)} - 3$$

$$= \frac{1}{n}\breve{K}(X_i) + \frac{3(n-1)}{n} - 3 = \frac{1}{n}\left(\breve{K}(X_i) - 3\right) = \frac{1}{n}K$$

8.6   APPENDIX G: DROST AND NIJMAN THEOREM

Theorem 1 (Drost and Nijman (1993))   *If the volatility of monthly returns follows a GARCH(1, 1) process, then 12-month volatility also follows a GARCH(1, 1) process but with the following parameters:*

$$\sigma_{[annual],\ t}^2 = \omega_{[annual]} + \beta_{[annual]}\sigma_{[annual],\ t-1}^2 + \alpha_{[annual]} \left(\sum_{i=1}^{12} \varepsilon_{t-12-i} \right)^2$$

with

$$\omega_{[annual]} = 12\omega \frac{1 - (\beta_{[monthly]} + \alpha_{[monthly]})^{12}}{1 - (\beta_{[monthly]} + \alpha_{[monthly]})}$$

$$\alpha_{[annual]} = (\beta_{[monthly]} + \alpha_{[monthly]})^{12} - \beta_{[annual]}$$

and $\mid \beta_{\text{annual}} \mid < 1$ *1 gives a solution of the quadratic equation*

$$\frac{\beta_{[\text{annual}]}}{1 + \beta^2_{[\text{annual}]}} = \frac{a(\beta_{[\text{monthly}]} + \alpha_{[\text{monthly}]})^{12} - 12}{a(1 + (\beta_{[\text{monthly}]} + \alpha_{[\text{monthly}]})^{24}) - 2b}$$

where

$$a = 12(1 - \beta_{[\text{monthly}]})^2 + 312 \frac{(1 - \beta_{[\text{monthly}]} - \alpha_{[\text{monthly}]})^2(1 - \beta^2_{[\text{monthly}]} - 2\beta_{[\text{monthly}]}\alpha_{[\text{monthly}]})}{(K_{[\text{monthly}]} + 2)(1 - (\beta_{[\text{monthly}]} + \alpha_{[\text{monthly}]})^2)}$$

$$+ 4 \frac{(11 - 12(\beta_{[\text{monthly}]} + \alpha_{[\text{monthly}]})^{12})(\alpha_{[\text{monthly}]} - \alpha_{[\text{monthly}]}\beta_{[\text{monthly}]}(\beta_{[\text{monthly}]} + \alpha_{[\text{monthly}]}))}{1 - (\beta_{[\text{monthly}]} + \alpha_{[\text{monthly}]})^2}$$

$$b = (\alpha_{[\text{monthly}]} - \alpha_{[\text{monthly}]}\beta_{[\text{monthly}]}(\beta_{[\text{monthly}]} + \alpha_{[\text{monthly}]})) \times \frac{1 - (\beta_{[\text{monthly}]} + \alpha_{[\text{monthly}]})^{24}}{1 - (\beta_{[\text{monthly}]} + \alpha_{[\text{monthly}]})^2}$$

Part III

Implicit Value-at-Risk

9

The Best Choice Implicit
Value-at-Risk

Depending on the point of view, the average coefficient of determination of regressions on individual hedge funds may be seen as a weakness or as a strength of the Style Model. Indeed, compared to the explanatory power at individual hedge funds level of other factorial models (such as those used by hedge funds clones), the quality of fit of the Style Model is rather good. However, the average adjusted R-square of 0.31 (from 2000 to 2006) is quite disappointing, particularly when compared to the results of Style analysis on individual mutual funds. Moreover, with about 40% of the volatility explained by the Style factor on average, the contribution of the Style Model within the Style Value-at-Risk may be quite limited for the majority of hedge funds. This may lead to a significant underestimation of the total risk of a multi-managers portfolio when the idiosyncratic risk is consolidated under the assumption of independence (see Chapter 11): the idiosyncratic risk may quickly be diluted.

Trying to improve the average R-square is therefore the natural next step in any attempt to find an efficient Value-at-Risk for investors in hedge funds. But obviously this is not an easy task: the disappointing results of the models underlying the hedge funds clones tend to show that a lot of work remains to be done to determine explicitly the individual hedge funds sensitivity to the traditional risk factors. On the other hand, the improvement of the quality of fit through the Style Model shed some lights on one possible direction for future research. As we will see in this chapter, the Style Model enables us to build implicitly, through the hedge funds indices, a basket of non-linear and dynamic exposure to traditional risk factor that more efficiently matches the exposures of any given hedge fund. Moreover, through the non-negativity constraint on parameters, the model enables an automated selection of some relevant factors from a larger set of exogenous variables. An automated selection process is particularly relevant for a universe of heterogeneous variables such as the returns of individual hedge funds.

As a consequence, the model proposed later in this chapter, called the Best Choice Implicit Model (BCIM), aims to exploit more efficiently these two fundamental properties of the Style Model for hedge funds: i.e. implicit factors obtained through aggregation of hedge fund returns, and the automated selection from a large set of regressors. The term Best Choice reflects the property that the automated selection process that is used is not path-dependent, contrary to stepwise regression.

9.1   ALTERNATIVE STYLE ANALYSIS AND BCI MODEL

As a matter of fact, the low average coefficient of determination can be explained by the omission of true factors. This is not surprising for hedge funds. Indeed, Chapter 3 was devoted to showing that a suboptimal classification with a large number of classes dominates an optimal restrictive classification. This high level of heterogeneity between hedge funds requires a large set of regressors: 10 alternative style indices are apparently not enough to capture the myriad of investment approaches implemented by hedge fund managers.

The congruence of a non-exhaustive set of alternative style indices, combined with a high level of heterogeneity, implies a second undesirable effect: each group average gathers returns of such fundamentally different hedge funds that the strategy features have been diversified. Out of a sample of 356 hedge funds with a 36-month track (as at December 2006) that enter into the computation of a CS/Tremont substyle index, 47.5% are more correlated with another CS/Tremont alternative investment style index than with the one used in the valuation. In other words, slightly less than half of the constituents of the indices are closer to other strategies than the one that they are supposed to represent. This[1] casts some heavy doubts on the relevance of the Style Model applied to hedge funds to track style drift: considering as 'a cat anything behaving as a cat[2]', cannot be applied to hedge funds. The style risk factors are so badly defined and so misrepresented (as if the only thing we knew of a cat was that it is an animal), that any change in the relation between a given hedge fund and a style factor cannot be interpreted as a style drift signal. This is clearly confirmed by the month to month changes in betas for a large set of hedge funds. Indeed, a relative stability in betas from one month to the next is required for the Style Value-at-Risk. As illustrated by Figure 9.1, such steadiness

---

[1] Combined with the non-representativeness of hedge fund active indices as discussed in Chapter 4.

[2] Sharpe (1988) uses the sentence, 'The manager behaves as if ...'

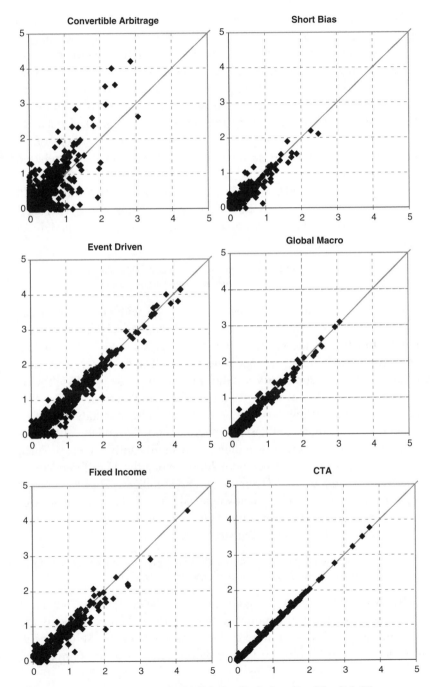

Figure 9.1   Changes in betas for 2162 hedge funds from Jan-05 to Feb-05

exists: each chart gathers the betas of 2162 hedge funds relative to a given strategy from January 2005 to February 2005. The vast majority of dots are located near the identity line exhibiting some monthly stability. However, for convertible arbitrage, almost all managers experienced important changes in beta. Under the assumption of a style drift model, the regular occurrence of this feature would mean that almost all hedge funds do the same style drift at the very same time. It seems more reasonable to consider these perturbations either as modifications of the representiveness of the style factors or as changes in the correlation structure of the indices.

This leads us to address the last reason why the Style Model both provides a disappointing coefficient of determination at the individual hedge fund level and cannot be considered as a style drift model. As stated by Sharpe (1992)

> Asset class returns should have either low correlations with one another or, in cases in which correlations are high, different standard deviations.

If the second part of the sentence is connected with constraint of coefficients smaller than 1, this assessment qualitatively describes the indetermination of the solution to a style analysis model when factors are linear combinations of other style factors. The over-diversification[3] of alternative investment style indices naturally leads to strongly correlated indices. Moreover, due to an opportunistic increase of the level of commonality during the equity rally between hedge funds, and as financial assets respond to the same macro-economic fundamentals, correlations between alternative indices have significantly increased since 2002. For instance, as of December 2006, among the 45 different correlations between the 10 CS/Tremont sub-style indices, 22 (49%) are not significantly lower than 0.7 (in absolute value) and 44 (75%) are not significantly inferior to 0.6. As pointed out by Lobosco and DiBartolomeo (1997), with such an association structure,

> Without explicit confidence intervals on the style weights, the damage done to reliability of the analysis can go undetermined and undetected.

Because of the non-negative constraint on the coefficients, the usual measure of the level of confidence that the individual coefficients are significantly different from zero does not apply to the Style Model. Lobosco and DiBartolomeo (1997) therefore propose to approximate

---

[3] As a result of a classification that does not match the level of heterogeneity between hedge funds.

the standard deviation of the estimates by the following formula

$$\frac{\sigma_\varepsilon}{\sigma_i \sqrt{36 - k - 1}} \tag{9.1}$$

where σ_ε is the standard deviation of the residual of the style analysis, k denotes the number of indices with non-zero coefficients, and σ_i is the standard deviation of the residuals of index i relative to the remaining indices. With such a measure, a backward elimination approach may be implemented in order to obtain a model composed only of indices with significant style weights. Obviously, conducting such analysis also reduces the average R-square and numerous hedge funds are simply not modelled by the style analysis.

At this stage we may wonder what is the real value of the Style Model applied to hedge funds. If the style interpretation is given up, the approach proposes to model hedge fund returns against some over-diversified portfolios that contain some residual exposures of what is performed by the hedge funds that compose these portfolios, in other words, to investment strategies with some dynamically managed non-linear exposures to traditional risk factors. In that context, the starting set of possible regressors does not need to be really different (and they are not): the constraint on the coefficient enables a few relevant ones to be pre-selected, as stated in Lobosco and DiBartolomeo (1997),

> By placing these constraints on the values of weights, we also somewhat mitigate the multicollinearity problem of traditional regression. Placing bounds on the weights reduces the likelihood that high correlations between the independent variables will cause the coefficient to blow up to unrealistic value.

In such an implicit framework, where the constraints are justified by an automated pre-selection process,[4] the proxy of the standard deviation of the estimates should be

$$\frac{\sigma_\varepsilon}{\sigma_{i,k} \sqrt{36 - k - 1}}$$

where $\sigma_{i,k}$ is not the standard deviation of the residuals of index i relative to the $k - 1$ other indices with a non-zero coefficient. Obviously, as

---

[4] Actually, under the style drift model framework, the non-negative constraint on the coefficient is hard to justify. For instance, in the merger arbitrage space, it is well known that some managers are short the deal, if they believe that the merger will not materialize. In other words, these managers initiate the reverse positions of the general acceptance of the strategy and often of most hedge funds managers. We already saw in Chapter 4 that the Dow Jones Convertible Bond investable index has experienced a fair amount of long equity exposure and short convertible exposure. These exposures are exactly the reverse of those entailed in pure convertible arbitrage.

$\sigma_{i,k} \geq \sigma_i$, it eases the acceptance of significant variables for a given estimate.

9.2   THEORETICAL FRAMEWORK OF BCIM

A good average coefficient of determination compared to other factor models thus holds for the Style Model only if it is considered as an implicit model with an automated pre-selection process. These two features reflect the complexity and diversity of hedge fund strategies. The target of the Best Choice Implicit Model is to exploit these two aspects of the Style Model in a more efficient way.

Best Choice Models start with a large set $\aleph_\zeta$ of ζ variables. Then, γ factors that provide the best fit[5] to the exogenous variable are selected, given that all coefficients should be significantly different from zero. Generally, two kinds of automatic selection methods are used: forward[6] stepwise and all-possible-regressions. While the first is path-dependent, as looking only one step forward at any point, the second soon requires a large number of estimations: for 36 factors, more than 68 billion regressions should be performed.

When the factors are implicit, the complexity of the automatic selection is drastically reduced as the factors are either orthogonal, or an orthogonal projection can be implemented on them without any loss of information. In such a framework, as established in a following Lemma, factors with the highest correlation in absolute value are the ones that will contribute more strongly to an improvement in the fit of the model. Thus, in the previous example of 36 potential regressors, the maximum number of regressions shrinks to 36.

In its pure form, the extraction of γ implicit orthogonal factors for a small number of monthly returns could be obtained through techniques based on Generalized Linear Latent Variable Models such as the one recently developed by Huber et al. (2004) or Huber and Victoria-Feser (2007). However, Factor Analysis focuses on the part of the total variance that is shared by the variables, while our target is to maintain the highest level of heterogeneity. Moreover, as Generalized Linear Latent Variable Models are fairly complex, they are quite difficult to implement. The methodology that follows proposes a theoretically less accurate, but

---

[5] The quality of adjustment is thereafter measured by the adjusted coefficient of determination, but statistics such as Mallows Cp penalizing more heavily for increasing the number of factors may also be used.

[6] A backward stepwise method is not possible for large $\aleph_\zeta$ as it would require that we start with more regressors than observations.

more simple way to obtain a Best Choice Implicit Model and ends up with very good results.

The first step of the approach consists at period T of extracting from a set $\aleph_\zeta$ of ζ alternative style indices a subset $\aleph_\varsigma$ of $\varsigma < \zeta$ indices. With the target being a subset $\aleph_\varsigma$ as heterogeneous as possible, the opposite of a single-linked hierarchical clustering is performed: we start with a correlation matrix associated with ζ indices, the $\varsigma \times \varsigma$ matrix with the lowest correlations in absolute value. Actually, a quite similar approach was used in Chapter 3 to build a classification with a large number of clusters. But here we go one step further as the style indices are now seen as implicit risk factors and thus a Principal Component Analysis (PCA) on $\aleph_\varsigma$ is performed. Generally, PCA is used to transform the original set of variables into a smaller set of linear combinations in order to reduce the size of the original set. Considering the high level of heterogeneity between hedge funds, such a reduction is not our aim here, but the complete orthogonal projection of a heterogeneous set of style indices is targeted. This will considerably ease the automated selection process. Moreover, PCA seems more convenient than Factor Analysis when interested in maintaining the highest level of heterogeneity: as already mentioned, Factor Analysis focuses on the part of the total variance that is shared by the variables, while PCA is interested in the total variance.

The second step constitutes the automated selection of the γ_s variables among the ς factors that explain, through a linear model and more efficiently, the last ξ monthly returns of hedge fund s. Obviously this is performed taking into account the orthogonality of the implicit factors. Moreover, no special constraints are put on the coefficients as, first the factors are implicit (with possible negative weighings) and the model, by construction, does not face any collinearity problems.

Below, we propose a formal and general presentation of the Best Choice Implicit Model process.

9.2.1 Implicit Factors

As a starting point, consider the set $\aleph_\zeta = \{z_i(T)\}_{i=1,\dots,\zeta}$ where $z_i(T) = (z_{i,t})_{t=1,\dots,T}$ denotes the vector of the T monthly returns of variable z_i. Then compute the correlations $\rho_{i,j}$ between the ζ variables for the last $\xi \leq T$ returns, i.e. between the vectors $z_i(T, \xi)$ that contain the last ξ coordinates of $z_i(T)$). Construct the subset $\aleph_{\zeta-1} = \aleph_\zeta - \{z_j(T)\}$

such that

$$\forall \, (z_i(T), z_{i'}(T)) \in \aleph_{\zeta-1}^2 \, i \neq i', \mid \rho_{i,i'} \mid \leq \max_{i''} \mid \rho_{j,i''} \mid$$

$$z_{i''}(T) \in \aleph_{\zeta-1} \quad \text{with} \quad \max_{i'''} \mid \rho_{i''',i''} \mid \leq \max_{i''''} \mid \rho_{i'''',j} \mid$$

$$\text{for} \, (z_{i'''}(T), z_{i''''}(T)) \in \aleph_{\zeta-1}^2, \, i''' \neq i'', \, i'''' \neq i''$$

Applying the same methodology on $\aleph_{\zeta-1}$ enables us to construct $\aleph_{\zeta-2}$ and the operation should be repeated until $\aleph_\varsigma$ with $\xi \geq \varsigma$ is reached. Then the $\varsigma \times \varsigma$ correlations matrix $\Sigma(\aleph_\varsigma)$ is such that for $i \neq i'$

$$\min_j \{\max_{j'} \mid \rho_{j,j'} \mid\} \geq \max_{i,i'} \mid \rho_{i,i'} \mid$$

for $z_j(T) \in \aleph_\zeta, z_{j'}(T) \in \aleph_\zeta - \aleph_\varsigma, (z_i(T), z_{i'}(T)) \in \aleph_\varsigma^2$

The next step consists of extracting the $\eta \leq \varsigma$ implicit factors through a principal component analysis. First compute the eigenvalues λ_i (for $i = 1, \ldots, \varsigma$) of the matrix $\Sigma(\aleph_\varsigma)$ ordering them by degree of magnitude. As the correlation matrix is computed on the ξ last returns of the $\varsigma \leq \xi$ styles indices, $\Sigma(\aleph_\varsigma)$ is symmetric definite positive and so $\lambda_i > 0 \, \forall i$.

Then consider the $\varsigma \times \varsigma$ matrix $V(\varsigma) = (v_i(\varsigma))_{i=1,\ldots,\varsigma}$ composed by the ς orthogonal eigenvectors $v_i(\varsigma)$ associated to the eigenvalues λ_i and denote the matrices $Z(\varsigma, T) = (z_i(T))_{i=1,\ldots,\varsigma}$ and $Z(\varsigma, T, \xi) = (z_i(T, \xi))_{i=1,\ldots,\varsigma}$. The standardized implicit factors are obtained by the projection of the standardized monthly returns on the eigenvector. Please note that the standardization should be performed by subtraction of the average of the last ξ monthly returns and division by the square root of the sum of the squared return for the last ξ months. Thus, each factor is not centralized for complete tracks but for the last ξ returns only, and the factors will be orthogonal only for the last ξ returns.

So, the $T \times \varsigma$ matrix $\tilde{G}(\varsigma, T) = (\tilde{G}_i(T))_{i=1,\ldots,\varsigma}$ of the centralized factor is obtained by

$$\tilde{F}(\varsigma, T) = \left(Z(\varsigma, T) - \frac{1}{\xi}\iota(T)\iota'(\xi)Z(\varsigma, T, \xi) \right)$$

$$\times \left(\sum_{i=1}^{\varsigma} \frac{\sqrt{\xi}}{\|z_i(T, \xi) - \frac{1}{\xi}\iota(\xi)\iota'(\xi)z_i(T, \xi)\|} e_i(\varsigma) e_i'(\varsigma) \right) V(\varsigma)$$

where $e_i(j)$ denotes the i basic coordinate vectors (canonical vectors or versors) of the j-dimensional space and $\iota(T)$ the $T \times 1$ sum vector.

In order to express these implicit factors with the same location and scaling as the initial variables, the matrix $\tilde{G}(\varsigma, T) = (\tilde{G}_i(T))_{i=1,\ldots,\varsigma}$ is decomposed into two blocks: the first one denoted $\tilde{G}(\varsigma, T, 1, T - \xi + 1)$ contains the $T - \xi + 1$ first coordinates of each vector $\tilde{G}_i(T)$ for $i = 1, \ldots, \varsigma$, while the second block denoted $\tilde{G}(\varsigma, T, \xi)$ contains the last ξ coordinates of each vector $\tilde{G}_i(T)$, i.e.

$$\tilde{G}(\varsigma, T) = \begin{pmatrix} \tilde{G}(\varsigma, T, 1, T - \xi + 1) \\ \cdots \\ \tilde{G}(\varsigma, T, \xi) \end{pmatrix}$$

So, the implicit factors matrix $G(\varsigma, T)$ is defined by

$$G(\varsigma, T) = \begin{pmatrix} G(\varsigma, T, 1, T - \xi + 1) \\ \cdots \\ G(\varsigma, T, \xi) \end{pmatrix} = (G_i(T))_{i=1,\ldots,\varsigma} \quad (9.2)$$

with

$$G(\varsigma, T, 1, T - \xi + 1)$$

$$= \left(\tilde{G}(\varsigma, T, 1, T - \xi + 1) - \frac{1}{\xi - T + 1} \right.$$

$$\times \iota(\xi - T + 1)\iota'(\xi - T + 1)\tilde{G}(\varsigma, T, 1, T - \xi + 1) \Bigg)$$

$$\times \left(\sum_{i=1}^{\varsigma} \frac{\sqrt{v_i'(\varsigma)}\Omega(\varsigma, 1, T - \xi + 1)v_i(\varsigma)(T - \xi + 1)}{\|\tilde{F}_i(T, 1, T - \xi + 1)\|} e_i(\varsigma) e_i'(\varsigma) \right)$$

$$+ \frac{1}{T - \xi + 1}\iota(T - \xi - 1)\iota'(T - \xi + 1)Z(\varsigma, 1, T - \xi + 1) V(\varsigma)$$

and

$$G(\varsigma, T, \xi) = \tilde{G}(\varsigma, T, \xi) \left(\sum_{i=1}^{\varsigma} \frac{\sqrt{v_i'(\varsigma)}\Omega(\varsigma, \xi)v_i(\varsigma)\xi}{\|\tilde{G}_i(T, \xi)\|} e_i(\varsigma) e_i'(\varsigma) \right)$$

$$+ \frac{1}{\xi}\iota(\varsigma)\iota'(\xi)Z(\varsigma, \xi) V(\varsigma)$$

where $\tilde{G}_i(T, \xi)$ and $\Omega(\varsigma, \xi)$ respectively denote the vector of the last ξ coordinates of $\tilde{G}_i(T)$ and the variance-covariance matrix of the ς initial variables $z_i(T)$ computed on the last ξ returns, while $\tilde{G}_i(T, 1, T - \xi + 1)$ contains the first $T - \xi + 1$ coordinates of $\tilde{G}_i(T)$ and $\Omega(\varsigma, 1, T - \xi + 1)$ is the variance-covariance matrix of the ς initial variables computed on the first $T - \xi + 1$ returns.

The last step consists simply of choosing η factors among the ς extracted ones. An obvious choice would be to take the η first factors as the eigenvalues ordered by degree of magnitude. Then the restriction on $\eta < \varsigma$ may be reasonable as the factor associated with lowest eigenvalue may be difficult to determine, as $\lambda_\varsigma \to 0$.

9.2.2   Coefficient of Determination and Independent Variables

One of the motivations of an Implicit Factor Model relies on the simplicity of an automatic selection of uncorrelated regressors, due to the property presented in the following Lemma.

Lemma 1   *Consider the model*

$$y_t = \alpha + \beta_1 x_{1,t} + \cdots + \beta_K x_{K,t} + \varepsilon_t \qquad t = 1, \ldots, T \qquad (9.3)$$

where x_k and $x_{k'}$ are uncorrelated, $k, k' = 1 \ldots K$, $k \neq k'$. Then the coefficient of determination is equal to the sum of the squared empirical coefficients of correlation

$$R^2 = \hat{\rho}_1^2 + \cdots + \hat{\rho}_K^2$$

where

$$\hat{\rho}_k = \frac{\sum_{t=1}^T (x_{k,t} - \bar{x}_k)(y_t - \bar{y})}{\sqrt{\sum_{t=1}^T (x_{k,t} - \bar{x}_k)^2} \sqrt{\sum_{t=1}^T (y_t - \bar{y})^2}} \qquad k = 1, \ldots, K$$

Proof: First consider the partitioned model

$$y = X\beta + \varepsilon = X_0 \beta_0 + X_1 \beta_1 + \varepsilon$$

The normal equations are

$$X'X\hat{\beta} = X'y \Longleftrightarrow \begin{cases} X_0'X_0\hat{\beta}_0 + X_0'X_1\hat{\beta}_1 = X_0'y \\ X_1'X_0\hat{\beta}_0 + X_1'X_1\hat{\beta}_1 = X_1'y \end{cases}$$

As $\hat{\beta}_0 = (X_0'X_0)^{-1}(X_0'y - (X_0'X_1)\hat{\beta}_1)$, we can solve for $\hat{\beta}_1$

$$X_1'X_1\hat{\beta}_1 - X_1'X_0(X_0'X_0)^{-1}X_0'X_1\hat{\beta}_1 = X_1'y - X_1'X_0(X_0'X_0)^{-1}X_0'y$$

that is

$$\hat{\beta}_1 = (X_1' M_0 X_1)^{-1} X_1' M_0 y$$

where $M_0 = I - X_0(X_0'X_0)^{-1}X_0'$ with I_T is the identity matrix of order T. In the particular case where $X_0 = \iota$ the sum vector, we get $M_0 = I_T - (1/T)\iota\iota'$.

Then recall that estimating the slope coefficients of equation (9.3) by ordinary least squares (OLS) is equivalent to estimating the model when all variables are expressed in deviation from their mean

$$\tilde{y}_t = \beta_1 \tilde{x}_{1,t} + \cdots + \beta_K \tilde{x}_{K,t} + \tilde{\varepsilon}_t \qquad t = 1, \ldots, T \qquad (9.4)$$

where $\tilde{y}_t = y_t - \bar{y}, \tilde{x}_{k,t} = x_{k,t} - \bar{x}_k, k = 1, \ldots, K$. Model (9.4) is simply equation (9.3) multiplied by the matrix $M_0 = I_T - (1/T)\iota\iota'$. In matrix form

$$M_0 \, y = M_0 \, X \, \beta + M_0 \, \varepsilon$$

where

$$y = [y_t]_{t=1,\ldots,T}, \qquad X = [x_t']_{t=1,\ldots,T} = [x_{1,t}, \ldots, x_{K,t}]_{t=1,\ldots,T},$$
$$\beta' = (\beta_1, \ldots, \beta_K)$$

The OLS estimator is given by

$$\hat{\beta} = (X' M_0 X)^{-1} X' M_0 y$$

As x_k and $x_{k'}$ are uncorrelated,

$$\frac{1}{T} \sum_{t=1}^{T} (x_{k,t} - \bar{x})(x_{k',t} - \bar{x}_{k'}) = 0, \qquad k \neq k',$$

and we get

$$(X' M_0 X) = \mathrm{diag}[\sum_{t=1}^{T} (x_{k,t} - \bar{x}_k)^2]_{k=1,\ldots,K}$$

and thus

$$(X' M_0 X)^{-1} = \mathrm{diag}\left[\left(\sum_{t=1}^{T} (x_{i,t} - \bar{x}_i)^2 \right)^{-1} \right]_{i=1,\ldots,K}.$$

Noting that $X'M_0 y = [\sum_{t=1}^{T}(x_{i,t} - \bar{x}_i)(y_t - \bar{y})]_{i=1,...,K}$, it comes

$$\hat{\beta} = \left[\frac{\sum_{t=1}^{T}(x_{k,t} - \bar{x}_k)(y_t - \bar{y})}{\sum_{t=1}^{T}(x_{k,t} - \bar{x}_k)^2} \right]_{k=1,...,K} \tag{9.5}$$

and thus the slopes are independent of each other.

In this context, the coefficient of determination of model (9.3) can be written as

$$R^2 = 1 - \frac{\tilde{S}S}{y'M_0 y}$$

where $\tilde{S}S/y'M_0 y = 1 - y'M_0 X\hat{\beta}/y'M_0 y$. By (9.5), we have

$$\tilde{S}S/y'M_0 y = 1 - \sum_{k=1}^{K} \frac{\left(\sum_{t=1}^{T}(x_{k,t} - \bar{x}_k)(y_t - \bar{y})\right)^2}{\sum_{t=1}^{T}(x_{k,t} - \bar{x}_k)^2 \sum_{t=1}^{T}(y_t - \bar{y})^2} = 1 - \sum_{k=1}^{K} \hat{\rho}_k^2 \quad \square$$

9.2.3   Automatic Selection of the Best Choice Implicit Model

The above Lemma significantly reduces the complexity of the selection of independent regressors. Indeed for a given number of endogenous variables, the more correlated ones to the exogenous variables are the regressors that provide the best fit. As the implicit factors are orthogonal, Lemma 1 applies.

So, let us consider $y_s(\xi)$, a ξ column vector. Then, re-rank the η implicit factors according to the absolute value of correlations $\rho_{i,s}$ between $y_s(\xi)$ and $F_i(T, \xi)$, i.e.

$$|\rho_{1,s}| \geq |\rho_{2,s}| \geq \ldots \geq |\rho_{\eta,s}|$$

Then, for any given number K of regressors, select the K implicit factors with the highest (absolute) correlation and estimate the parameters of the following regression through OLS:

$$y_s(\xi) = \left[\iota(\xi) \vdots G_1(T, \xi) \vdots \cdots \vdots G_K(T, \xi) \right] \begin{pmatrix} \alpha_s^{[K]} \\ \beta_{1,s} \\ \vdots \\ \beta_{K,s} \end{pmatrix} + \varepsilon_s^{[K]}$$

$$= X_s^{[K]} \beta_s^{[K]} + \varepsilon_s^{[K]}$$

where the vector of errors $\varepsilon_s^{[K]}$ is distributed according to a zero mean and a variance denoted by $\sigma_{\varepsilon_s^{[K]}}^2$.

Then compute for $k = 1, \ldots, K$

$$t_{k,s}^{[k]} = \frac{\mid \hat{\beta}_{k,s} \mid \; \|G_{i_s=k}(T, \xi) - \frac{1}{\xi}\iota(\xi)\iota(\xi)'G_{i_s=k}(T, \xi)\|}{\sqrt{\frac{1}{\xi-m-1}\left(X_s^{[k]'}X_s^{[k]}\right)^{-1}_{m+1,m+1}} \; \varepsilon_s^{[k]'}\varepsilon_s^{[k]}}$$

and perform a t-test[7] on $\beta_{k,s}$ at the 5% level. If all the coefficient $\beta_{k,s}$ for $k = 1, \ldots, K$ are significantly different from zero, then the adjusted coefficient of determination is computed

$$\bar{R}_{K,s}^2 = 1 - \frac{\xi - 1}{\xi - K - 1}\left(1 - \sum_{k=1}^{K}\hat{\rho}_k^2\right)$$

Then, consider the set Υ of adjusted coefficients of determination for regressions with all slopes significantly different from zero, considering the model with $K = 1, \ldots, \gamma^*$ regressors, where γ^* denotes the chosen possible maximum number of regressors. The Best Choice Implicit Model is simply the model with γ_s significant regressors that provides the highest adjusted R-square, i.e. γ_s is such that $\bar{R}_{\gamma_s,s}^2 = \max \Upsilon$.

9.3   BEST CHOICE IMPLICIT VaR

The first step of the Implicit Value-at-Risk consists of applying the Best Choice Implicit Model methodology previously described to the set $\aleph_{\zeta=194}$ of the $\zeta = 194$ alternative investment style indices described in Appendix A in Chapter 3. Following the approach described in section 9.2.1, extract for each month t the $\varsigma = 36$ more heterogeneous indices as computed by the absolute correlation on the last $\xi = 36$ months. Then the matrix $F(\varsigma = 36, t)$ of equation (9.2) is computed through both a Principal Component Analysis and the location and the relevant scaling adjustment on the $\xi = 36$ initial implicit factors. As there may be some computation problems for the eigenvector associated with the lowest eigenvalue, only the first $\eta = 35$ factors are retained.

Finally, for each hedge fund s, the Best Choice Implicit Model is determined with regressions on the last $\xi = 36$ monthly returns with $\gamma^* = 10$ maximum number of regressors. In that framework, a synthetic

---

[7] If the Durbin Watson statistics indicates first-order autocorrelation in the residual of the regression, the spectral variance should be used to perform the significance test.

track for each hedge fund can be computed with

$$\hat{r}_s(t) = \left[\iota(\xi) \vdots G_1(t) \vdots \cdots \vdots G_{\gamma_s}(t) \right] \begin{pmatrix} \hat{\alpha}_s^{[\gamma_s]} \\ \hat{\beta}_{1,s} \\ \vdots \\ \hat{\beta}_{\gamma_s,s} \end{pmatrix}$$

and the synthetic Value-at-Strategy-Risk is

$$\text{VsR}_s^{\text{Synthetic and Implicit}} = \text{VaR}_{\text{EVT}}(\hat{r}_s(t))$$

If a closed form risk attribution is desired, a risk consolidation similar to the one that was exposed in section 7.3.1 can be used. However, some slight modifications should be implemented. First, the γ_s slope estimations $\hat{\beta}_{k,s}$ should be searched for within the space of the $\eta = 35$ implicit factors. Moreover, as we will see later, because the risk asymmetry is taken into account in the risk consolidation, it will be useful to define a non-negative beta vector denoted by $\tilde{\hat{\beta}}_s = (\tilde{\hat{\beta}}_{s,i})_{i=1,...,70}$ as

$$\begin{aligned} \tilde{\hat{\beta}}_{s,i} &= \hat{\beta}_{s,i} & \text{for } i \leq 35 \text{ and } \hat{\beta}_{s,i} > 0 \\ &= -\hat{\beta}_{s,i-35} & \text{for } i = 36, \ldots, 70 \text{ and } \hat{\beta}_{s,i} < 0 \\ &= 0 & \text{otherwise} \end{aligned}$$

Then using the tail dependence system as defined by equation (7.10), the Implicit Value-at-Strategy-Risk is defined as

$$\text{VsR}_s^{\text{Implicit}} = \hat{\mu}' \tilde{\hat{\beta}}_s + \sqrt{\tau_s' \, \Xi \, \tau_s + \sum_{i=1}^{70} \tau_s^{[i]'} \, \Theta^{[i]} \, \tau_s} \qquad (9.6)$$

with

$$\hat{\mu} = \frac{1}{t}(G(\eta = 35, t) \vdots - G(\eta = 35, t))' \, \iota(t)$$

$$\tau_s = (\tau_{s,i})_{i=1,\ldots,35} \left(\left(\tilde{\hat{\beta}}_{s,i} \, (\text{VaR}_{\text{EVT}}(G_i(t)) - \hat{\mu}_i) \right)_{i=1,\ldots,35} \right.$$

$$\left. \vdots \left(\tilde{\hat{\beta}}_{s,i} \, (-\text{VaR}_{\text{EVT}}(G_i(t)) + \hat{\mu}_i) \right)_{i=36,\ldots,70} \right)$$

and $\Xi = (\tilde{\tilde{\chi}}_{i,j})$ defined with

$$\tilde{\tilde{\chi}}_{i,j} = \tilde{\tilde{\chi}}_{i,j} \quad \text{if } \tilde{\tilde{\chi}}_{i,j} \geq 0$$
$$= 0 \quad \text{otherwise}$$

and $\Theta^{[i]} = (\theta^{[i]}_{i',j})$ defined with

$$\theta^{[i]}_{i',j} = -\tilde{\tilde{\chi}}_{i,j} \quad \text{if } i = i' \text{ and } \tilde{\tilde{\chi}}_{i,j} < 0$$
$$= 0 \quad \text{otherwise}$$

and $\tau_s^{[i]} = (\tau^{[i]}_{s,i'})_{i'=1,\dots,70}$

$$\tau^{[i]}_{s,i'} = -\tilde{\tilde{\beta}}_{s,i} \, (\text{VaR}_{\text{EVT}}(G_i(t)) - \hat{\mu}_i) \quad \text{if } i = i' < 36$$
$$\quad -\tilde{\tilde{\beta}}_{s,i} \, (\text{VaR}_{\text{EVT}}(-G_i(t)) + \hat{\mu}_i) \quad \text{if } i = i' > 35$$
$$= 0 \quad \text{otherwise}$$

Finally, if we define the Implicit Value-at-Idiosyncratic-Risk as

$$\text{ViR}_s^{\text{Implicit}} = \hat{\alpha}_s^{[\gamma_s]} + \text{VaR}_{\text{EVT}}\left(r_s(t, \xi = 36) - \hat{r}_s(t, \xi = 36)\right) \tag{9.7}$$

and the Implicit Value-at-Risk for hedge fund s as

$$\text{VaR}_s^{\text{Implicit}} = \hat{\alpha}_s^{[\gamma_s]} + \hat{\mu}' \tilde{\tilde{\beta}}_s + \sqrt{\left(\text{ViR}_s^{\text{Implicit}} - \hat{\alpha}_s^{[\gamma_s]}\right)^2 + \left(\text{VsR}_s^{\text{Implicit}} - \hat{\mu}' \tilde{\tilde{\beta}}_s\right)^2} \tag{9.8}$$

Analogically, the Synthetic Implicit Value-at-Risk is defined as

$$\text{VaR}_s^{\text{Synthetic and Implicit}}$$

$$= \hat{\alpha}_s^{[\gamma_s]} + \hat{\mu}' \tilde{\tilde{\beta}}_s + \sqrt{\left(\text{ViR}_s^{\text{Implicit}} - \hat{\alpha}_s^{[\gamma_s]}\right)^2 + \left(\text{VsR}_s^{\text{Synthetic and Implicit}} - \hat{\mu}' \tilde{\tilde{\beta}}_s\right)^2} \tag{9.9}$$

9.4 EMPIRICAL TESTS

The empirical tests below were performed according to the following rule. As the set $\aleph_{\zeta=194}$ of the $\zeta = 194$ alternative investment style indices[8] gathers hedge fund indices from different sources, the common starting date is not 1994 but January 1997. Taking into account the exclusion of August, September and October 1998, the first month when

---

[8] See Appendix A in Chapter 3 for a detailed description of the database of hedge fund indices.

implicit factors may be computed is March 2000. Then, for each month until December 2006, we select again the most heterogeneous indices, we compute the $\xi = 35$ implicit factors and determine the Best Choice Implicit Model of each hedge fund belonging to the testing sample with a 36-month track. Over the whole period, we examine the adjusted R-square of 138 943 Best Choice Implicit Models.

The first Implicit Value-at-Risk is computed in December 2002, so the backtesting of the Implicit Value-at-Risk is conducted over the period from January 2003 to December 2006. When possible, Extreme Value Moves of the Implicit Factors and Tail Dependence Estimators are computed on 96 monthly returns, as in the backtesting of the New Style Model. However, for months before March 2005, estimations were performed on smaller samples as the starting date for index sampling is January 1997.

9.4.1   Quality of the BCI Model

The average adjusted coefficient of determination from 2003 to 2006 is 0.74, while the average R-square is 0.81; for the same period and for the Style Model, the average adjusted R-square is 0.31 and the R-square is 0.42. Clearly, the quality of the fit is substantially improved. Table 9.1 compares the annual average of the adjusted R-square between the Style Model and the Best Choice Implicit Model.

In section 6.3.3 we explained that one source of risk underestimation of the Original Style Model was the poor fit of the regression model. As an illustration, consider the 1951 regressions for December 2006. For 48% of the hedge funds, the Style Model explains less than 40% of the historical returns, while the R-square exceeds 0.7 for only 13% of the investment vehicles. By contrast, the Best Choice Implicit Model

Table 9.1   Average annual R^2 and $\overline{R}^2$ for the Style Model and the Best Choice Implicit Model excluding August to October 1998 data. Years impacted by the reduction of the sample are followed by an asterisk

		2000*	2001*	2002	2003	2004	2005	2006	Total
BCI Model	R^2	0.80	0.80	0.82	0.81	0.81	0.81	0.81	0.81
	$\overline{R}^2$	0.72	0.73	0.75	0.74	0.73	0.74	0.74	0.74
Style Model	R^2	0.47	0.45	0.42	0.42	0.40	0.41	0.41	0.42
	$\overline{R}^2$	0.37	0.34	0.30	0.30	0.29	0.30	0.32	0.31

Table 9.2 Coefficients of determination distributions for 1951 hedge funds as of December 2006

R^2	Style Model	Implicit Model
[0%;10%[	9.23%	0.05%
[10%;20%[	11.74%	0.05%
[20%;30%[	12.97%	0.00%
[30%;40%[	13.84%	0.51%
[40%;50%[	12.25%	0.41%
[50%;60%[	14.30%	1.18%
[60%;70%[	12.51%	5.69%
[70%;80%[	9.12%	32.85%
[80%;90%[	3.49%	48.80%
[90%;100%[	0.56%	10.46%

provides a coefficient of adjustment higher than 0.7 for 97.8% of the hedge funds. Table 9.2 tells the story.

9.4.2 Backtesting

Out of the 3126 hedge funds providing a testing period, 367 experienced at least one Value-at-Risk exception, i.e. 11% in four years. Among them, only 28 investment vehicles had more than two exceptions. Table 9.3 details the percentage of exceptions from 2003 to 2006 and compares the results of the Original Model and the New Style Model. For the four years, the average exception rate of the Implicit Value-at-Risk is 0.55% and 0.41% for the Implicit Synthetic Value-at-Risk. As for the New Style Value-at-Risk, these levels of exceptions are significantly lower than 1%. However, we may consider that these exception rates are downside biased. Indeed, as we will see in Chapter 12, there exists some empirical evidence that some managers of our sample who have stopped reporting performance, may have suffered a Value-at-Risk exception after exiting from the sample.

Table 9.3 Annual exception rates

	2003	2004	2005	2006	Total
Implicit VaR	0.80%	0.63%	0.51%	0.31%	0.55%
Synthetic Implicit VaR	0.56%	0.43%	0.37%	0.33%	0.41%
New Style VaR	0.21%	0.18%	0.31%	0.36%	0.27%
Synthetic Style VaR	0.26%	0.32%	0.76%	0.59%	0.51%
Original Style VaR	0.51%	0.87%	1.37%	1.77%	1.16%

Table 9.4   Number of changes in the annual modification of the set of 36 indices

	2004	2005	2006
New indices	7	6	4

9.4.3   Steadiness

One major weakness of the Implicit Model as formulated lies in the high level of volatility of the underlying risk factor from one month to another. Indeed, contrary to the Style Model, the past track of the style factors change every month, as the set of 36 hedge fund indices on which the implicit analysis is performed is altered each month and also as the Principal Component Analysis is updated each month. In other words, it is as if, for each month, the set of style-based factors were never the same. Obviously, this process will end with a highly volatile Value-at-Risk.

One way to circumvent this instability lies in imposing the set of 36 indices on which the Principal Component Analysis is performed. For instance, the implicit factors can be computed on the same 36 hedge fund indices each month of the same year. This initial set of 36 indices can be constructed as follows. First conduct the reverse cluster analysis for each month of the previous year. This ends up with 12 sets of 36 indices. Then select the 36 indices that are more frequently included in these 12 sets. As a consequence the set of 36 indices on which the Principal Component Analysis is performed is altered only at the beginning of the year. Table 9.4 reveals that, on average, 5.6 indices are excluded per year.

10

BCI Model and Hedge Fund Clones

The objective of the Best Choice Implicit Model is to represent information in a space defined by a set of orthogonal implicit variables called principal components. For hedge funds, these principal components can be seen as projections or as an average of alternative investment strategies active indices. Obviously, the drawback of this approach lies in its lack of legibility. The hedge funds making up the constituencies of each index are not directly known (one would need to know all components of all underlying indices). Moreover, as hedge funds indices may be difficult to interpret with respect to traditional risk factors, the interpretation of the principal components is even harder: the implicit approach applied to the risk measure may be particularly exposed to hidden risk. If the next chapter provides some tools to reduce this risk for large investors in hedge funds through homogeneity analysis, this chapter aims to provide an explicit understanding of these principal components with regard to the traditional risk factors. The idea is to apply two different methodologies that are clearly connected with the model used for hedge funds clones. As we will see, if some factors can be easily explained by these approaches, some cannot. In other words, the level of heterogeneity and complexity of hedge funds requires the Best Choice Implicit Model to be a good model at the individual investment vehicle level. The fact that the clones model can duplicate only a small part of the set of alternative risk factors simply illustrates that these methodologies are too restrictive for the hedge funds universe.

10.1 THE TEN-FACTOR MODEL

Fung and Hsieh (2004) proposed to model the excess return (in excess of the risk-free rate) of a diversified hedge fund with seven factors representing four traditional buy-and-hold and four primitive trend-following (PTS) strategies. The Fung and Hsieh (2004) factors are S&P 500 excess return (S&P $-$ rf), Wilshire small cap minus large cap return (SC – LC), change in the constant maturity yield of the 10-year Treasury (BD10RET), change in the spread of Moody's Baa minus the 10-year Treasury (BAAMTSY) and the return of primitive trend-following strategies on bonds (PTFSBD), currencies (PTFSFX), and commodities (PTFSCOM). Fung and Hsieh (2001) modelled Primitive Trend-Following as a portfolio of lookback straddles. More recently, the primitive trend-following strategy on short-term interest (PTFSST) as well as the buy-and-hold strategy on emerging markets have been added. All data are available on http://faculty.fuqua .duke.edu/~dah7/DataLibrary/TF-FAC.xls. Finally, following Agarwal and Naik (2000a), the Fama–French's book-to-market (HML) factor was added.

To try to interpret the principal components of the BCIM, we conduct 1023 regressions[1] (on the last 36 months) for each of the 35 implicit factors (C_k) as of December 2005 in order to reflect all possible combinations of the 10 factors. Then the model with the highest R-square and with all slope coefficients significatively different from zero is selected. Table 10.1 shows, for each of the 35 principal components, the results of this process as well as the percentage of hedge funds significantly exposed to the implicit factors.

Out of the 35 factors, 12 cannot be explained by the model (no significant coefficient), while the average adjusted coefficient of determination rises to 0.17 for the model with at least one significant slope. The adjusted R-square is larger than 0.30 for only two components. Remember that the implicit factors consists of an average of indices, and as such the idiosyncratic risk is diversified away. The low quality of fit cannot be explained by specific exposures. As the system defined by the principal components enables us to explain a large universe of hedge funds, the average low R-square value of the 10 factors model is implied by the omission of important risk factors that drive the performance of the alternative investment strategies.

Not surprisingly, at the individual hedge fund level, the quality of fit of the 10-factor model is also disappointing. Indeed, the average adjusted coefficient of determination[2] for 2238 hedge funds with at least a 36-month track record as of December 2005 is 0.33, i.e. half of the quality of fit of the Best Choice Implicit Model. Table 10.2 exhibits the distribution of adjusted R-square for the 10-factor model and for the

---

[1] The all possible regression process has the advantage of being not path dependent.

[2] For regressions with significant slope coefficient computed with backward regressions.

Table 10.1 $\bar{R}^2$ of model with slope coefficients significantly different from zero. % in hedge funds relates to the rate of hedge funds among 2238 hedge funds that have a significant exposure to the principal component

	% in HF	$\bar{R}^2$	Significant
C_1	85%	0.62	PTFSFX, S&P$-rf$, SC$-$LC, BAAMTSY, HCL
C_2	51%	0.26	PTFSBD, SC$-$LC, BAAMTSY
C_3	47%	0.53	PTFSBD, PTFSCOM, S&P$-rf$, SC$-$LC, BD10RET, BAAMTSY
C_4	39%	0.26	PTFSBD, SC$-$LC, HCL
C_5	27%	0.14	BD10RET
C_7	34%	0.06	PTSSTK
C_8	36%	0.07	PTFSBD
C_9	38%	0.27	PTFSBD, PTFSFX, BAAMTSY, HCL
C_{11}	38%	0.09	HCL
C_{13}	29%	0.25	PTFSFX, SC$-$LC, BAAMTSY
C_{14}	28%	0.05	BD10RET
C_{15}	30%	0.12	PTFSBD, BAAMTSY
C_{17}	30%	0.11	PTFSFX, S&P$-rf$
C_{18}	21%	0.13	PTFSFX, PFTSST
C_{21}	26%	0.14	PTFSBD, PTFSCOM
C_{22}	21%	0.22	PTFSCOM, PTFSSR, HCL
C_{23}	26%	0.08	PTFSSTK
C_{24}	17%	0.13	PTFSFX, PTFSSTK
C_{26}	21%	0.05	PTFSST
C_{28}	18%	0.23	PTFSST, PTFSSTK
C_{30}	19%	0.09	BAAMTSY
C_{31}	16%	0.08	PTFSSR
C_{35}	16%	0.08	PTFSCOM

Table 10.2 Adjusted coefficients of determination distribution for 2238 hedge funds as of December 2005

$\bar{R}^2$	10 factors	Best Choice Implicit Model
[0%; 10%[	16.91%	0.00%
[10%; 20%[	15.17%	0.00%
[20%; 30%[	15.70%	0.13%
[30%; 40%[	16.06%	0.45%
[40%; 50%[	12.89%	1.52%
[50%; 60%[	10.47%	6.44%
[60%; 70%[	6.76%	26.94%
[70%; 80%[	4.03%	37.40%
[80%; 90%[	1.70%	25.28%
[90%; 100%[	0.31%	1.83%

BCI Model: while 47.79% of $\bar{R}^2$ are below 0.4 for the former, 91.45% are above 0.7 for the latter.

10.2   THE NON-LINEAR MODEL

In order to capture the potentially non-linear sensitivities between hedge funds and factor returns, we use the methodology proposed by Diez de los Rios and Garcia (2006). Their approach is an extension of the classical non-linear model by Merton (1981) that was used to test the existence of market-timing skills among mutual fund managers. The idea is to replicate the hedge fund return pattern with two explanatory variables: the factor itself, and a call option on the factor returns. Contrary to Merton (1981), who set the strike price equal to the risk-free rate, Diez de los Rios and Garcia (2006) allow the strike price to be determined directly from the data. The model can be written as follows:

$$r^*_{s,t} = \alpha_s + \beta_{i,s} I_{i,t} + \delta_{i,s} \max(I_{i,t} - S_{i_s}, 0) + \varepsilon_{s,t}$$

where $\beta_{i,s}$ denotes the proportion invested in the factor, $\delta_{i,s}$ can be interpreted as the number of options held by the hedge fund, and S_{i_s} is the data-driven strike price. $r^*_{s,t}$ and $I_{i,t}$ are monthly excess returns over the risk-free rate. While modelling the payoff of only one option may seem restrictive, the model can capture many different option strategies. For instance, a short position in a put option is obtained when $\beta_{i,s} > 0$ and $\delta_{i,s} = -\beta_{i,s}$. Moreover, a straddle can be defined as follows: $\beta_{i,s} < 0$ and $\delta_{i,s} = 2\beta_{i,s}$.

After estimating the model parameters, we can make different hypothesis tests. The first and most important one consists in knowing if there is any relationship between the hedge fund and the factor returns. This corresponds to a joint test defined as:

$$H_0^1 : \delta_{i,s} = \beta_{i,s} = 0$$

In case this test is rejected, the sensitivity between the hedge fund and the corresponding factor can be considered as significant. We set the critical *p-value* at 10%. We can then determine whether the relation is non-linear:

$$H_0^2 : \beta_{i,s} = 0$$

or linear:

$$H_0^3 : \delta_{i,s} = 0$$

Table 10.3 $\bar{R}^2$ of the Diez de los Rios and Garcia (2006) model whose joint test is rejected

Implicit	Factor	$\bar{R}^2$	β	δ	S	Implicit	Factor	$\bar{R}^2$	β	δ	S
C_1	MSEM	0.72	-0.91	0.03	0.11%	C_{19}	EM	0.06	0.15	0.00	1.12%
C_2	HML	0.11	0.47	0.04	0.35%	C_{20}	RICI	0.11	0.15	-0.13	-5.01%
C_3	MOM	0.37	0.40	0.00	-0.35%	C_{21}	EM	0.11	-0.47	0.62	0.17%
C_4	MSEAP	0.32	0.15	0.80	6.24%	C_{22}	BEM	0.07	-0.14	0.69	2.85%
C_5	EUR	0.14	-0.30	0.01	-0.98%	C_{23}	RICI	0.07	0.17	-0.18	-6.24%
C_6	BEU	0.13	-0.84	-0.21	0.85%	C_{24}	DEF	0.03	0.51	-1.35	0.42%
C_7	SMB	0.03	0.54	-0.70	-1.64%	C_{25}	DEF	0.00	-0.05	-0.06	-0.27%
C_8	BEU	0.16	-0.06	-2.37	0.85%	C_{26}	VIX	0.08	0.01	0.01	-5.77%
C_9	HML	0.14	0.48	-0.05	0.02%	C_{27}	SMB	0.04	0.02	0.32	2.83%
C_{10}	S&P	0.10	-2.23	2.31	-2.00%	C_{28}	YEN	0.03	0.09	-0.02	-1.41%
C_{11}	MOM	0.07	0.05	-1.16	3.10%	C_{29}	HML	0.02	0.08	-0.00	1.66%
C_{12}	BUS	0.06	0.15	0.15	-1.60%	C_{30}	MSEU	0.05	0.01	0.04	-2.05%
C_{13}	RICI	0.25	-0.05	-0.13	2.51%	C_{31}	MOM	0.02	-0.03	-0.01	-1.44%
C_{14}	BEU	0.11	-0.37	0.07	0.53%	C_{32}	RICI	0.05	-0.00	0.03	0.10%
C_{15}	DEF	0.17	-1.35	-0.07	0.35%	C_{33}	YEN	0.14	0.10	0.01	0.54%
C_{16}	HML	0.10	0.22	-1.00	0.98%	C_{34}	MSEU	0.00	-0.04	0.04	-2.72%
C_{17}	YEN	0.09	0.06	0.09	-2.22%	C_{35}	DEF	0.06	-2.26	2.30	-0.27%
C_{18}	EUR	0.12	-0.38	0.52	-2.48%						

If the strike S_{i_s} was set to a constant, these hypothesis tests could be implemented with a classical Wald statistic. However, the problem is a little more subtle here because S_{i_s} is data-driven and fixed to a level which minimizes the variance of the model residuals. For this reason, the test is based on the supremum of the Wald statistic over all possible strike prices. The distribution of this supremum under the null hypothesis is non-standard, and requires a simulation analysis.

We apply this model to the 35 implicit factors as of December 2005 for a set of 17 factors covering different asset classes, geographic areas and style orientation: the returns of the S&P 500 (S&P), the MSCI Europe index (MSEU), the MSCI Asia Pacific index (MSEAP), the MSCI Emerging index (MSEM), Fama–French's book-to-market factor (HML), Fama–French's small over big cap factor (SMB), high over low momentum factor (MOM), US government bonds with a 3–10 year maturity index (BUS), European government bonds with a 3–10 year maturity index (BEU), long-term corporate bonds over government bonds (DEF), long-term over small-term government bonds (TERM), JP Morgan Emerging Market Bond index (BEM), Euro in US dollar (EUR), Yen in USD (JPY), a basket of Emerging currencies (EM) and the percentage change in the RICI index (RICI) and in the VIX. Table 10.3 provides the maximum coefficient determination for regressions whose joint test is rejected. As for the 10-factor model, the average quality of fit is low (0.12): if 72% of the first factor, 37% of the third implicit and 32% of the fourth principal component are explained by the model, the R-square values are below 0.2 for the other exogenous variables. If

Table 10.4 Maximum adjusted coefficients of determination distribution for 2238 hedge funds as of December 2005. The Non-Linear Model gathers regression whose joint test is rejected

$\bar{R}^2$	Non-Linear Model	Best Choice Implicit Model
[0%; 10%[	23.73%	0.00%
[10%; 20%[	17.29%	0.00%
[20%; 30%[	16.18%	0.13%
[30%; 40%[	15.19%	0.45%
[40%; 50%[	11.35%	1.52%
[50%; 60%[	8.22%	6.44%
[60%; 70%[	5.45%	26.94%
[70%; 80%[	1.79%	37.40%
[80%; 90%[	0.49%	25.28%
[90%; 100%[	0.31%	1.83%

we consider only the model whose joint test is rejected and with two significant slope coefficients (tested individually), nine of the principal components are not explained and the average fit decreases to 0.08.

Finally, we apply the model to the 2238 hedge funds as of December 2005. Again, the average quality of fit at the individual hedge fund level is disappointing. Table 10.4 exhibits the distribution of adjusted R-square values first for the model whose joint test is rejected. The average adjusted coefficient of determination is 27.63%.

11

Risk Budgeting

One major effect of the institutionalization of the hedge funds industry lies in the contraction in the interquartile spreads of multi-manager portfolios. As shown in section 2.5, the annual return spreads between the best fund in the bottom quartile and the worst fund in the top quartile decreased to 4.12% on average. Then, a multi-manager portfolio composed partly of a highly diversified portfolio and partly of a few allocations concentrated on risky hedge funds can easily move from the top to the bottom quartile of its own peer group. At the end of their first quarter of 2008, some multi-manager funds of funds recorded year-to-date losses larger than 10% mainly due to excessive exposure to some hedge funds that were highly impacted by the financing crisis and/or had too aggressive directional exposure. Given the increasingly tough competitive environment, some of these funds of funds had to close down or to activate their gate redemption, which is almost the equivalent in the fund of funds industry of postponing the end of their operations. Today's market environment therefore argues in favour of portfolio management that sizes exposure according to the likelihood of the managers' moving the fund of funds.

For a long period of time, portfolio managers of funds of funds used to look at actual return attributions to modify their risk exposures: applying the prudent rule of gains realization, they effectively tended to decrease allocation of the largest contributors. This was equivalent to assessing that a hedge fund that contributed 400 basis points to the performance of the portfolio, could have made the portfolio lose these 400 basis points. However, return attribution is an ex-post measure and risk management based on it assumes a symmetric distribution of return. Risk budgeting based on the Style Value-at-Risk or the Implicit Value-at-Risk is more appropriate as it consists of computing ex-ante indicators of the potential loss contribution.

Indeed, assessing portfolios in terms of risk allocation is the key to risk budgeting. In a household budget, budgeting consists of assigning parts of the resource to different elements of the spending. For portfolio managers, risk budgeting is a process of decomposing risk and assigning risk budgets to each element of the portfolio. Portfolios are no longer considered in terms of asset allocation, but in terms of risk allocations. For a portfolio of hedge funds, this consists of allocating a maximum risk attribution to each manager and to each strategy.

In this chapter, we first address the issue of how to compute a Value-at-Risk at the multi-manager portfolio level. Then, two ways of computing risk attribution are examined. The first one is the least subtle but is particularly convenient for synthetic Value-at-Risk. The second methodology to compute risk components is based on the linear marginal analysis and enables us to express risk attribution in a closed form, which drastically reduces the amount of computation.

11.1 VALUE-AT-RISK OF A MULTI-MANAGERS PORTFOLIO

Consider a multi-managers portfolio p composed by n hedge funds. Then at time t, the portfolio return p_t is

$$p_t = \sum_{s=1}^{n} \omega_s r_{s,t} \qquad (11.1)$$

where $\omega_{s,t}$ denotes the allocation to hedge fund s at the beginning of month t. The risk consolidation at the portfolio level relies on both the consistency and the transparency principles: as a hedge fund can be considered as a portfolio, a multi-managers portfolio Value-at-Risk should be computed in the same way as an individual hedge fund risk. So, basically, equations (7.8) to (7.13) for the Style Value-at-Risk and equations (9.6) to (9.9) for the Implicit Value-at-Risk have to be adapted for the multi-managers portfolio. However, one major issue of this type of risk consolidation lies in the aggregation of idiosyncratic risk. As independence is assumed between specific risks, the diversification may quickly dilute these idiosyncratic contributions. This explains why a model with a good average quality of fit, such as the Best Choice Implicit Model, is an important condition for efficient risk budgeting.

11.1.1 Style Model

Within the style analysis framework, the return of hedge fund s is modelled as

$$r_{s,t} = \alpha_s + \sum_{i=1}^{10} \beta_{s,i} I_{i,t} + \varepsilon_{s,t} \qquad (11.2)$$

Using equation (11.2) in equation (11.1)

$$p_t = \sum_{s=1}^{n} \omega_{s,t}\, \alpha_s + \sum_{s=1}^{n} \omega_{s,t} \sum_{i=1}^{10} \beta_{s,i}\, I_{i,t} + \sum_{s=1}^{n} \omega_{s,t}\, \varepsilon_{s,t}$$

$$p_t = a + \sum_{i=1}^{10} b_i\, I_{i,t} + e_t$$

with $b_i = \sum_{s=1}^{n} \omega_s \beta_{s,i}$. Then a similar approach as that described in section 7.3.1 can be used to compute the New Style Value-at-Risk of the multi-managers portfolio. First consider the synthetic track of the portfolio

$$\hat{p}_t = \hat{a} + \sum_{i=1}^{10} \hat{b}_i\, I_{i,t}$$

then define the portfolio Value-at-Strategy-Risk as

$$\text{VsR}_p = \sum_{i}^{10} \hat{b}_i\, \hat{\mu}_i + \sqrt{\sum_{i=1}^{10} \sum_{j=1}^{10} \tilde{\bar{\chi}}_{i,j}\, \hat{b}_i \left(\tilde{F}_i^{[j]} - \hat{\mu}_i \right) \hat{b}_j \left(\tilde{F}_j^{[i]} - \hat{\mu}_j \right)}$$

where $\tilde{F}_i^{[j]}$ and $\tilde{\bar{\chi}}_{i,j}$ are defined by equations (7.9) and (7.10). Assuming independence between hedge funds' idiosyncratic risk, the portfolio Value-at-Idiosyncratic-Risk is

$$\text{ViR}_p = \hat{a} + \sqrt{\sum_{s=1}^{n} \omega_s^2\, \text{VaR}_{\text{EVT}}^2 (r_s - \hat{r}_s)}$$

Finally the portfolio Value-at-Risk is

$$\text{VaR}_p = \hat{a}_+ \sum_{i}^{10} \hat{b}_i \hat{\mu}_i + \sqrt{\left(\text{ViR}_p - \hat{a} \right)^2 + \left(\text{VsR}_p - \sum_{i}^{10} \hat{b}_i\, \hat{\mu}_i \right)^2} \tag{11.3}$$

The portfolio Synthetic Value-at-Strategy-Risk is

$$\text{VsR}_p^{\text{Synthetic}} = \text{VaR}_{\text{EVT}}(\hat{p})$$

where $\hat{p}$ denotes the portfolio synthetic track computed with the coefficients $(\hat{\alpha}_p, (\hat{\beta}_{p,i})_i)$ and thus

$$\text{VaR}_p = \hat{\alpha}_p + \sum_i^{10} \hat{\beta}_{p,i} \hat{\mu}_i$$

$$+ \sqrt{\left(\text{ViR}_p - \hat{\alpha}_p\right)^2 + \left(\text{VsR}_p^{\text{Synthetic}} - \sum_i^{10} \hat{\beta}_{p,i} \hat{\mu}_i\right)^2}$$

11.1.2 Best Choice Implicit Model

First define a non-negative beta vector denoted $\tilde{b} = (\tilde{b}_i)_{i=1,\dots,70}$ as

$$\tilde{b}_i = \sum_{s=1}^n \omega_s \hat{\beta}_{s,i} \qquad \text{for } i \le 35 \text{ and } \sum_{s=1}^n \omega_s \hat{\beta}_{s,i} > 0$$

$$= -\sum_{s=1}^n \omega_s \hat{\beta}_{s,i-35} \text{ for } i = 36, \dots, 70 \text{ and } \sum_{s=1}^n \omega_s \hat{\beta}_{s,i} < 0$$

$$= 0 \qquad\qquad\qquad \text{otherwise}$$

where $\hat{\beta}_{s,i}$ are the BCIM coefficients[1] of hedge fund s.

Then using the tail dependence system as defined by equation (7.10), the Implicit Value-at-Strategy-Risk is defined as

$$\text{VsR}_s^{\text{Implicit}} = \hat{\mu}'\tilde{b} + \sqrt{\tau_p' \, \Xi \, \tau_p + \sum_{i=1}^{70} \tau_p^{[i]'} \, \Theta^{[i]} \, \tau_p}$$

with

$$\tau_p = (\tau_{p,i})_{i=1,\dots,70} = \left(\left(\tilde{b}_i \left(\text{VaR}_{\text{EVT}}(G_i(t)) - \hat{\mu}_i\right)\right)_{i=1,\dots,35} \vdots \right.$$
$$\left. \left(\tilde{b}_i \left(\text{VaR}_{\text{EVT}}(-G_i(t)) + \hat{\mu}_i\right)\right)_{i=36,\dots,70} \right)$$

---

[1] In this framework, the 70 slope coefficients of the portfolio are non-negative, while at the individual hedge fund level, these coefficients may be negative.

and $\tau_p^{[i]} = (\tau_{p,i'}^{[i]})_{i'=1,...,70}$

$$\tau_{p,i'}^{[i]} = -\tilde{b}_i \ (\mathrm{VaR_{EVT}}(G_i(t)) - \hat{\mu}_i) \quad \text{if } i = i'$$
$$= 0 \qquad\qquad\qquad\qquad\qquad \text{otherwise}$$

Finally, if we define the portfolio Implicit Value-at-Idiosyncratic-Risk as

$$\mathrm{ViR}_p^{\mathrm{Implicit}} = \tilde{a} + \sqrt{\sum_{s=1}^{n} \omega_s^2 \, \mathrm{VaR}_{\mathrm{EVT}}^2 \, (r_s(t, \xi = 36) - \hat{r}_s(t, \xi = 36))}$$

with

$$\tilde{a} = \sum_{s=1}^{n} \omega_{s,t} \, \hat{\alpha}_s^{[\gamma_s]}$$

the portfolio Implicit Value-at-Risk is

$$\mathrm{VaR}_p^{\mathrm{Implicit}} = \tilde{a} + \hat{\mu}'\tilde{b} + \sqrt{\left(\mathrm{ViR}_p^{\mathrm{Implicit}} - \tilde{a}\right)^2 + \left(\mathrm{VsR}_p^{\mathrm{Implicit}} - \hat{\mu}'\tilde{b}\right)^2} \tag{11.4}$$

Analogically, the portfolio Synthetic Implicit Value-at-Risk is defined as

$$\mathrm{VaR}_p^{\mathrm{Synthetic\ and\ Implicit}} = \tilde{\alpha}_p + \hat{\mu}'\tilde{\beta}_p$$
$$+ \sqrt{\left(\mathrm{ViR}_p^{\mathrm{Implicit}} - \tilde{\alpha}_p\right)^2 + \left(\mathrm{VsR}_p^{\mathrm{Synthetic\ and\ Implicit}} - \hat{\mu}'\tilde{\beta}_p\right)^2}$$

where

$$\mathrm{VsR}_p^{\mathrm{Synthetic\ and\ Implicit}} = \mathrm{VaR}_{\mathrm{EVT}}(\hat{p})$$

with

$$\hat{p} = (\hat{p}_t) = \left(\tilde{\alpha}_p + \sum_{i=1}^{35} \tilde{\beta}_{p,i} \, I_{i,t}\right)$$

11.2 RISK DECOMPOSITION: 'BEFORE AND AFTER' ATTRIBUTION

The 'before and after' risk attribution does not require knowledge of the risk parameters of the n individual hedge funds that compose the portfolio. The risk attribution of hedge fund s is simply deduced from the difference in Value-at-Risk of the actual portfolio and of the same portfolio excluding hedge fund s. In other words, the Value-at-Risk before and after exclusion of hedge fund s are compared. This type of approach is particularly suitable when the portfolio risk is computed on a synthetic track. Indeed, the risk decomposition is obtained through comparison of historical simulations, which are the only input of the Synthetic Value-at-Risk.

Unfortunately, the 'before and after' approach has some drawbacks. First, it requires computing the risk for $n + 1$ portfolios. Moreover, the sum of the risk attribution does not necessary equal the portfolio Value-at-Risk. A common trick consists of reallocating the risk shortfall across positions pro rata to the original risk attributions.

11.3   RISK DECOMPOSITION: CLOSED FORM ATTRIBUTION

The portfolio Value-at-Risk is a linear homogeneous function of the positions in managers (or in any relevant instruments): the same proportional change in all positions will proportionally change the Value-at-Risk. Mathematically, if we denote portfolio $p(\omega)$ with $\omega = (\omega_s)_{s=1,\ldots,n}$ as the vector of allocation, then $\text{VaR}_{p(\lambda\omega)} = \lambda\text{VaR}_p$ for $\lambda > 0$. This property allows us to provide an explicit formula of risk attribution or Value-at-Risk component ($C\text{VaR}$). Indeed, Euler's theorem stipulates that any function that is homogeneous of degree 1 can be decomposed as the sum of each partial derivative multiplied by each related endogenous variable, i.e.

$$\text{VaR}_p(\omega) = \sum_{s=1}^{n} \frac{\partial \text{VaR}_p}{\partial \omega_s} \omega_s = \sum_{s=1}^{n} C\text{VaR}_s$$

Thus by definition, the Value-at-Risk component satisfies the property of additivity.

Finally, in order to assess portfolios not in terms of monetary allocation, but rather of risk allocation, we should consider the relative risk attribution, i.e. the percentage contribution to portfolio risk of hedge fund s:

$$\frac{(\partial \text{VaR}_p/\partial \omega_s)\omega_s}{\text{VaR}_p} = \frac{C\text{VaR}_s}{\text{VaR}_p}$$

11.3.1 New Style Attribution

To ease the presentation of the computation of the risk component for the New Style Model, equation (11.3) can first be written as

$$\text{VaR}_p = \hat{a} + \sum_{i}^{10} \hat{b}_i \hat{\mu}_i$$

$$+ \sqrt{\sum_{s=1}^{n} \omega_s^2 \, \text{VaR}_{\text{EVT}}^2 (r_s - \hat{r}_s) + \sum_{i=1}^{10} \sum_{j=1}^{10} \tilde{\bar{\chi}}_{i,j} \, \hat{b}_i \left(\tilde{F}_i^{[j]} - \hat{\mu}_i \right) \hat{b}_j \left(\tilde{F}_j^{[i]} - \hat{\mu}_j \right)}$$

Then the risk attribution is

$$\frac{\partial \text{VaR}_p}{\partial \omega_s} \omega_s = \left\{ \hat{\alpha}_s + \sum_{i=1}^{10} \hat{\beta}_{s,i} \mu_i + \frac{\omega_s \, \text{VaR}_{\text{EVT}}^2 (r_s - \hat{r}_s)}{\sqrt{\text{VaR}_p - \hat{a} - \sum_{i}^{10} \hat{b}_i \hat{\mu}_i}} \right.$$

$$\left. + \frac{\displaystyle\sum_{i=1}^{10}\sum_{j=1}^{10} \tilde{\bar{\chi}}_{i,j} \hat{\beta}_{s,i} (\tilde{F}_i^{[j]} - \hat{\mu}_i) \hat{b}_j (\tilde{F}_j^{[i]} - \hat{\mu}_j) + \displaystyle\sum_{i=1}^{10}\sum_{j=1}^{10} \tilde{\bar{\chi}}_{i,j} \hat{b}_i (\tilde{F}_i^{[j]} - \hat{\mu}_i) \hat{\beta}_{s,j} (\tilde{F}_j^{[i]} - \hat{\mu}_j)}{2 \sqrt{\text{VaR}_p - \hat{a} - \displaystyle\sum_{i}^{10} \hat{b}_i \hat{\mu}_i}} \right\} \omega_s$$

As the matrix of tail dependence is not symmetric, the two double sums cannot be consolidated in one, contrary to the Original Style Model whose risk component for hedge fund s is

$$\frac{\partial \text{VaR}_p^{\text{Original Style}}}{\partial \omega_s} \omega_s = \frac{\displaystyle\sum_{i=1}^{10}\sum_{j=1}^{10} \hat{\rho}_{ij} \hat{\beta}_{s,i} \hat{b}_j \, F_i \, F_j + 2.33^2 \, \omega_s \, \hat{\sigma}_{s,\hat{\varepsilon}}}{\sqrt{\text{VaR}_p^{\text{Original Style}}}} \omega_s$$

11.3.2 BCIM Attribution

First, rewrite equation (11.4)

$$\text{VaR}_p = \tilde{\hat{a}} + \hat{\mu}' \tilde{\hat{b}} + \sqrt{\sum_{s=1}^{n} \omega_s^2 \, \text{VaR}_{\text{EVT}}^2 (r_s - \hat{r}_s) + \tau_p' \, \Xi \, \tau_p + \sum_{i=1}^{70} \tau_p^{[i]} \, \Theta^{[i]} \, \tau_p}$$

Then the first derivative is

$$\frac{\partial \text{VaR}_p}{\partial \omega_s} = \hat{\alpha}_s^{[\gamma_s]} + \hat{\beta}_s' \mu$$

$$+ \frac{2\,\omega_s\,\text{VaR}_{\text{EVT}}^2\,(r_s - \hat{r}_s) + 2\,\tau_s'\,\Xi\,\tau_p + \sum_{i=1}^{70}\left(\tau_s^{[i]'}\,\Theta^{[i]}\,\tau_p + \tau_p^{[i]'}\,\Theta^{[i]}\,\tau_s\right)}{2\,\sqrt{\text{VaR}_p - \tilde{\hat{a}} - \hat{\mu}'\tilde{\hat{b}}}}$$

12

Value-at-Risk Monitoring

It is popular to say that portfolio management is about risk management. In practice, however, portfolio managers are often not aware of the benefits of understanding and exploiting the quantitative risk measures related to the investment vehicles that make up a hedge fund of funds portfolio. In particular, assessing how big the losses of a specific holding might be can be gauged by examining how bad the underlying hedge fund behaved over some relevant period of time.

This again might sound trivial but in the context of hedge funds, the point is crucial as the risk may be as high as the fund's collapse. The aim of any well-defined risk measure such as the Value-at-Risk is about helping portfolio managers to avoid such a scenario and to lead them to act accordingly.[1] In other words, the question is to determine if a risk indicator such as the Style Value-at-Risk provides relevant information about how bad a fund might perform in the future. Is a Value-at-Risk exception a signal for underperformance? Is there a tendency for hedge fund managers to go bankrupt after some Value-at-Risk violations?

12.1 ANALYSING GRAVEYARDS AND HEDGE FUNDS DEMISE

Incorporating so-called dead funds is not only important to reduce the survivorship bias of any statistical analysis of the hedge funds world, but graveyard databases can also be exploited to test leading indicators for poor performing funds. Indeed, it is well known that hedge fund managers only report to databases on a voluntary basis. The intuition says that some managers may suddenly drop from databases because of poor performance. Besides, the higher the risk, the weaker the fund's viability and the lower is the probability of reporting to database providers. We first examine the truth of this statement and then investigate the specific relevance of the Style Value-at-Risk.

---

[1] Obviously, liquidity constraints may limit the ability to be reactive.

For a start, we may simply look at the proportion of dead funds that experienced losses in excess of the Value-at-Risk before going out of business. In the context of the graveyard sample defined in section 12.3, only 91 vehicles among the 1016 dead funds violated the Value-at-Risk, meaning that 925 dead funds did not report any loss in excess of the Value-at-Risk over the last 36 months before exiting the databases. The conclusion is that more funds died whilst having complied with the Value-at-Risk rule than those violated that rule. Does this imply that Value-at-Risk does not provide useful insights about the probability of a fund's collapse? As discussed below, this conclusion misses the important explanatory factors of a fund's demise and, consequently, turns out to be misleading.

12.2   THE PROBIT MODEL

Assuming that a fund that stops reporting performance has gone out of business, the model is about explaining the dependent variable y_i that takes the value 1 if the fund i is considered to be dead and 0 if the fund i is still active

$$y_i = \begin{cases} 1 & \text{if fund } i \text{ is dead,} \\ 0 & \text{if fund } i \text{ is still alive.} \end{cases}$$

From an econometric point of view, explaining a dichotomous variable such as y_i requires a specific treatment. Indeed, fitting y_i to a set of regressors using the linear regression framework, e.g. $y_i = x_i'\beta + \varepsilon_i$, is inappropriate as it yields fitted values that are not restricted to lie between 0 and 1, as required by the definition of the dependent variable.

One way to comply with this rule is to use a distribution function of the set of regressors, say $F(x_i'\beta)$. In this context, the so-called probit model is the one that is obtained when using a Gaussian distribution, that is $F(x_i'\beta) = \Phi(x_i'\beta)$, where $\Phi(.)$ denotes the cumulative distribution function of the standard normal distribution.

Specifically, the probit model assumes that the probability of y_i being equal to 1 is given by

$$P(y_i = 1|x_i, \beta) = \Phi(x_i'\beta).$$

Therefore, we have

$$P(y_i = 0|x_i, \beta) = 1 - \Phi(x_i'\beta).$$

Hence, the essence of the probit model for hedge funds demise is to see the probability of a fund being dead as a function of some explanatory variables $x_i' = (x_{1,i}, \ldots, x_{K,i})$. Interestingly, we get

$$E(y_i|x_i, \beta) = \Phi\left(x_i' \beta\right)$$

and the probit model can be written in the form of the regression equation

$$y_i = \Phi\left(x_i' \beta\right) + \varepsilon_i$$

where ε_i is the residual representing the deviation of the binary variable y_i from its conditional mean. Then we get

$$E(\varepsilon_i|x_i, \beta) = 0,$$
$$V(\varepsilon_i|x_i, \beta) = \Phi\left(x_i' \beta\right)\left(1 - \Phi\left(x_i' \beta\right)\right).$$

The parameters of the probit model are typically estimated by maximizing the log-likelihood function with respect to β. As the first-order conditions for this likelihood are non-linear, no closed end form is available for $\hat{\beta}$ and parameter estimates are obtained by an iterative solution

$$\hat{\beta} = \arg\max_{\beta} \sum_{i=1}^{N} \left[y_i \log \Phi\left(x_i' \beta\right) + (1 - y_i) \log\left(1 - \Phi\left(x_i' \beta\right)\right) \right].$$

For statistical inference, the asymptotic covariance matrix can then be estimated by using the inverse of the Hessian evaluated at the maximum likelihood estimates.

Different statistics can be computed to assess the goodness of fit of the probit model. The *LR* statistic or model χ^2 is similar to the overall significance test that is used in a linear regression framework. The idea is to test the null hypothesis that all slope coefficients except the intercept are equal to zero. In practice, the statistic takes the form $-2[l(\tilde{\beta}) - l(\hat{\beta})]$ where $l(\tilde{\beta})$ is the maximized log-likelihood function under the null hypothesis while $l(\hat{\beta})$ is the log-likelihood function evaluated at $\hat{\beta}$ as defined above.

As the name suggests, the pseudo-R^2 or McFadden R^2 is an analog to the R^2 reported in the linear regression model. In particular, it has the property of always lying between 0 and 1. In practice, the statistic is computed as $1 - l(\hat{\beta})/l(\tilde{\beta})$, where $l(\hat{\beta})$ and $l(\tilde{\beta})$ are defined as in the *LR* approach. Note that the pseudo-R^2 can be used to compare different specifications of the model but is not good at comparing models with different data sets.

The percent correct predictions statistic assumes that if the resulting probability $\hat{y}$ is greater than or equal to 0.5 then the event is expected to occur, and not occur otherwise. By assigning 1 or 0 to these probabilities and comparing these to the actual 0 and 1 values, the percentage of correct yes, correct no, and the overall correct scores are calculated. They can then serve to assess the model.

12.3   EMPIRICAL EVIDENCE

12.3.1   Return and Volatility

In what follows, a dead fund is a fund that has a track record made up of at least 36 rates of return and has stopped reporting performance at the end of July 2006. Proceeding in this way, we come up with a sample of 3000 vehicles from which 1016 are considered to be dead, that is, about one-third of the sample. Note that the style distribution within the dead funds does not significantly differ from the style distribution of living funds.

Following Malkiel and Saha (2005), we model the probability of the fund's demise as a function of the fund's return and standard deviation over the final 12 months before the fund exited the database. Estimating the original specification suggested by these authors yields coefficients that are highly significant, but the first quarterly return does not show up with the expected sign.

As the outcome of the original specification is somehow difficult to interpret, we re-estimate the model with the overall 12-month cumulative return in place of the four quarterly returns suggested by Malkiel and Saha (2005). The results are displayed in Table 12.1. Here again, the estimated coefficients are strongly significant but they all present the expected sign. Lower return and higher risk figures tend to make it more likely that the fund will drop from the database.

Considering another point of view, we may argue that the return and risk variables have to be constructed from a relative standpoint. Indeed, comparing the reported performance to zero implies that hedge

Table 12.1   Probit regressions, cumulative return approach

Variable	Coefficient	Std error	z-Statistic
Constant	−0.41	0.036	−11.24
12-month return	−0.01	0.002	−5.77
12-month volatility	0.01	0.003	2.77

Table 12.2 Probit regressions, erosion approach

Variable	Coefficient	Std error	z-Statistic
Constant	0.17	0.086	2.01
12-month/36-month return	0.00	0.002	0.87
12-month/36-month volatility	−0.60	0.085	−7.10

funds belonging to the same category would all exit the database during particularly severe conditions for the strategy. For instance, long/short equity managers with a long bias should mostly have disappeared from databases during the bear market of 2001 under this absolute approach. In that regard, we may think that a fund is likely to exit databases for performance reasons if the more recent rates of return are substantially lower than the ones the fund reported previously. As such, the probit model was re-estimated with return and volatility statistics as defined as the difference between the cumulative return over the last 12 months and the last 36 months before the fund dropped from the databases. The results of this approach (which will be referred to as the erosion approach) are displayed in Table 12.2. It is shown that the coefficients present the wrong sign. Furthermore, the return indicator is not statistically different from zero.

If the past history of a manager cannot define his own benchmark, the manager has to be evaluated relatively to the standards for the industry. In this respect, consider the probit model where the last 12-month performance and standard deviation are expressed in deviation from the CS/Tremont index of the strategy to which the fund belongs.[2] The results of such a practice, which we will define as the relative approach, are disclosed in Table 12.3. The estimated coefficients present the expected sign and are highly significant. Clearly, lower return and higher risk figures than the industry's averages tend to make it likely that the fund will drop from the database.

The goodness-of-fit measures for the three specifications are reported in Table 12.4. The relative approach displays the highest McFadden R^2 and percent correct predictions statistic. Then come the cumulative and the erosion approaches.

---

[2] Note that Malkiel and Saha (2005) compare the performance of the fund to all other funds in the same category through another explanatory variable, but surprisingly the latter does not appear to be significantly different from zero.

Table 12.3 Probit regressions, relative approach

Variable	Coefficient	Std error	z-Statistic
Constant	−0.50	0.027	−18.50
12-month return in dev. from CS	−0.01	0.002	−7.66
12-month volatility in dev. from CS	0.02	0.003	5.63

Table 12.4 Probit regressions, goodness of fit

Approach	Model χ^2	McFadden R^2	% correct
Cumulative	35.7	0.01	66.3
Erosion	51.5	0.01	66.1
Relative	75.1	0.02	66.9

12.3.2 Value-at-Risk

We now investigate whether the number of exceptions – that is, the number of violations of the Value-at-Risk – also produces a leading indicator of a hedge fund demise. Adding this variable to the set of regressors described above, we get the results displayed in Tables 12.5 and 12.6. Note that the erosion approach has not been considered further in view of its less appealing goodness of fit measures. Interestingly, the coefficient of the additional variable shows up with the expected sign but fails to be statistically different from zero.

Table 12.5 Probit regressions, cumulative approach with exceptions

Variable	Coefficient	Std error	z-Statistic
Constant	−0.42	0.037	−11.34
12-month return	−0.01	0.002	−5.61
12-month volatility	0.01	0.003	2.73
Number of exceptions	0.16	0.102	1.56

Table 12.6 Probit regressions, relative approach with exceptions

Variable	Coefficient	Std error	z-Statistic
Constant	−0.51	0.027	−18.48
12-month return in dev. from CS	−0.01	0.002	−7.54
12-month volatility in dev. from CS	0.02	0.003	5.58
Number of exceptions	0.15	0.103	1.45

Table 12.7   Probit regressions, goodness of fit with exceptions

Approach	Model χ^2	McFadden R^2	% correct
Cumulative with exceptions	38.2	0.01	66.2
Relative with exceptions	77.3	0.02	66.7

Table 12.7 reports the measures of fit for the two specifications, and shows that the relative approach outperforms the cumulative approach.

12.4   IMPLICATIONS FOR PORTFOLIO MANAGEMENT

This analysis confirms the intuition that managers are most likely to exit databases on the grounds of risk and performance issues. However, the violations of the Value-at-Risk does not appear with a coefficient statistically different from zero. This finding is indeed disappointing but in fact not surprising as this might be the direct consequence of the decision of the manager not to report to the database if he experiences a big loss that would ultimately mean a Value-at-Risk exception. The notorious short-comings of hedge funds databases set here again the limits of the investigation.

Beyond the incomplete coverage of hedge funds databases, the experience proves that monitoring the Value-at-Risk of any investment vehicle that make up a hedge funds portfolio gives instructive insights of who might be about to go out of business in the future. The manager may choose not to report to the database but have no choice to inform his investors about where he actually stands. In other words, the Value-at-Risk analysis and its conclusions can still be done provided the fund remains in the portfolio.

The empirical evidence also shows that hedge fund managers are selected on a comparative basis. Admittedly, any hedge fund classification used in such a practice is flawed due to the peculiar properties of any hedge fund manager. Indeed, the notion of benchmark and any alternative investment style classification has to be interpreted with caution, as discussed in detail in Chapter 3. Yet, investors do look at peers or benchmarks to assess the relative attractiveness of a particular investment vehicle.

13

Beyond Value-at-Risk

The financing crisis that started during the second part of 2007 (while we were completing the redaction of this book) strongly impacted traditional assets as well as alternative investments. In the beginning of March 2008, Edgar de Picciotto, pioneer of the hedge funds industry and chairman of UBP (Union Bancaire Privée), described in *Le Temps* (10 March 2008) the roots of the 2007–2008 financing crisis as follows:

> Even before the end of the first half of 2007, we had been aware for some time that sooner or later the world was in for a massive shock. The market turmoil of August 2007 was nevertheless unexpectedly severe. This shock, which is still to reveal its full impact, is a product of the era of the financial model, which has led to all kinds of excesses.
>
> The first model to serve as a basis for a universal monetary system was conceived at Bretton Woods in 1944, shortly before the end of the Second World War. Devised to regulate and support the western world's economic aims, the system centred on the US dollar, while guaranteeing that the other countries' dollar reserves were convertible into gold. This model proved effective during the all-important post-war reconstruction, but was later demolished by President Nixon. On 15 August 1971, the President declared that he was taking the dollar off the gold standard, thus abrogating America's treaty commitments and enabling the dollar to float freely. Aided by formidable economic and political power, the US entered the age of unlimited credit. In 1998, the LTCM crisis was the first major accident in this system. The bankruptcy of this hedge fund, which was based on a model created by winners of the Nobel Prize in economics and had a leverage ratio of 1 to 100, represented the first failure in the credit and leverage model.
>
> In 2001, a model based on money creation and low interest rates enabled the economy to steer its way through the dangers of the dot.com crisis. The perverse effects of this model seeped through to the housing market, where the structured credit models engineered by banks broadened the market and made credit almost universally available. This model began to crack in 2006 and finally shattered in August 2007, thrusting us into a financial crisis entailing huge losses, with results that are still surfacing in early 2008. Some banks have faced a dramatic capital meltdown and the whole financial industry has been plunged into a downward spiral of capital destruction.

During 2007, subprime mortgages and related mortgage-backed securities experienced significant losses that cast some doubts on the valuations of credit innovative products. This triggered a large number of sell orders and purchasing reluctance of collateral debt obligations (CDOs) whose quality of super-senior tranches was suddenly impacted. This uncertainty spread to other complex credit instruments (collateralized loan obligations), asset-backed securities (such as asset-backed commercial papers) and high-yield bonds. Prices were pushed down affecting the valuation of firms' assets. Quickly, liquidity overall dried up on the markets.

For risk management practices, this period was full of insights. As pointed out by the Senior Supervisors Group (2008) of financial supervisors from France, Germany, Switzerland, the United Kingdom and the United States:

> Because these and other innovative products had been created during the prior period of more benign market conditions, banks and securities had not observed how such products would have behave during a significant market downturn and found their risk management practices tested to various degrees.

For instance, some models circumvent the problem of the short price history of super-senior tranches of CDOs by the use of AAA-rated corporate bonds as a proxy. As a matter of fact, that assumption led to a substantial understatement of risk.

13.1   2007–2008 LIQUIDITY CRISIS AND HEDGE FUNDS

During the end of 2007 and the first months of 2008, the hedge funds suffering most significantly were those that exhibited the largest mismatch between the liquidity of their assets and that of their liabilities. Obviously, this is the same reason that caused the nationalization of Northern Rock. The credit crunch led to a financing and liquidity crisis and then to a solvency crisis.

For hedge fund managers, the risk attached to prospective cash flows over a defined time horizon period can be measured by Cash-Flow-at-Risk, also known as Liquidity-at-Risk. In order to reflect the asset and liability mismatch, the results should be interpreted with respect to the liquidity-adjusted Value-at-Risk of the recent market turmoils. These results speak in favour of a risk measure that reflects illiquidity.

However, even in the long-only and fully transparent world this is not an easy task. As pointed out by Dowd (2005):

> There are many ways we could estimate liquidity adjusted Value-at-Risk. These vary in their degrees of sophistication in their ease (or otherwise) of implementation and there is no single 'best' method. However, sophisticated approaches are not necessarily more useful than more basic ones and the 'best' method, even if we could establish what it is, is not necessarily better than a collection of 'inferior' ones.

and one of the conclusions by Finger (2008) about the recent liquidity crisis was

> For liquidity in general, that we do not have any perfect models is acceptable. That we do not have any established models, with a history of failures, successes and dialogues is not. [...] we need to get on with implementing what we have, gaining experience and making things better.

For hedge fund investors, the relevance of Value-at-Risk mainly based on the risk of the alternative strategy may be questionable in such an environment. Stress tests and analysis scenarios or liquidity-adjusted Value-at-Risk seem to be convenient. The choice mainly depends on the perception of the 2007–2008 events: was there an exogenous shock or an endogenous one?

13.2   MECHANICAL STRESS TEST

Should the financial system enter an area of dislocation and should all the fundamental relationships fail, Value-at-Risk would obviously fail to provide efficient loss expectations. Remember that Value-at-Risk aims to capture the loss that will be exceeded under stable market conditions, due to the stochastic behaviour of the financial market, without exogenous shocks. On the other hand, stress tests are supposed to capture the risk exposure due to a breakdown in normal relationships, in this state of business and economic cycles, in the recent level of volatility. Stress tests also provide information on the risk associated with the extreme region of the tail that is not described by the Value-at-Risk.[1] Finally, by focusing on maximum loss over a long time horizon, stress tests could identify non-linear expositions that may not appear in normal market conditions.

---

[1] Expected Shortfall may also fail to correctly describe these areas of the tail as the underlying level risk can be dampened by the smoothing effect of averaging.

One simple stress test consists of collecting the worst price movements for each relevant underlying risk factor and aggregating them in the most conservative way. This mechanical stress test can be seen as a proxy of the maximum loss a fund can experience when facing a massive exogenous shock. Based on the two methodologies presented in the previous chapter, two types of stress test may be defined. The first, which relates to the New Style Model for hedge fund s, is

$$\text{MTS}_s^{\text{New Style}} = \sum_{i=1}^{10} \hat{\beta}_{s,i} \max_t(I_{i,t}) + \max_t(\hat{\varepsilon}_{s,t}) + \max(\hat{\alpha}_s, 0)$$

For the Implicit Model, the stress test is

$$\text{MTS}_s^{\text{Implicit}} = \sum_{i=1}^{35} \tilde{\hat{\beta}}_{s,i} \max_t(G_i(t)) + \sum_{i=36}^{70} \tilde{\hat{\beta}}_{s,i} \min_t(G_i(t))$$
$$+ \max_t(\hat{\varepsilon}_{s,t}) + \max(\hat{\alpha}_s, 0)$$

This mechanical stress test finally consists of taking into account all the available crises and selecting among them the one that was most painful for the underlying risk factor. For hedge funds, this approach mainly focuses on the behaviour of CS/Tremont alternative investment style indices during the late 1998 crisis when liquidity drastically dried up.[2] So the New Style mechanical stress test can also be interpreted as a liquidity crisis scenario analysis and could be written, quite simply.

13.3 LIQUIDITY-ADJUSTED VALUE-AT-RISK

On the other hand, we may consider, as Edgar de Picciotto, that the events of the second part of 2007 are only one element of a sequence of accidents caused by Nixon's decision to abrogate the dollar gold parity. As the financing crisis of 1998, the dislocation of 2007–2008 may be entirely caused by a monetary system based on a money with no intrinsic value. This financing crisis can be seen as an endogenous

---

[2] It should be noticed that not all financial market crises are dominated by liquidity risk, as was shown by the 2000 technology bubble bust and the corporate scandals. Moreover, some CS/Tremont substyle indices recorded gains in August 1998, some for fundamental reasons (such as short sellers) that are likely to happen again, some by luck, such as CTAs. Indeed, we may argue that long-term trend followers recorded positive returns in August 1998 because they were correctly provisioned in July 1998. Moreover, since then more and more managers have initiated large exposure to equity futures. We can imagine the diversification effect if a sudden liquidity crisis happens just after the confirmation of a long-term equity trend.

shock and enters the set of events that should be correctly forecasted by Value-at-Risk.

As already mentioned in section 6.3.1, General Equilibrium Theory confirms the existence of endogenous shocks even in a very simple supply and demand system. But this rigorous and highly general economic approach also casts some particular lights on any monetary system based on bona fide money. Indeed, Samuelson (1958) pointed out that the introduction of bona fide money is a way to achieve optimality in a model[3] where the exchange opportunities are limited by an intertemporal structure. On the other hand, an economy based on money without any intrinsic value may also generate a continuum of equilibria that seems to converge to a long-term equilibrium while it faces drastic dynamic changes. In other words, even in a very simple intertemporal monetary framework, beside endogenous shocks occuring, a relatively quiet path of monetary equilibria may face drastic breakdowns and generate a liquidity crisis that morphs into a solvency crisis until a new monetary system is devised.[4]

13.3.1 Non-Myopic Risk Measures

One obvious consequence of this theoretical result lies in the fact that myopic risk measures are not appropriate for forecasting risk during a liquidity crisis. As pointed out by Fung and Hsieh (2006):

> Between the end of 1987 and September 1998, credit spreads had stayed in a narrow range relative to the earlier years. [...] As the credit spread widened after the Russian debt default in August 1998, fixed-income hedge funds suffered large losses. While the increase in credit spreads [in August 1998] was large relative to the experience of the previous ten years, the spreads were not especially large against the backdrop of a much longer time period.

Risk measurements on the basis of short time periods are inappropriate in such an environment. Age-weighted methodology (or a conditional approach) may help after the breakdown: typically, even if

---

[3] The General Equilibrium Theory first formulated by Walras (1954) and Arrow and Debreu (1954) considers a universal market with heterogeneous agents. Because of the abstraction and the widespread insight of this framework, any implementation of time does not seem to be relevant. A correct interpretation of the commodities according to not only physical but also spatial or temporal characteristics is sufficient to regard an infra-temporal model as a simple extension of the static case. However, an inter-temporal model that differs from the static general equilibrium framework is the overlapping generation model of Samuleson (1958), since both an infinite horizon and demographic assumptions are implemented: as some generations will never meet and some markets are definitely closed to certain generations, the model incorporates a certain level of incompleteness. It is therefore not surprising that contrary to the static case, equilibria may not be Pareto Optimal.

[4] For more detailed analysis on the overlapping generation model, see Ghiglino and Tvede (1995, 2000).

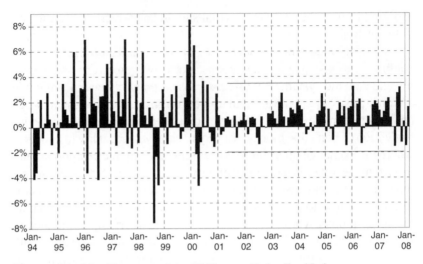

Figure 13.1   Monthly returns of the CS/Tremont Hedge Fund Index

GARCH models or exponentially weighted models are quickly adapted after the occurrence of turmoil markets, they will fail to predict the level of breakdown. In practice, risk management is not rocket science and practitioners tend to recalibrate their models when the level of volatility is particularly low. A more relevant approach consists of sticking to the long-term volatility or, in a conditional approach, to use estimates of the current level only if it is larger than the long-term one. Some anecdotic evidence tend to show that many risk managers have changed the parameters of their models after the first sign of the subprime collapse, even for the models that are tracking the risk level of assets not directly correlated with asset-backed markets. For traditional assets, the extreme move forecasts are no longer computed on the last two years, but on a more volatile period such as 2002–2004 or on the last nine years.

For hedge funds, Figure 13.1 shows that the volatility of returns has drastically decreased since the end of 2000. This reflects various phenomena: institutionalization and pasteurization of the hedge funds industry,[5] over-diversification of the CS/Tremont indices due to the increase of components,[6] and a deceiving recent average level of risk. Not surprisingly, as shown in Table 7.14, the Original Style Model, whose underlying risk is computed on the previous 36 months, exhibited

---

[5] See section 2.5.2.
[6] See Chapter 3.

a high level of exception rate in August 2007 and November 2007: 13.2% and 15.3% on average and 31.8% for Fixed Income managers in August and 38.2% for Convertible Arbitrage in November. The New Style Model and Implicit Value-at-Risk exhibited a higher level of robustness during these two difficult months. However the level of exception rates and the proximity between the two different months[7] also reveals that these models, despite being based on longer time windows, are not formulated to properly capture the risk attached to such an environment. A liquidity add-on is required.

13.3.2 Liquidity Adjustment Based on Replication

It is a well-known fact that during market turmoils, in the long-only world, the only thing that rises is correlation. Empirical evidence proves that hedge funds are exposed to the same correlation convergence risk. This is more surprising as, for instance, such a convergence of correlation with respect to the equity market for long/short managers assumes that at the same time the correlation of the long book rises to 1 while the correlation of the short book goes to -1 (with a cumulative loss effect). More generally, taking into account the heterogeneity of alternative investment styles, this convergence of correlation is hard to understand. Fung et al. (2008) advocates that if we assume that hedge fund managers invest in different ways, there is one thing they share:

> They borrow from the same small group of investment banks.

For them, basic risk management should not focus only on the risk of the investment strategy implemented by hedge funds, but also on the risk related with the terms of their leverage. Alternative investment styles combine location (what is traded), strategy (how these assets are traded) and leverage. Value-at-Risk cannot spare the measure of the combined risk of these three parameters. Fung and Hsieh (2004) observed that

> The cost of financing the positions will also depend on the overall liquidity of the marketplace, which is also reflected in the credit spread variable.

Thus credit spreads can be seen as the relevant single factor to incorporate explicitly liquidity effect in the Strategy Value-at-Risk. One advantage of this approach lies in the very long history of the Baa/treasury spread, as data go back to 1920.

---

[7] January 2008 and March 2008 were also difficult months for the alternative industry.

Table 13.1 Exception rate during two difficult months of 2007 for each style

	August 2007			November 2007		
	Original Style VaR	New Style VaR	Adjusted New Style VaR	Original Style VaR	New Style VaR	Adjusted New Style VaR
Total	13.2%	3.84%	1.15%	15.3%	4.70%	1.47%
Convertible Arb.	21.7%	0.0%	0.0%	38.2%	0.0%	0.0%
Short Bias	0%	0.0%	0.0%	0.0%	0.0%	0.0%
Emerging Markets	5.7%	4.3%	1.4%	6.8%	0.0%	1.7%
Eq. Market Neutral	11.5%	8.2%	3.3%	4.0%	0.0%	0.0%
Event-Driven	15.9%	3.7%	0.0%	25%	5.1%	0.0%
Fixed Income	31.0%	12.6%	3.4%	17.1%	3.9%	2.6%
Global Macro	21.3%	5.0%	1.3%	13.8%	4.6%	6.2%
Long/Short	8.0%	0.9%	0.9%	17.0%	7.3%	1.5%
Managed Futures	13.0%	8.7%	2.6%	0.0%	0.0%	0.0%
Multi-Strategy	20.0%	6.0%	0.0%	11.5%	3.4%	2.3%

Let us first compute a beta to credit spread changes for each hedge fund and each CS/Tremont substyle index as of July 2007 and October 2007. Then, the credit spread sensitivity is extracted from the tracks of the hedge fund and of the indices, simply by considering the residuals of the regressions. Reflecting the other side of the balance sheet, the tracks of all the time series are de-autocorrelated. Style analysis are then performed on this new data set and the Value-at-Risk are computed. Such a Value-at-Risk can be considered as a risk indicator net of all liquidity and funding effects. Then the liquidity (and funding) adjusted Value-at-Risk is obtained simply by adding to the former Value-at-Risk both the increase in volatility (multiplied by 2.33) due to the de-smoothing process and the long-term Extreme Value Theory Move on credit spread changes multiplied by the beta of each hedge fund (if there is a short exposure to credit spread changes).

Table 13.1 provides the results of the backtest of this add-on for the New Style Value-at-Risk. Obviously for August, the Fixed Income exception rate significantly decreases with the liquidity-adjusted indicator.

13.4   LIMIT OF LIQUIDITY-ADJUSTED VALUE-AT-RISK AND LIQUIDITY SCENARIO

However, these two approaches have two main weaknesses. The first is methodological: as already shown, the individual hedge fund clones model exhibits a low quality of fit. Second, if we only apply the illiq-uidity add-on to those hedge funds whose liquidity adjustment is more significant, then the backtesting results remain almost unchanged. Con-trary to 1998, the events of 2007 and 2008 do not reflect a systemic crisis at the hedge funds level. The 2007–2008 financing crises mainly im-pacted the funding liquidity and is thus mainly specific. Two managers that perform the same strategy may be impacted in a completely different way depending on the quality and nature of their financing. Sometime before 2007, we saw some hedge funds performing illiquid strategies such as direct lending, and negotiating fixed terms with banks in order to borrow money for the next 10 years. Despite the fact it impacts the level of return, it did not change the nature of the strategy. However, having negotiated better conditions in terms of rate and a marginal requirement to protect them against the effect of the liquidity crisis on the financing part of the strategy, it gave them an obvious competitive advantage.

In our opinion, the assumption that the quality and nature of the current financing of complex strategies may appear in its historical track, is a 'false premise'. Of course, liquidity risk tends to compound other risks, particularly credit risk, but fixed income spreads (credit, convertible-treasury or mortgage treasury) tend to simultaneously widen and some long-term primitive convergence strategies (modelled by short positions in a lookback straddle) exhibit high correlation with the related fixed income spread. This is caused more by the nature of the bets and the relationship between fundamentals than by the way positions are funded; also, the correlation between fixed income arbitrage indices and credit spread may be high.

Thus, the choice and the interpretation of the risk indicators during the 2007–2008 financing crisis requires a preliminary step: the quali-tative knowledge of the conditions of financing for each hedge fund. This knowledge is necessary to correctly assess if applying a liquidity-adjusted Value-at-Risk to a particular hedge fund, based on conditions that are no longer structurally prevalent, makes sense or not. More than ever, none of the four dimensions of the risk management for hedge funds investors[8] can afford to neglect the others.

---

[8] See Chapter 5.

Bibliography

Agarwal, V. and Naik, N.Y. (2000a). On taking the alternative route: Risks, reward, style and performance persistence of hedge funds, *Journal of Alternative Investments*, **2**, 6–23.

Agarwal, V. and Naik, N.Y. (2000b). Multi-period performance persistence analysis of hedge funds, *Journal of Financial and Quantitative Analysis*, **35**(3), 327–342.

Agarwal, V. and Naik, N.Y. (2000c). Performance evaluation of hedge funds with option-based and buy-and-hold strategies, *Journal of Financial and Quantitative Analysis*, Sept., 1–52.

Agarwal, V. and Naik, N.Y. (2000d). Generalized style analysis of hedge funds, *Journal of Asset Management*, **1**(1), 93–109.

Agarwal, V. and Naik, N.Y. (2000e). Flows and performance in the hedge fund industry, Working Paper, Centre for Hedge Funds Research and Education.

Agarwal, V. and Naik, N.Y. (2003). Risk and portfolio decisions involving hedge funds, *Review of Financial Studies*, **17**, 63–98. (published in 2004).

Agarwal, V., Daniel, N.D. and Naik, N.Y. (2003). Flows, performance and managerial incentives in hedge funds, CFR Working Paper No. 04–04.

Amenc, N. (2007). Three early lessons from the subprime lending crisis: A French answer to President Sarkozy, Working Paper, EDHEC Risk and Asset Management Centre.

Amenc, N. and Goltz, F. (2006). A reply to the CESR recommendations on the eligibility of hedge fund indices for investments of UCITS, Working Paper, EDHEC Risk and Asset Management Research Centre.

Amenc, N. and Kat, H.M. (2002). Welcome to the dark side: Hedge fund attrition and survivorship bias over the period 1994–2001, Working Paper, EDHEC Risk and Asset Management Centre.

Amenc, N. and Martellini, L. (2003). The brave new world of hedge funds indices, Working Paper, EDHEC Risk and Asset Management Research Centre.

Amenc, N. and Meyfredi, J.C. (2007). *Emerging Alternatives to Hedge Funds*. EDHEC Risk and Asset Management Research Center, EDHEC Asset Management Days 2007 presentation.

Amenc, N., El Bied, S. and Martellini, L. (2002). Evidence of predictability in hedge fund returns and multi-style multi-class tactical style allocation decisions, Working Paper Series, USC Marshall School of Business.

Arrow, K. and Debreu, G. (1954). Existence of equilibrium for a competitive economy, *Econometrica*, **22**, 265–290.

Balasko, Y. (1988). *Foundations of the Theory of General Equilibrium*, Academic Press, Boston.

Balasko, Y. and Ghiglino, C. (1995). On the existence of endogenous cycles, *Journal of Economic Theory*, **67**, 566–577.

Balkema, A.A. and de Haan, L. (1974). Residual life time at great age, *Annals of Probability*, **2**, 792–804.

Barone-Adesi, G., Bourgoin, F. and Giannopoulos, K. (1998). Don't look back, *Risk*, **11**, 100–103.

Basle Committee on Banking Supervision (1996). *Amendment to the Capital Accord to Incorporate Market Risks*, Basle: Basle Committee on Banking Supervision, Bank for International Settlements, January.

Blum P., Dacorogna, M. and Jaeger, L. (2003). Performance and risk measurement challenges for hedge funds: Empirical considerations, in *Euromoney Books*, Ed., L. Jaeger.

Capocci, D. and Hubner, G. (2004). Analysis of hedge funds performance, *Journal of Empirical Finance*, **11**, 55–89.

Carhart, M. (1997). On persistence in mutual fund performance, *Journal of Finance*, **52**, 57–82.

Castillo, E. and Hadi, A. (1997). Fitting the Generalized Pareto Distribution to data, *Journal of the American Statistical Association*, **92**(440), 1609–1620.

Christensen, R. (1990). *Log-Linear Models*, Springer Verlag, New York.

Christoffersen, P.F., Dielbold, X. and Schuermann, T. (1998). Horizon problems and extreme events in financial risk Management, *Federal Reserve Bank of New York Economic Policy Review*, October, 109–118.

Christopherson, J. (1995). Equity style classifications, *Journal of Portfolio Management*, **21**(3), 32–43.

Coles, S. (2001). *An Introduction to Statistical Modeling of Extreme Values*, Springer-Verlag, London.

Coles, S., Heffernan, J. and Tawn, J. (1999). Dependence measures for extreme value analyses, *Extremes*, **2**(4), 339–365.

Compte-Sponville, A. (2004). *Le Capitalisme est-il moral?*, Albin Michel, Paris.

Cowell, A., Martin, B., Mill, J. and Rajan, A. (2007). Convergence and divergence: New forces sharing the investment universe, Working Paper, KPMG.

Cremer, M. and Petajisto, A. (2006). *How Attractive is Your Fund Manage? A New Measure that Predicts Performance*. International Center for Finance, Yale School of Management.

Dacorogna, M.M., Pictet, O.V., Muller, U. A. and de Vries, C.G. (2001). Extremal forex returns in extremely large datasets, *Extremes*, **4**(2), 105–127.

Daul, S. and Finger, C. (2007). *Capturing Risk in Hedge Funds: Moving from Positions to Strategy*, RiskMetrics Group, EDHEC Alternative Investments Days 2007 presentation.

Davidson, A.C. and Smith, R.L. (1990). Models for exceedances over high thresholds, *Journal of the Royal Statistical Society*, Ser. B, **52**, 393–442.

Diez de los Rios, A. and Garcia, R. (2006). Assessing and valuing the non-linear structure of hedge fund returns. Working Papers, 06–31, Bank of Canada.

Dowd, K. (2002). *An Introduction to Market Risk Measurement*, John Wiley & Sons, Ltd, Chichester.

Dowd, K. (2005). *Measuring Market Risk* (second edition), John Wiley & Sons, Ltd, Chichester.

Drost, F.C. and Nijman, T.E. (1993). Temporal aggregation of GARCH process, *Econometrica*, **61**, 909–927.

Duc, F. (2004a). Hedge fund indices: Status review and user guide, Working Paper, 3A.

Duc, F. (2004b). Investable indices: A viable alternative to funds of funds?, Working Paper, 3A.

Duc, F. (2004c). Investable hedge fund indices: Illusion or reality?, Working Paper, 3A.

Duc, F. and Schorderet, Y. (2007). Assessing hedge fund risk with extreme value theory, Union Bancaire Privée, Working Paper.

Dupuis, D.J. (1998). Exceedances over high thresholds: A guide to threshold selection, *Extremes*, **1**(3), 251–261.

Embrechts, P., Kluppelberg, C. and Mikosch, T. (1997). *Modelling Extremal Events for Insurance and Finance*, Spring-Verlag, Berlin.

Fama, E.F. and French, K. (1992). The cross-section of expected stock returns, *Journal of Finance*, **67**, 427–465.

Feffer, S. and Kundro, C. (2003). Valuation issues and operational risk in hedge funds, Working Paper, Capco.

Finger, C.-C. (2006). How historical simulation makes me lazy, *Monthly Research*, April, RiskMetrics Group.

Finger, C.-C. (2008). The SSG and my two brains, *Monthly Research*, March, RiskMetrics Group.

Fung W. and Hsieh, D.A. (1997). Empirical characteristics of dynamic trading strategies: The case of hedge funds. *Review of Financial Studies*, **10**, 275–302.

Fung W. and Hsieh, D.A. (2000). Performance characteristics of hedge funds and commodity funds: Natural versus spurious biases. *Journal of Financial and Quantitative Analysis*, **35**(3).

Fung, W. and Hsieh, D.A. (2001). The risk in hedge fund strategies: Theory and evidence from trend followers. *Review of Financial Studies*, **14**, 313–341.

Fung, W. and Hsieh, D.A. (2002). Hedge funds benchmarks: Information content and biases. *Financial Analyst Journal*, **58**(1), 22–34.

Fung, W. and Hsieh, D.A. (2004). Hedge fund benchmarks: A risk-based approach. *Financial Analyst Journal*, **60**(5), 65–80.

Fung, W. and Hsieh, D.A. (2006). *Hedge Funds: An Industry in its Adolescence*, Federal Bank of Atlanta.

Fung, W., Hsieh, D.A. and Naik, V. (2008). Synthetic hedge funds accessing alternative beta returns, Presentation for 2008 Hedge Fund Programme, London Business School.

Géhin, W. and Vaissié, M. (2004). Hedge fund indices: Investable, non-investable and strategy benchmarks, Working Paper, EDHEC Risk and Asset Management Research Centre.

Geltner, D. (1991). Smoothing in appraisal-based returns. *Journal of Real Estate Finance and Economics*, **4**(3), 327–345.

Geltner, D. (1993). Estimating market values from appraised values without assuming an efficient market, *Journal of Real Estate Finance and Economics*, **8**(3), 325–345.

Getmansky, M., Lo, A.W. and Makarov, I. (2003). An econometric model of serial correlation and illiquidity in hedge fund returns, *Journal of Financial Economics*, **74**, 529–609.

Ghiglino, C. and Tvede, M. (1995). Endowments, stability and fluctuations in OG models, *Journal of Economic Dynamics and Control*, **19**, 621–653.

Ghiglino, C. and Tvede, M. (2000). Optimal policies in OG economies, *Journal of Economic Theory*, **90**(1), 62–83.

Gilli, M. and Këllezi, E. (2005). An application of extreme value theory for measuring financial risk, Working Paper, Department of Econometrics.

Goltz, F. (2007). *Long Only Absolute Return Fund*, EDHEC Risk and Asset Management Research Centre, EDHEC Asset Management Days 2007 presentation.

Goltz, F., L. Martellini, L. and Vaissié, M. (2007). Hedge fund indices: Reconciling investability and representativity, *European Financial Management*, **13**, 257–286.

Grimshaw, S.D. (1993). Computing maximum likelihood estimates for the Generalized Pareto Distribution, *Technometrics*, **35**, 185–191.

Hasanhodzic, J. and Lo, A.W. (2006). Can hedge funds returns be replicated?, Working Paper, MIT.

Henriksson, R.D. and Merton, R.C. (1981). On market timing and investment performance II: Statistical procedures for evaluating forecasting skills, *Journal of Business*, **54**(4), 513–533.

Hosking, J.R.M. and Wallis, J.R. (1987). Parameter and quantile estimation for the Generalized Pareto Distribution, *Technometrics*, **29**(3), 339–349.

Hosking, J.R.M., Wallis, J.R. and Wood, E.F. (1985). Estimation of the Generalized Extreme-Value Distribution by the method of probability-weighted moments, *Technometrics*, **27**, 251–261.

Huber, P., Ronchetti, E.M. and Victoria-Feser, M.-P. (2004). Estimation of generalized latent trait models, *Journal of the Royal Statistical Society*, **66**(4), 893–908.

Huber, P. and Victoria-Feser, M.-P. (2007). Estimation procedure of a factor model for the construction of hedge funds indices, Working Paper, Cinetics Asset Management, Geneva and University of Geneva.

Ineichen, A.L. (2003). *Absolute Returns: The Risk and Opportunities of Hedge Funds Investing*, John Wiley & Sons, Inc., New York.

Israelsen, C. L. and Cogswell, G.F. (2007). The error of tracking error. *Journal of Asset Management*, **7**(6), 419–424.

Jaeger, L. (2002). *Managing Risk in Alternative Investment Strategies*, Prentice Hall, London.

Joe, H. (1993). Parametric family of multivariate distributions with given margins, *Journal of Multivariate Analysis*, **46**, 262–282.

Joe, H. (1997). *Multivariate Models and Dependence Concepts*, Chapman & Hall, London.

Jorion, P. (2007). *Value at Risk: The New Benchmark for Controlling Market Risk*, McGraw-Hill, New York.

Kahn, R. and Rudd, A. (1965). Does historical performance predict future performance?, *Financial Analysts Journal*, **51**(6), 43–52.

Kat, H.M. and Manexe, F. (2003). Persistence in hedge funds performance: The true value of a track record, *Journal of Alternative Investments*, **5**(4), 66–72.

Kat, H.M. and Palero, H.P. (2005). Hedge funds returns: You can make them yourself, Working Paper, Cass Business School.

Kaufman, L. and Rousseeuw, P. (1990), *Finding Groups in Data*, John Wiley & Sons, Inc., New York.

Kazemi, H., Martin, H. and Schneeweis, T. (2001). Understanding hedge fund performance: Research results and rules of thumb for institutional investor, Working Paper, Lehman Brothers.

Kupiec, P. (1995). Techniques for verifying the accuracy of risk management models, *Journal of Derivatives*, 373–384.

Lamont, O.A. (2003). Go down fighting: Short sellers vs. firms, Working paper, University of Chicago.

Lhabitant, F.S. (2001). Assessing market risk for hedge funds and hedge funds portfolio, *Journal of Risk Finance*, Spring, 2001, 1–17.

Lhabitant, F.S. (2002a). Assessing market risk of hedge funds. *Financial Risk and Financial Risk Management*, **16**, 417–449.

Lhabitant, F.S. (2002b). *Hedge Funds: Myths and Limits*, John Wiley & Sons, Ltd, Chichester.

Lhabitant, F.S. (2003). Evaluating hedge fund investments: The role of pure style indices, Working Paper, EDHEC Risk and Asset Management Centre.

Lhabitant, F.S. (2004). *Hedge Funds: Quantitative Insights*, John Wiley & Sons, Ltd, Chichester.

Lhabitant, F.S. (2006a). *Handbook of Hedge Funds*. John Wiley & Sons, Ltd, Chichester.

Lhabitant, F.S. (2006b). Les indices de hedge funds doivent-ils être éligibles ou non aux fonds grand public. Autorité des Marchés Financiers, Les cahiers scientifiques no. 2.

Lhabitant, F.S. and Learned, M. (2003). Hedge fund diversification: How much is enough?, *Journal of Alternative Investments*, **5**(3), 23–49.

Liew, J. (2003). Hedge fund index investing examined, *Journal of Portfolio Management*, **6**(1).

Lo, A. (2001). Risk management for hedge funds: Introduction and overview, Working Paper, MIT Sloan School of Management.

Lobosco, A. and DiBartolomeo, D. (1997). Approximating the confidence intervals for Sharpe style weights, *Financial Analysts Journal*, **53**(4), 80–85.

Lowenstein, R. (2000). *When Genius Failed: The Rise and Fall of Long-Term Capital Management*, Random House, New York.

Malkiel, B.G. and Saha, A. (2005). Hedge funds: Risk and return, *Financial Analysts Journal*, **61**(6), 80–88.

Martinelli, L., Vaissié, M. and Goltz, F. (2004). Hedge fund indices from an academic perspective: Reconciling investability and representativity, Working Paper, EDHEC Risk and Asset Management Research Centre.

Merton, R.C. (1981). On market timing and investment performance I: An equilibrium theory of value for market forecasts hedge funds: Quantitative insights, *Journal of Business*, **54**, 363–406.

Neftçi, S.N. (2000). Value at Risk calculations, extreme events, and tail estimation, *The Journal of Derivatives*, Spring, 1–15.

Ofek, E., Richardson, M. and Whitelaw, R.F. (2003). Limited arbitrage and short sales restrictions: Evidence from the options market, NBER Working Paper 9423.

Pickands, J. (1975). Statistical inference using extreme order statistics, *The Annals of Statistics*, **3**, 119–131.

Pole, A. (2007). *Statistical Arbitrage Algorithm Trading Insights and Techniques*, John Wiley & Sons, Inc., Chichester.

Poon, S., Rockinger, M. and Tawn, J. (2002). Modelling extreme-value dependence in international stock markets, Working Paper, University of Strathclyde.

Popper, K.R. (1998). *Des sources de la connaissance et de l'ignorance*, Payot &Rivages, Paris.

Porter, G.E. and Trifts, J.W. (1998). Performance persistence of experienced mutual fund managers, *Financial Service Review*, **7**(1), 57–68.

Rahl, L. (2000). *Risk Budgeting: A New Approach to Investing*, Risk Books, London.

Rahl, L. (2003). *Hedge Fund Risk Transparency*, Risk Books, London.

Reiss, R.D. and Thomas, M. (1997). *Statistical Analysis of Extreme Values with Applications to Insurance, Finance, Hydrology and Other Fields*, Birkhäuser Verlag, Basel.

Reynolds Parker, V. (2000). *Managing Hedge Fund Risk*, Risk Books, London.

Samuelson, P.A. (1958). An exact consumption-loan model of interest with or without the social contrivance of money, *Journal of Political Economy*, **79**, 1002–1011.

Scherer, B. (2002). *Portfolio Construction and Risk Budgeting*, Risk Books, London.

Schneeweis, T. (1998). Dealing with myths of hedge funds, *Journal of Alternative Investments*, Winter, 11–15.

Senior Supervisors Group (2008). Observations on risk management practices during the recent market turbulence, 6 March report, Federal Reserve Bank of New York.

Sharpe, W.F. (1988). Determining a fund's effective asset mix, *Investment Management Review*, **2**(6), 59–69.

Sharpe, W.F. (1992). Asset allocation: Management style and performance measurement, *Journal of Portfolio Management*, **18**(2), 7–19.

Sidani, R. and Soueissy, M. (2003). The risks underlying hedge funds strategies, Working Paper, HEC, Université de Lausanne.

Singer, B., Staub, R. and Terhaar, K. (2002). Determining the appropriate allocation to alternative investments, *AIMR Conference Proceedings*: Hedge Fund Management (AIMR).

Spurgin, R. (1999). A benchmark for commodity trading advisor performance, *The Journal of Alternative Investements*, **2**(1), 11–21.

Tajvidi, N. (1996a). *Confidence intervals and accuracy estimation for heavy-tailed Generalized Pareto Distribution*, Thesis Article, Chalmers University of Technology.

Tajvidi, N. (1996b). *Design and Implementation of Statistical Computations for Generalized Pareto Distributions*, Technical Report, Chalmers University of Technology.

Till, H. (2007). The Amaranth collapse: What happened and what have we learned thus far?, Working Paper, EDHEC Risk and Asset Management Research Centre.

Trzcinka, C. (1995). Comment on equity style classifications (Christopherson), *Journal of Portfolio Management*, **21**(3), 44–46.

Vidyamurthy, G. (2004). *Pairs Trading Quantitative Methods and Analysis*, John Wiley & Sons, Inc., Chichester.

Walker, G.A. and Saw, J.G. (1978). The distribution of linear combination of t-variables, *Journal of the American Statistical Association*, **732**(364), 876–878.

Walras, L. (1954). *Element of Pure Economics*, Allen & Unwin, London.

Walshaw, D. (1990). Discussion of models for exceedances over high thresholds, by Davidson, A. C. and Smith, R. L., *Journal of the Royal Statistical Society*, Ser. B, **52**, 393–442.

Index

Index compiled by Terry Halliday